MUSIC AND FAITH

MUSIC AND FAITH

CONVERSATIONS IN A POST-SECULAR AGE

JONATHAN ARNOLD

THE BOYDELL PRESS

First published 2019
The Boydell Press, Woodbridge

ISBN 978 1 78327 260 0

The Boydell Press is an imprint of Boydell & Brewer Ltd
PO Box 9, Woodbridge, Suffolk IP12 3DF, UK
and of Boydell & Brewer Inc.
668 Mt Hope Avenue, Rochester, NY 14620-2731, USA
website: www.boydellandbrewer.com

A catalogue record for this book is available from the British Library

This publication is printed on acid-free paper

MIX
Paper from responsible sources
FSC® C013056
FSC www.fsc.org

Typeset by BBR Design, Sheffield
Printed and bound in Great Britain by TJ International Ltd, Padstow, Cornwall

In memory of John Milne, singer, musician and friend

CONTENTS

ILLUSTRATIONS

The author and publishers are grateful to all the institutions and individuals listed for permission to reproduce the materials in which they hold copyright. Every effort has been made to trace the copyright holders; apologies are offered for any omission, and the publishers will be pleased to add any necessary acknowledgement in subsequent editions.

INTERVIEWEES

NICK BAINES

Before becoming the Bishop of Leeds in 2014, the Rt Revd Nick Baines was Bishop of Bradford (2011–14), and before that, Bishop of Croydon (2003–11). He read German and French at Bradford University and, before ordination, worked as a Russian linguist at GCHQ. He speaks regularly at conferences in Germany (in German), and is a member of the House of Lords. He is also a broadcaster (often heard on BBC Radio 4's *Thought for the Day* and the *Chris Evans Breakfast Show* on BBC Radio 2), an author (of seven books), a blogger and tweeter (with 14,500 followers). He is married to Linda (an artist and health visitor) and they have three adult children and three grandchildren.

RONALD BLYTHE

In a long and distinguished career, Ronald Blythe's work includes *Akenfield* – his classic study of English village life, poetry, fiction, essays, short stories, history and literary criticism. His work has been filmed, widely translated, awarded literary prizes and his 'voice' recognised as one of special originality. He is President of the John Clare Society and has always taken part in the cultural life of his native countryside. He lives in the Stour Valley in the farmhouse Bottengoms, which was once the home of his friend John Nash.

JANET BOULTON

Janet Boulton studied painting at Camberwell School of Art London in the 1950s. She has held a number residencies and shown widely in solo and mixed exhibitions. From 1980 she was a regular exhibitor in Cork Street London, represented by the Mercury Gallery and subsequently the Redfern Gallery. In 2009 after an extensive show at the Edinburgh Festival 'Remembering Little Sparta' (The Sculpture Court, ECA) she held further exhibitions in London, Abingdon and Oxford. Her contribution to gardening was marked in 2014 by the publication of *Foreground/Background: About Making a Garden* and film of the same title, shown at the Garden Museum with an exhibition of her garden paintings 1982–2012. Recently the retrospective 'A Seeming Diversity' was held at Swindon Museum & Art Gallery, accompanied by an illustrated catalogue and a film showing her working processes. This exhibition brought together the various strands of Boulton's work, including her ongoing 'Eye/Music'. Her work is held in private and public collections in the UK, Italy, Japan, Canada and USA.

MICHAEL BOURDEAUX

Michael Bourdeaux was born in 1934 in Cornwall. During his National Service he trained as a Russian interpreter. He read Modern Languages and Theology at Oxford University. In 1959 the British Council selected him as a member of the first-ever exchange programme with the Soviet Union. During his year at Moscow University persecution of religion recommenced under Nikita Khrushchev. After ordination in the Church of England, he founded the Keston College in 1969, aiming to institute systematic study of all aspects of church–state relations in the Soviet Union, which highlighted the revival of religion in Russia. He is author of about a dozen books. In 1984 he received the Templeton Prize for Progress in Religion. He became an honorary canon of Rochester in 1989, and in 1996 the Archbishop of Canterbury awarded him a Lambeth Doctorate of Divinity. The archive of Keston College is now at Baylor University, Texas: the 'Michael Bourdeaux Keston Center'.

NICHOLAS BROWN

Nick grew up in Dorset, where he sang in and then played the organ at a parish church, which maintained a weekly choral evensong. After studying music at Royal Holloway University of London he studied the effect of the Reformation on music in parish churches alongside work as a teacher and church musician. Following an excursion that saw him running a railway company he returned to study theology prior to ordination. Since ordination he has undertaken a curacy in Wiltshire and is now Team Rector of a market town in Lincolnshire, which continues to support regular choral music in the liturgy, as well as serving as Rural Dean of a rural area on the east coast. Having recently completed an MA exploring music and theology in the Anglican tradition, he is continuing this work with further research through Durham University.

CHRISTOPHER CAMPLING

Christopher Campling was born in 1925 and educated at Lancing College and, after a spell in the Navy, St Edmund Hall, Oxford. He was ordained in

1952 and began his career with a curacy in Basingstoke, after which he was a Minor Canon at Ely Cathedral and Chaplain to the King's School, Ely. He was appointed Chaplain of his old school in Lancing and was later Vicar then Rural Dean of Pershore, Worcestershire. He was appointed Archdeacon of Dudley in 1975, a post he held jointly with his role as director of education for the Anglican Diocese of Worcester and priest-in-charge of St Augustine's Church, Dodderhill, Droitwich. Then, in 1984, he was appointed Dean of Ripon. He is author of *Food of Love*, a book about music and faith. He is now retired and living in Worthing. He continues to preach and lecture occasionally.

QUINTON DEELEY

Dr Deeley is Senior Lecturer in Social Behaviour and Neurodevelopment at the Institute of Psychiatry, Psychology, and Neuroscience (IOPPN), King's College London. He is also Consultant Neuropsychiatrist in the National Autism Unit and Neuropsychiatry Brain Injury Clinic at the Maudsley and Bethlem Hospitals. Dr Deeley chairs the Maudsley Philosophy Group, and Social and Cultural Neuroscience Group at the IOPPN. Dr Deeley has researched the relations between culture, cognition and brain function since his qualifications in Theology and Religious Studies from Cambridge University, and later medicine at Guys and St Thomas' Medical School, London, and psychiatry at the Maudsley and Bethlem Hospitals. Dr Deeley brings cognitive neuroscience research methods into dialogue with humanities scholarship to improve understanding of religious cognition, experience and behaviour. Current research topics include researching voice hearing in patient groups and cultural practitioners, and how cognitive and brain processes involved in the formation of beliefs and experiences can be influenced by cultural practices such as ritual.

BALÁZS DÉRI

Balázs Déri is Head of the Department of Latin at Eötvös Loránd University of Sciences. His research interests include classical philology (Christian Poetry, especially Prudentius); medieval Latin philology (Lexicography, the Bible in Medieval Latin Literature, St Gerard Bishop of Csanád); musicology and liturgy (Gregorian Chant, Oriental [Coptic, Syriac], Byzantine [Serbian], Jewish Liturgical Music and Liturgy); and Catalan literature (R. Llull, A. March, Modern Catalan Literature). He has won the Lénárt Sándor-Prize (1999) of the Hungarian Society for the Study of the Ancient World (Ókortudományi Társaság); Niveau-Prize of the Hungarian Radio (Magyar Rádió) (1999); Our

Mother Tongue-Prize (Édes Anyanyelvünk-díj) of the Ministry of the National Cultural Heritage, II. degree for Poetry (for the volume *Kézírás*, 2004); and the Ürményi József-Prize for education awarded by Eötvös Loránd University, Budapest, Faculty of Humanities (2012).

ROBIN DUNBAR

Robin Dunbar gained his MA from the University of Oxford and PhD from Bristol University. He is currently Professor of Evolutionary Psychology at the University of Oxford, and an emeritus Fellow of Magdalen College. He has held Research Fellowships and Professorial Chairs in Psychology, Biology and Anthropology at the University of Cambridge, Stockholm University, University College London and the University of Liverpool. He is an elected Fellow of the British Academy, and was co-Director of the British Academy's Centenary Research Project. His principal research interests focus on the evolution of sociality in mammals (with particular reference to ungulates, primates and humans). He is best known for the social brain hypothesis, the gossip theory of language evolution and Dunbar's Number (the limit on the number of relationships that we can manage). His current project focuses on the mechanisms of social cohesion, and uses a range of approaches from comparative analysis and cognitive experiments to neuroimaging to explore the mechanisms that allow humans to create large-scale communities. His popular science books include *The Trouble with Science*; *Grooming, Gossip and the Evolution of Language*; *The Human Story*; *How Many Friends Does One Person Need? Dunbar's Number and Other Evolutionary Quirks*; *The Science of Love and Betrayal*; and *Human Evolution*.

ELISABETH DUTTON

Elisabeth Dutton is Professor of Medieval English at the University of Fribourg, Switzerland. She has published widely on medieval religious writings, especially Julian of Norwich, and on early English theatre. Her research on drama is informed by her work as a theatre director. She heads the Early Drama at Oxford project, which examines plays written and performed in Oxford colleges between 1485 and 1642, and, with Olivia Robinson and Matthew Cheung-Salisbury, the Medieval Convent Drama project, exploring plays written and performed by nuns in England, France and the Low Countries. She also leads the Multilingual Shakespeare project at the University of Fribourg: the project experiments with translation which reflects the multilingual Swiss environment to create productions of a 'Swiss Shakespeare'.

SHANIKA RANASINGHE

Shanika Ranasinghe is a 30-year-old PhD music student based in London. Born into a Sinhalese Roman Catholic family, she attended a convent school in West London (2000–7) before reading music at Worcester College, University of Oxford (2007–10). In her final year at Oxford, she experienced life-changing transformations to her health and, subsequently, her faith. Though she remains a practising Roman Catholic, she is unable to attend church due to severe ongoing mental health issues; instead, she expresses and experiences her faith through music and art, as well as reading and writing about female mystics. She is a member of the Student Christian Movement and writes occasional blog posts for them.

FIROOZEH WILLANS

Firoozeh Willans is a qualified Integrative Counsellor and a member of the Association of Christian Counsellors. She attended International schools in many different, and often politically sensitive, countries before going to boarding school. After a degree in French, she became a Montessori teacher and then Primary school teacher. Her strengths lay in working with the more vulnerable pupils. This led her to pursue counselling. She is holistic in her outlook and interested in all aspects of emotional, physical, psychological and spiritual life. She is involved with CRUSE, a national bereavement charity, and youth counselling.

PREFACE

In 2014 I published *Sacred Music in Secular Society*. It was a kind of therapy for me. Having worked for nearly two decades as a professional singer with choirs such as The Sixteen, Polyphony, The Gabrieli Consort, The Tallis Scholars and St Paul's Cathedral Choir, I had spent the first part of my working life performing high-quality sacred music in both liturgical and non-liturgical settings. When I retired from my full-time singing career to become a priest, chaplain and writer, I had the opportunity to reflect upon the state of sacred music in secular Western Europe, and so I undertook a series of interviews with renowned professional composers, performers, theologians and philosophers to try to understand the relationship between faith, music and secularism in the modern world. There have been many helpful reviews of that work. One positive criticism that I have taken on board is that the book gave no voice to the non-professional listener: someone who listens to sacred music in a concert, in a church service or through any of the varied digital media available. This work seeks to address that omission by interviewing people who have a broad range of interests in three main categories: the arts, the human mind and society, and religious belief, including atheists, church laity (both Protestant and Catholic) and clergy. The chosen interviewees are not representative of Western society or any particular section of it and, indeed, I do not promise a sociological approach, either qualitatively or quantitatively, to analysing data arising from the talks. However, I hope that their musical, artistic, psychological and neurological, as well as theological, interests, however oblique, may be of interest to anyone concerned with the nature of faith and its relationship, in the post-modern West, to music.

Moreover, since the publication of *Sacred Music in Secular Society* the notion of post-secularism has been more and more at the forefront of my thoughts. Through the interviews with a variety of writers, artists, scientists, historians, atheists, church laity and clergy, it became clear to me that the term post-secular (a term explained in the introduction below) was a more accurate description of the relationship between faith, religion, spirituality, agnosticism and atheism in the West today. I explore this phenomenon within the context of wider reflections on natural, implicit and trans-rational theologies, apophaticism and current scholarship relating theology and music by Jeremy Begbie, David Brown, Gavin Hopps, June Boyce-Tillman,

Anthony Monti, Frank Burch Brown and many others. In this work I have also, very deliberately, included the word 'faith' in the title, by which I mean, for the purposes of this book, Christian faith. I hope it will soon be clear that by faith I do not just mean Christian belief. The temporal, linear, relational, communal process of experiencing faith is closely related, I hope to show, to music, but not necessarily so closely akin to the presumed certainties of propositional belief. I hope you enjoy this sequel to *Sacred Music* and that it offers hope for the place of faith and music in today's post-secular Western world.

ACKNOWLEDGEMENTS

I would like to thank all those who have helped and encouraged the completion of this book, especially those who kindly gave their time by agreeing to be interviewed: Nick Baines, Ronald Blythe, Janet Boulton, Michael Bourdeaux, Nicholas Brown, Christopher Campling, Quinton Deeley, Balázs Déri, Robin Dunbar, Elisabeth Dutton, Shanika Ranasinghe and Firoozeh Willans. I am immensely grateful to them for their insights and wisdom, without which this book would have been impossible. As I explain in the introduction, they have been chosen not as sociological guinea pigs but because each one has experience of and/or expertise in exploring the nature of music's relationship with faith, either as believers, agnostics or atheists, but all with an eye to religious, theological and ontological questioning.

My sincere appreciation goes to Worcester and Magdalen colleges in Oxford, where the research allowance, both financial and temporal, has allowed me to complete this work while continuing my work in those places as Chaplain and Dean of Divinity respectively. Thank you to those who completed the 'Experience of Music' survey and to those who have helped me by reading extracts from my book and offering criticism and advice, including Spencer Klavan, Kathryn King, James Crockford, Emma Pennington, Matthew Cheung-Salisbury and Carol Harrison. I am deeply grateful to Emily DiDodo and Geoffrey Pascoe for transcribing the interview material, which has saved me an enormous amount of time. I am very grateful to Joan Jones for her painstaking proofreading, editing and sound advice, and to Michael Middeke and Megan Milan, my editors at Boydell and Brewer, for all their support and help, as well as the anonymous peer-reviewers who offered such helpful guidance on the proposal. Their work has assisted me immeasurably and any mistakes that remain are entirely my own.

As with any project I undertake, it would get nowhere without the love, support and faith of Emma, and the constantly stimulating company of our children, Thomas and Katie. During the writing of this work I have found that walks in the Oxfordshire countryside with Flossy the dog have helped me think things through, often in conversation with Emma. Our new cat, Smudge, has taken over the role of chief walker across the computer keys, and may Amy rest in peace.

Lastly, I would like to thank all those who, whether religious believers, agnostics or fervent atheists, have shared in the faith process by joining me in sharing the experience of music and its power to transform and heal our lives.

INTRODUCTION: FAITH, BELIEF AND POST-SECULARISM

> Faith is love, and therefore it creates poetry and music. Faith is joy, and therefore it creates beauty. Cathedrals are not medieval monuments but living buildings where we feel 'at home': we find God and we meet others. Neither is great music – Gregorian chant, or Bach, or Mozart – a thing of the past, for it lives in the vitality of the liturgy and our faith. If faith is alive, Christian culture does not become 'past' but remains living and present. And if faith is alive, today too we can answer the enduring imperative of the Psalms: 'Sing to Him a new song.'[1]

Listen. You are about to eavesdrop on some fascinating, thoughtful and honest conversations about people's journey of faith, whether Christian believers or not, and how music has played an important part in that journey. Many of the people interviewed for this book have encountered the darkness of life and lived with it through their Christian faith – the 'conflict, drama, suffering, on fallen-ness' of humanity, as Michael Symmons Roberts puts it.[2] Some of the voices you will hear are from those who engage with the counter-cultural project of the Christian faith today and who find, through being bound to the sacrificial 'tension, that struggle, that completeness in the midst of incompleteness.'[3] Others are not Christian but nevertheless find immense meaning and mystery in music. Intended as a companion volume to *Sacred Music in Secular Society*, which focused on composers, performers, philosophers and theologians and their relationship to music and Christianity, this book is centred on those who, by and large, are not professional musicians, philosophers or theologians, but who find that music and faith are bound up with each other and with their own lives. Very often, as the interviews reveal, the results of this 'binding' are transformative, whether it be in outpourings of artistic expression of another kind, or greater involvement with issues of social justice, or becoming ordained to serve within the Church. Even those interviewed who do not have a Christian faith find that sacred music has a transformative effect on the mind and the body and even, to use a word deliberately employed by Richard Dawkins, the 'soul.'[4]

It is important to stress that this book is not a work of sociology, neither is it academically or personally objective. It is written from a perspective of faith, and it is for those who either have faith of some kind or are interested in the phenomenon of faith. It is also borne out of a double vocation to music and ordained ministry. As a professional singer for two decades I sang for concert audiences and made many recordings with The Sixteen, Polyphony, the Gabrieli Consort, The Tallis Scholars and others. I also sang in countless religious services with St Paul's Cathedral Choir, among other church, cathedral and chapel choirs. Following my ordination and subsequent ministry in the Church and College Chaplaincy, I have a deep personal interest in both music and faith.

At the heart of the conversations in this book is a simple question: how do we know, encounter and experience the divine? I will reveal a little more about the interviews and interviewees at the end of this introduction, but first I wish to reflect upon how the relationship between aesthetic experience and faith has developed and changed over the centuries and where we might be now.

AESTHETICS AND FAITH

In late medieval Europe aesthetic experience, and music in particular, was a gateway to the numinous and transcendent: 'Medievals ... tended to look upon nature as a reflection of the transcendent world ... they possessed a sensibility capable of fresh and vivid responses to the natural world, including its aesthetic qualities.'[5] There are many accounts of how music could 'precipitate a supernatural happening' or be 'conjuration, exorcism and miraculous cure', among other positive effects.[6] There was a sense that music possessed a powerful efficacy that operated beyond itself. Late medieval writers on music recognised what has been described today as the 'extravagance' in the generosity of God's creation, which flows out through the world, through nature and the arts, that allowed people to be 'open to the divine'. Indeed, the root of this word 'extravagance' is medieval itself: *extra vagari*, meaning 'wayward, wandering and straying outside limits'.[7] No art form arguably was, and is, better for 'spiritual expression and religious resonance' despite, or rather because of, its non-verbal essence.[8] Nothing better conveys religious meaning and 'communicates to our senses and to our reflection what little we can grasp of the naked wonder of life'.[9]

However, Renaissance humanists' criticisms of Church musicians partially contributed to a renewed emphasis on the predominantly literary, verbal, era where the revelation of God through the Word (*logos*) of Christ as revealed in the Scriptures dominated over medieval, devotional, aesthetic religious expressions. This 'logocentric' rationalist route to knowledge has characterised Reformation thought and reformed theology ever since. But in the modern secularised and post-secular West, increasing levels of biblical and religious illiteracy along with decline in membership of institutional religions has seen a concurrent increase in the appetite for aesthetic religious, or quasi-religious, experiences, where 'spirituality becomes process, with notions of God replaced by notions of being-ness'.[10] In this book we will explore how this search for the numinous, mystical and transcendent, through musical aesthetics, has parallels with pre-Reformation devotional religion and ask what the implications are for the future of institutional Christian religion in the West.

As Giles Fraser has written, 'The best theologians are musicians. And Christianity is always better sung than said. To the extent that all religion exists to make raids into what is unsayable, the musicians penetrate further than most.' Moreover, 'It's not propositional. It's a cry from the depths of his [the musician's] being. Longing, joy, hope, hopelessness, the call for justice – all these get expressed by religious music in ways that religious words can only partially capture ... It is in the hands of such musicians that the church is at its most emotionally compelling.'[11]

With the twentieth-century wane in membership of institutional religion in Western Europe, increased secularisation and decline in biblical literacy,[12] artistic endeavour, whether in visual art, poetry or music, has developed a new vocabulary, one step removed from the word-centred legacy of Reformation Europe and its cultural inheritors, especially when seeking to express spirituality, for 'wordlessness is allied to music'.[13] I will argue that the 'explicit theology' of the Word (creeds, biblical teaching, articles of religion, doctrine and tradition) can be deeply and richly nourished by an 'implicit theology' that attends not so much to the rationality of our cognitive belief, but to the less explicit, more opaque and numinous area of our relational faith – relational to the divine, to the beauty of the world around us and to each other.[14] As Martyn Percy has written: 'Music moves us; it is not merely an accompaniment to faith, but rather, an actual expression of it.'[15]

But before we think about faith, I want to begin with a story: a human story. A very wise theologian and a great man, Professor John Bowker, once came to spend some time back at his old college, Worcester College in Oxford, at my invitation, when I was Chaplain there. During his stay I am afraid that, despite his age and failing eyesight, I put him to work! He preached for Remembrance Sunday in Chapel, he gave a talk at a dinner I had arranged, and he agreed to talk to a group of students at my weekly discussion group. At the latter event,

I remember one phrase that has never left me. He said, 'If you want to know the God story, start with the human story.' He went on to explain a little of what he meant with his own tale – 'a tale of woe' as Mr Rochester would have it[16] – of an unhappy childhood and a subsequent inability to accept love in adult life. However, the persistent love of one individual, no matter how many times he pushed that love away, eventually transformed his existence as he began to find that he was accepted and loved, just as he was. That person happened to be the wonderful Margaret, an excellent ecclesiastical historian, who has now been John's wife for many years. But in a sense, the encounter, the relationship, the experience of being loved, which transformed one man's spirit, could have been with anybody.

The point, for me, was not only that God's love is 'like' human love but magnified in a way that is beyond our knowing and our comprehension; not only that human love reflects divine love, from which we can extrapolate a vision of God's love from an example and episode of human love that makes us marvel at the generosity, persistence and unconditionality of God's love; not only that the story has implications for how we might perceive the final judgement of God upon us, if we believe in such a thing, not in terms of wrathful punishment but loving forgiveness. No. What struck me at the time, and has stayed with me all these years is that, in the human story that we inhabit, the story we live every minute of every day, we have the opportunity to find a power greater than ourselves – something that some call spirituality, some call love, some call God – at almost every moment of relationship, encounter and experience. Our human story is one that we might believe was also shared by God, in the form of Christ, limited like us to time and space and the messy complexity of everyday relationships. But either way the story brought me back to the ideas of relationship, encounter and experience as the ways in which, through other people and the world around us, we might glimpse the divine.

The arts, and music in particular, offer one important way into finding a transcendent (a word explored below)[17] path which can take our experience of the world and help us to perceive the reality and mystical truth of something greater beyond ourselves. In relationships we may perceive a spark of divinity, or spirit, and in art we might take that experience one stage further and intuit a deep knowledge of the spiritual life that cannot be found by reasoned argument or deductive thinking. This is not to say that numinous emotionalism, as it were, is all we need for Christian salvation or atonement for instance, where doctrine is inevitably important, but that music and the arts can help us encounter theological truths at the deepest level of our human experience, often beyond cerebral knowledge. In this introduction I want to explore this further with some brief reflections on music's place in natural and apophatic theology. But first I want to emphasise the importance of community.

COMMUNITY AND THE DIVINE

We live in a world where community is more important than ever. In the United Kingdom since the 1980s there has been an increasingly individualist and consumerist approach to our wider communities which has led to increased poverty and a wider gap between the very rich and the very poor, for instance. But we are now moving into what is becoming labelled as a post-secular age, where individualism is giving way to a greater search for relationship and belonging. As Ian Mobsby writes:

> Our post-Reformation, post-Enlightenment inheritance is the cult of the individual, and in short we desire community but often have no idea how to seek it. As a result, our culture has become less humane. The Church has not escaped the scourge of rampant individualism. Some churches operate like depersonalized corporate communities, emphasizing the 'business' of conversion; others operate like imperialistic establishments ... Both forms of individualism gravely impoverish the quality of our spiritual communities.[18]

Post-secularism has grown in the rich soil of those who seek food for their spiritual lives and yet do not, for whatever reason, identify with any institutional religion. The secularisation of the past few decades has been described as 'the process of reducing religious, spiritual and philosophical belief in general society'. This pruning has allowed new post-secular shoots to emerge in 'a time when the forces of secularization have not only stopped, but where social forces have driven a renewed appreciation for the place of spirituality in general society'.[19] Holistic spirituality, a concept that includes 'the return to the importance of the subjective and experiential over the rational'; 'a return to the appreciation of the sacred and enchantment of life'; 'and a world view informed by postmodern sensibilities',[20] is flourishing while Sunday church attendance declines. Thus arises the phenomenon that a growing number of people want to label themselves as 'spiritual but not religious'. Nancy Ammerman has labelled such people as extra-theistic. Such people may be those who have never been to church; they might be those who have stopped attending church but who still seek meaning, joy and the fulfilment of their humanity, in nature and beauty, while seeking somehow to explain the mystery of existence.[21]

THE ARTS AND WAYS OF KNOWING

Ian Mobsby was brought up in a family rich in atheism and rationalism where knowledge was considered as the acts of reasoned argument concerning facts and deductive reasoning.[22] But he also found that there was a contradiction in that the family, who were also extremely artistic, who lived music and the arts, ironically ignored the arts as a type of intuitive knowledge.[23] Although the music and arts were enjoyed, the opportunity for finding in them an intuitive path towards an implicit knowledge of something beyond the materialistic was sadly lost.

It is this intuitive way of knowing that likewise touches myself and many others in today's post-secular world. It is through experience, encounter and relationship that knowledge of a deeper reality of self and other emerges, perhaps through music and the arts, perhaps through nature and the world around us, perhaps through relationships with people.[24] Ian Mobsby found that, through contemplation of art, he found something deeper and greater:

> Things were different for me: the arts touched my emotions and a deeper sense of self, and enabled me to see a legitimate place for spirituality; and from an early age my experience of and delight in the world enabled me to transcend my family's belief in atheism. These glimpses of the Divine, or rather 'knowing through artistic experiences', began with my sitting in our back garden encountering nature. My mother tells me that as a child I would sit for hours listening to birdsong and the sound of bees and insects, smelling flowers and trees, and sensing the warmth of the sun. Looking back I am sure that I encountered the Divine first through nature.[25]

Ian's experience reminds me of those powerful words by Rowan Williams concerning listening: 'To listen seriously is to learn what it means to live with and before God.'[26] Mobsby's experience of listening to nature, contemplating it, sensing its intense music at once gave him both a deep encounter with himself and the world around him.[27] He found a similar spiritual revelation through art:

> My next important memory, and my first real spiritual experience, was contemplating the Chagall stained-glass window in Chichester Cathedral ... it was full of mystery, beauty and awe. Chagall's window was an overpowering experience of bright colours and symbolism, which deeply moved me.[28]

Such experiences, for Mobsby, open up significant questions concerning epistemology, namely, 'How do we know what we know?' Since the Reformation and Enlightenment, the idea of knowledge in the Western world has been dominated by reason and argument, at the expense of knowing through experience, contemplation or intuition.[29] If we are to explore the relationship between music and faith we must acknowledge trans-rational ways of knowing, not only through music but other artistic and imaginative means, such as literature and storytelling. One of the greatest examples of trans-rational, imaginative storytelling is the Bible, so much of which was meant to be heard aurally, told aloud and passed on from one generation to the next through an oral tradition.[30] It is perhaps ironic, therefore, that post-Reformation exegesis has produced a tendency to explain the Bible so often in rational terms, as a book of facts to be learned, when so much of the Bible is poetic, 'imaginative experiential encounter'.[31] Great examples of this are the parables of Jesus, who answers rationalist questions with trans-rational stories:

> Parables subvert [the] desire to make faith simple and understandable. They do not offer the reader clarity, for they refuse to be captured in the net of a single interpretation and instead demand our eternal return to their words ... A parable does not primarily provide information about our world. Rather, if we allow it to do its work within us, it will change our world.[32]

The role of rational language, especially the logocentric emphasis of post-Reformation modernity, has brought with it a tendency to objectify God through language, leading, in some cases, to a dangerous fundamentalism.[33] But as Peter Rollins reminds us, 'God's revelation is always surrounded in mystery.'[34]

Marie McCarthy has asserted that access to this mysterious revelation, especially in the postmodern era, requires contemplative awareness:

> Awareness as a discipline opens us to levels of reality not immediately apparent. It enables us to see ourselves, our circumstances, our world without illusion. The discipline of awareness involves deep listening, which is marked by waiting, attending, and presence. We must sit in the stillness, wait, and listen deeply.[35]

For McCarthy, listening involves being silent. All deep listening eventually leads to silence. The Welsh poet and priest R.S. Thomas expressed this beautifully in his poem *A.D.*:

> But the silence in the mind
> is when we live best, within
> listening distance of the silence we call God.
>
> It is a presence, then,
> whose margins are our margins;
> that calls us out over our own fathoms.

But, as the composer John Cage, famous for his piece *4'33"* (*Four Minutes, Thirty-Three Seconds*, originally entitled *Silent Prayer*) wrote, 'Silence is all of the sound we don't intend. There is no such thing as absolute silence. Therefore silence may very well include sounds and more and more in the twentieth century does. The sound of jet planes, of sirens, et cetera.'[36] Silence has revelatory significance if we acknowledge the importance of listening to its sounds and its music. Revelation, whether through the sound of silence or composed music, is an important issue in our discussion of aesthetic experience, belief and the divine, and so I shall explore music's revelatory power in a little more detail now.

MUSIC AS REVELATION

In his most recent work, the pre-eminent scholar in music and theology Jeremy Begbie expresses his suspicion of those who argue that encounter with the divine happens where the limits of our language and verbal understanding end, especially scriptural language, wisdom and doctrine. Writing from a firmly reformed tradition, he asserts that:

> In a proper eagerness to make common cause with those of little or no explicit faith, we have too frequently lost a sense of the disturbing particularities and disruptive power of the vistas presented in the Old and New Testaments.[37]

But where does this leave God's ineffability, unknowability and transcendence? Begbie argues that God is indeed ineffable, but that language nevertheless remains at the heart of God for, as the New Testament demonstrates, 'human speech, embedded in the life of a community and culture, has been pulled into the momentum of God's rescue, assumed into the heart of the divine drama of liberation.'[38] In other words, it is in speech that God reveals himself, both as divine *logos*, the eternal Word of God with us, and in the particular incarnation and ministry of Jesus Christ. In Begbie's analysis, 'the reconciling self-communication of God' does not do away with the need for language, but we must also acknowledge that our human eloquence cannot be identified with nor enclose the divine.[39]

However, for David Brown, Begbie's approach is too restrictive and constraining because he sets limits on the ways in which God may be reached through music, and that composers whose work is found to be doctrinally or philosophically suspect by Begbie's standards are then inferior communicators of divine experience through music. The reason for this constraint, says Brown, is because Begbie is part of the Reformation 'legacy of Trinitarian doctrinal logocentricism, which leaves no place for the more experiential encounters with the divine through the natural world.'[40] For Brown:

> Begbie constrains our potential encounter with the divine through the God-given gift of music, by his insistence upon logocentric doctrinal scrutiny in order to assess its Trinitarian legitimacy.[41]

I shall return to this debate as we journey through the book and especially in the methodology and conclusion, because it represents an issue at the heart of scholarship concerning music and divine revelation today.[42] However, in order to delve deeper into whether music can be a vehicle for a devotional, spiritual or numinous experience for those who cannot necessarily assent to orthodox doctrinal propositions, and if so how, I suggest that we consider what 'faith,' especially in the context of musical encounter, might be. Thus, a brief definition of terms is important.

DEFINITIONS: MUSIC AND FAITH

For the purposes of this book, music is defined as broadly as possible, such as 'the art and science of combining vocal or instrumental sounds or tones in varying melody, harmony, rhythm, and timbre, especially so as to form structurally complete and emotionally expressive compositions.'[43] As David Aldridge has written, it is perhaps better to explain that we shall be exploring 'music*s*'. The notion of one universal music, or some high concept of Music, is not applicable here.'[44] Specifically I am concerned with Western Christian classical sacred music and with other Western worship music, such as contemporary worship bands, hymns, songs and ballads, as well as some secular popular music. I am not concerned in this volume with Eastern religions or music. I have previously explored the definition and nature of sacred music and will not rehearse the argument again here.[45]

With regard to 'faith,' we have to start with New Testament Greek and the word πίστις (*pistis*), which can mean either faith, trust or belief. The English word 'belief' often denotes a propositional aspect of assent to a particular idea or doctrine; for instance, 'I believe in Angels.' Emile Durkheim described religion as a 'unified system of beliefs relative to sacred things, that is to say, things set apart and forbidden.'[46] But, as Ed Sanders has persuasively written, the word 'faith' has a closer connection to 'belonging' rather than 'believing':[47]

> 'Faith' best translates [Saint] Paul's *pistis*, since 'belief' often connotes 'opinion', which is far from what Paul meant. But English has no verb which corresponds to 'faith', and so for Paul's verb *pisteuein*, English translators have to use 'believe' ... The resulting problems of translation can readily be exemplified. In Gal. 3: 6–7 Paul, quoting Gen. 15:6, wrote this (according to the RSV):
>
> Thus Abraham '*believed* God, and it was reckoned to him as *righteousness*'. So you see that it is people of *faith* who are the sons of Abraham. And the scripture, foreseeing that God would *justify* the Gentiles by *faith*, preached the gospel beforehand to Abraham. Paul did not actually change terms from 'believe' to 'faith' or from 'righteousness' to 'justify'. With regard to the first set, he used the verb *pisteuein* ('believe') when quoting Genesis to prove that people of *pistis* ('faith') are 'justified'.[48]

While Sanders may be going too far to say that 'opinion ... is far from what Paul meant', the inability of the English language to express a verb 'to faith' and the difference between that concept and the word 'believe' will become an important distinction as this book develops, as will a concept of music's ability to help us be transported beyond the realm of words, ideas and propositions towards the numinous, transcendent and unknowable divine.

Moreover, when we begin to examine further how the verb πίστεύω (I believe/trust) is employed in the New Testament, we find an even more nuanced picture. One example is in the Gospel of John, chapter fourteen. Verse one reads 'πιστεύετε εἰς τὸν Θεόν, καὶ εἰς ἐμὲ πιστεύετε (Put your trust/belief in God, and put your trust/belief in me)'. Then in verse ten, we have 'οὐ πιστεύεις ὅτι ἐγὼ ἐν τῷ πατρί (don't you believe that I am in the father?)'. While verse eleven reads 'πιστεύετέ μοι (believe (in) me)'. Each of these uses of the word πίστις (*pistis*) suggests a slightly different sort of relationship.[49] Likewise, in modern English the statement 'I believe you' is propositional, whereas 'I trust you' is relational, but the phrase 'I believe *in* you' can become less propositional, more relational and closer to the notion of trust or reliance that might be best expressed by a verb 'to faith', if such a verb existed.

Thus, one of the most important words in the Bible and in the history of the Judeo-Christian tradition, πίστις, is a word with many types of meaning, but held together in one unitary state of relationship, which can be looked at in multiple dimensions and from multiple viewpoints. To use Spencer Klavan's image, 'It's like we're turning a prism this way and that, refracting the light into different wavelengths, but the light remains one unified thing.' The unitary concept of πίστις has been divided into smaller concepts like faith, trust and belief in English, whereas the biblical Greek expresses a closer association between actions and relationships in one word. Interestingly, in the other biblical language, Hebrew, a word might often be either a verb or a noun: the same three-letter root can be altered to become a verb or a noun depending on which vowels are added to it. 'For instance, the verb אָמַן (*aman* – Abraham's action of trusting in Genesis) could just as easily be turned into a noun describing the relationship he has with God.' Moreover, there are other words that can be formed from the אָמַן root. One is a noun meaning 'faithfulness' or 'truth,' which is אֹמֶן (*omen*). Another is אָמֵן, which is pronounced *amen*, from which we derive the word 'amen' with the sense of 'yes indeed' or 'it is so,' but also 'so be it' or 'in this I trust.'[50]

But English and the Romance languages have been through a process of taking a word with a unitary concept, such as πίστις, and dividing it into different meanings. Owen Barfield, writing in 1928, perceived that there are many examples of words (in Biblical Greek for instance) with complex meanings and definitions unified within a single word. English translations of such words cannot be achieved by a single English word, but must be divided into more than one, to reflect the 'prism'-like nature of the original:

> Thus, even as recently as the date of composition of the Fourth Gospel (John, ch. 3, v and viii) we can hear in the Greek πνεῦμα [*pneuma*] an echo of just such an old, concrete, *undivided* meaning. This meaning (and therefore, in this case, practically the whole sense of the passage) is lost in the inevitable double English rendering of *spirit* (v) and *wind* (viii).[51]

If the word πνεῦμα has a double or even triple meaning (if we include the translation 'breath' as well), then πίστις also has at least a triple meaning for us today. Barfield laments the loss of this multi-layered sense of experience and relationship alongside the material, physical world, all contained within a single word. The original use of words like πνεῦμα and πίστις possessed a unity that has been lost. Now we have to search in order to find that sense of relationship that can only come when we recover the original unity between the different conceptual parts of the word that might now seem disparate to us, leaving us with an impoverished language which only the poets can restore:

> The language of primitive men reports them as direct perceptual experience. The speaker has perceived a unity, and is not therefore himself conscious of *relation*. But we, in the development of consciousness, have lost the power to see this one as one. Our sophistication has cost us an eye; and now it is the language of poets, in so far as they create true metaphors, which must *restore* this unity conceptually, after it has been lost from perception.[52]

The poet, for Barfield, has the ability to restore this lost element of meaning, because it engages the realm of imagination.[53] The musician, I argue, can also play an important part of this restoration project for, using its own non-verbal means of communication, music helps us to see the light shining through the prism of this one small word πίστις, where trust, belief, relationship, experience and encounter all combine. The world of faith, therefore, is far more rich and complex than some may suppose. We may assent to certain Christian propositions of doctrine, but when we meet as a body of people, we act out of trust in others and God; we contribute to the whole; we relate, we receive; we embody our faith through liturgy, prayer, singing, worship, listening, encountering. To lose any of these elements diminishes what we mean by a life of 'faith.' Music, I suggest, is often at the heart of a more holistic approach to faith. One of the activities we almost always do as Christians is sing and listen to music; music sustains and informs the life of faithful Christian community.

Andrew Brown and Linda Woodhead have acknowledged the importance of non-verbal actions in religion: 'In religious rituals, the essential nature of a religion is enacted in ways that cannot be contained in words.'[54] Of the three elements of religion they suggest (practice, ritual and belief), theological belief is perhaps the least important and is subservient to action:

> Theology ... is how you explain what you are doing, both to yourself and others. So it is dependent on what you actually do. This is a tremendously obvious insight which some forms of Christianity – and all forms of journalism – try more or less consciously to ignore. Pierre Bourdieu called it the 'scholastic fallacy' – the mistake which those who live in their heads make of assuming that everyone else does the same.[55]

These elements of practice, ritual and theology depend on each other, but are also independent: 'What matters most is to remember that practice is not just the outworking of theory, but has its own logic.'[56]

My working definition of faith, therefore, is also rooted in religious practice, ritual, community and Western Christian society, with an emphasis upon an orthopraxy as well as orthodoxy. As Kwame Anthony Appiah wrote for the 2016 Radio 4 Reith Lectures:

> Every religion has three dimensions: there's what you do – call that practice. There's who you do it with – call that community, or fellowship. And, yes, there's a body of beliefs. The trouble is that we tend to emphasize the details of belief over the shared practices and the communities that buttress religious life. We all know the word 'orthodoxy': it comes from a Greek word that means correct belief. But there's a less familiar word, 'orthopraxy', which comes from another Greek word, πρᾶξις (*praxis*), which means action. So orthopraxy is a matter not of *believing* right but of *acting* right.[57]

Thus, along with Appiah, I resist the temptation to focus on a definition of faith that only refers to adherence to a particular doctrine. For the practice of faith through music, whether as a listener or performer, is just one aspect of the way doctrines are shaped by practice:

> The priests and the scholars often want to insist that doctrine, which they are, after all, the masters of, drives practice. So it's easy to ignore the reverse process, the way doctrine is often *driven* by practice – by forms of worship, familiar feelings, traditions of social regulation. Practice changes, of course, over time, sometimes slowly, sometimes swiftly. And changed practice can lead to changed belief.[58]

Thus, if we acknowledge that the actions, practices, experiences and relationships involved in communal Christianity are crucial elements to any definition of faith, then the concept of faith itself becomes much richer than a simple insistence upon intellectual assent to one particular doctrine or another. Moreover, just as practice changes over time, so do the doctrinal emphases of faith, along with music's relationship with faith and how it is employed both within and outside the context of Christian worship.

CURRENT TRENDS IN CHRISTIAN FAITH AND BELIEF

Two books published in 2018 encapsulate key aspects of, and sides of, the current debate, that is: a defence of the role of traditional orthodox Trinitarian theology in interpreting the arts, and a counterargument in defence of a wider interpretation of musical encounter with the divine through music that is not constrained by the limits of Trinitarian, or any other, doctrine.[59] The first argument centres on the contention that recent talk concerning the role of transcendence through the arts has become vague and has therefore lost the true meaning of the Christian Gospel, even if the talk has the best of motives.[60] Jeremy Begbie suggests that we have, as it were, been putting the cart before the horse. We have put music and the arts as the starting point for divine encounter when, in fact, our interpretation of artistic truth, goodness and beauty (the traditional attributes of transcendence) should come after the explicit knowledge of creeds, the Bible, Christian history and doctrine.[61]

The growing number of those who call themselves 'spiritual but not religious' (explored in the introduction above) find that, in our post-secular climate, music restores something that has been lost, as Boyce-Tillman and Morgan acknowledged.[62] Music, particularly communal music, can help restore a transcendental sense of awe, wonder and mystery. But Begbie is not concerned with these transcendentals. Rather, he advocates the 'transcendence of the God of Israel testified in Scripture and made known in Jesus Christ'.[63] Begbie acknowledges that when we employ the language of transcendence, with words such as 'beyond', 'awe' and so on, we start to form an ontology. He is aware that one can unwittingly adopt a philosophically suspect view of music and the divine that is incoherent with Christian theology. David Brown and Gavin Hopps, on the other hand trust such language and experience, as if it were philosophically neutral. Begbie critiques this presumed authority, particularly claims to 'sublimity'.

A concept of the 'sublime' through music emerged in the eighteenth and nineteenth centuries.[64] This sublimity, according to Schopenhauer and Wagner, is a characteristic of music's ungraspable nature, beyond conceptual thought. It has meaning that is beyond representation. Likewise, according to Vladimir Jankélévitch (1903–85), music takes us to something ineffable, something 'other', beyond the limits of our words.[65] But Begbie will have none of this, because if the 'other' is only something unknowable it is no more than an empty void.[66] Jankélévitch's idea does not allow for a true apophatic theology, where God is active in the 'reconciling self-communication' of Himself, but which we cannot 'enclose' in our language.[67] Authentic apophaticism comes from our participation in the risen life of Christ and is about God's uncontainability, but which is nevertheless 'propelled' towards us by 'ceaseless love'.[68] 'Positive transcendence', Begbie suggests, is 'the covenant of God in action, bringing the integrity of creation to its fulfilment', not what *might* lie behind but what has been particularly enacted.[69] Therefore, if we are to talk about musical transcendence we must be 'explicit and assess' the theology of the claim;[70] we should not talk about a deity in general but one who specifically acts and generously creates.[71] Brown argues that, in the uncontainability of music's representative and perceptive abilities, one can find a portal to an experience of the divine, and that indeed this is a sign of God's own action towards creation by means of excessive generosity. Whereas Begbie emphasises that music is built into creation's capabilities and purposes. For both, therefore, music is at the heart of God's activity towards us, and not simply a neutral accident of nature or opportunity of human conniving. At the heart of both is the idea of God working through, deliberately, the existence of music and musicking.[72]

However, in reviewing Begbie's latest book, David Brown is critical of Begbie's Trinitarian doctrinal constraints. Access to the divine through music need not be 'transcendent' at all, Brown argues. For instance, in the works of Bruckner or Messiaen there is immanence, timelessness, peace and joy. Brown points to the theological implications of Schleiermacher's 'feeling of absolute dependence' or Rudolph Otto's 'awe before a disturbing mystery.'[73] Begbie's rejection of 'partial encounters' with God through music, 'where only some aspect of the divine is revealed,' is, for Brown, a constraint of our potential encounter with the divine through the God-given gift of music, by his insistence upon logocentric doctrinal scrutiny in order to assess its Trinitarian legitimacy. While belief in the propositional doctrinal elements of religion is no longer the norm for many people in Western Society, and indeed the number of those attending Christian services has fallen overall, many still declare some faith in God or a higher power. Writing in 1994, at the height of secularism, Grace Davie related this to the phenomenon of 'belonging without believing,' in which people are connected with, say, the national Church in some sense, and attend for significant annual occasions, but do not assent to all the creedal propositions of the Church.[74] As Charles Taylor puts it, 'The Churches are seen, one might say, as a crucial element in the historical-cultural identity.'[75] Davie calls this 'Christian nominalism,' where a militant atheism is relatively rare compared to being a nominal Christian.[76] Another expression of this is Davie's notion of 'vicarious religion,' in which people are connected with the institution of the Church, but at a distance, 'which they nevertheless cherish.'[77] With regard to music, the arts and the aesthetic, the question for Taylor is, 'Can the experience [of beauty, art and nature] be made sense of in an ontology excluding the transcendent?'[78] For Taylor, the answer is 'yes,' but only in part. For him, the sense of awe and wonder that any secularist may feel when confronted with beauty in the world is intensified when put into the context of religious transcendence.[79] Taylor also rejects the notion that we are drawn towards the beauty of great art, be it a cathedral or the music of Bach, merely by its connection with our religious and cultural past.[80] For Taylor, the element of faith remains key to our appreciation of, and spiritual engagement with, sacred music.

However, in a recent work that argues in favour of faith over belief, Robert Ellis has claimed that Christian 'faith ... excludes belief in revelation.'[81] Revelation through that natural world (including the arts), through the scriptures and through individual inspiration are all flawed, he argues. Ellis is interested in 'what moves people helpfully towards positions that can be recognised, justified, applied and practised in experience – and thus avoids the dogmas that interfere with that process.'[82] All belief is naïve, he claims, and fragile and always leads to division.

Ellis's objection to Christian belief is that it is absolute: 'Faith is simply a term for the more embodied and emotive aspect of belief.'[83] As such he seems to reject belief but also wishes to define faith as one characteristic of belief. However, the Greek word *pistis* is a prism of a word through which one can perceive trust, confidence, relationship, as well as faith and belief. It is in the twenty-first-century West that a whole spectrum of atheisms, agnosticisms, beliefs, faiths and differing spiritualties coexist. Thus, a new term has emerged for our current age, which forms the context for this volume – post-secularism, to which I now turn.

POST-SECULARISM AND THE ARTS

In *A Secular Age*, Charles Taylor argued that, although the sixteenth-century reformers Luther and Calvin were right to be suspicious of late medieval spiritual superiority, they 'inadvertently helped to produce, via another stage of "reform", today's secular world by leading us towards a 'more homogenous world of conformity to a hedonic principle',[84] where our immediate pleasure becomes the greatest goal and self-sacrificial lives dedicated to religious observance and humility have been marginalised and discredited to the point of Western secularisation. As I have argued briefly above, the Reformation led to the marginalisation of medieval religious aesthetic experience, to be replaced by an emphasis upon word-centred propositional and doctrinal Christianity, to which one can assent or choose to reject. The story of modernity is a shift away from a Western culture in which 'it was virtually impossible not to believe in God' to one in which 'belief in God is no longer axiomatic. There are alternatives.'[85] Taylor sees the process of secularisation, from the seventeenth and eighteenth centuries onwards, as one of individualisation of faith, where personal commitment becomes paramount.[86] As June Boyce-Tillman has noted, the danger of personal religious doctrinal certainty in opposition to atheist secular certainty is that it leads to a dogmatism on both sides that inhibits human flourishing by extinguishing the imagination.[87] Or, as Rowan Williams has asserted, ideally religion should be able to supply the vocabulary and practices that enable people to face and absorb 'disruption without panic' and 'allow imagination to flourish.'[88]

But despite the title of his work, Taylor uses the phrase post-secular to describe the West, as Boyce-Tillman has noted:

> What Charles Taylor meant by the term is not entirely clear – whether he was pointing out that Western society never did fully secularize or that a new phenomenon is appearing. The term reflects a society which is having to come to terms with the peaceful co-existence of sacred and secular world views and a shift from seeing the religious simply as a remnant of an older world order.[89]

Reflecting on Taylor's work, Michael Warner has asserted that 'secularity is not just a net reduction in religious belief or practice ... but a change in the very conditions of belief.'[90] The conditions have been considered by the social-philosophical writing of Jürgen Habermas, the most influential commentator on post-secularism, who argues for a greater dialogue between secular and religious people, as he marks a widespread rise in public awareness of religion in wealthy European societies and many other countries.[91] This growth, Habermas argues, has been fostered by the connections between religion and global conflicts, in which the religious element cannot be ignored, such as the increase in religious voices on 'value-laden civil and political issues and controversies,'[92] and increased immigration 'from countries with traditional cultural backgrounds.'[93] In the light of these developments, secular ideologies have to be 're-evaluated.'[94] It is in this sense that dialogue can flourish between those who regard themselves as secular and those who regard themselves as religious. Neither can be ignored: these 'groups need fully to recognize the right of each other to participate in and contribute to the wider civic and political life.'[95] There needs to be a 'complementary learning process'[96] because the growth of secularisation does not bring about with it a complementary retreat of religion, but rather is 'a phenomenon that often occurs concurrently with counterdevelopments in postinstitutional forms of religion and spirituality.'[97]

One of the problems with these categories of 'religious' and 'secular,' therefore, is the lack of recognition of the many people who do not neatly fall into either category, and that faith is not the same as ideological and doctrinal belief. As Bryan Turner has argued, 'Philosophers tend ... to concentrate on religious beliefs rather than on practice and they almost never look at religious objects.'[98] Thus, we must not only acknowledge the importance of faith practice, as well as belief, but also that the term post-secular can enable us to comprehend the relevance of religion in public culture.[99] It is into the realm of practice, or praxis, that culture and the arts fit so well.

CULTURE, THE ARTS AND RELIGIOUS IDENTITY

The idea of 'culture', however, brings with it certain difficulties. Alan Thomson has noted that there is a tendency in the social sciences to assume we can define culture in theologically neutral terms. However, Richard Niebuhr suggested otherwise in his important work, *Christ and Culture,* in which he defined culture as the social life of humanity, the environment created by human beings in the areas of 'language, habits, ideas, beliefs, customs, social organization, inherited artefacts, technical processes, and values.'[100]

Niebuhr examines three main ways in which people have sought to be Christians, while relating to the culture surrounding them: opposition to culture (Christ against culture), agreement between Christ and culture (Christ of culture), and a combination of both these views (Christ above culture). Moreover, the work of Charles Taylor, John Milbank and Jacques Derrida suggests that a theologically neutral view of culture is not a tenable view of our current world. Rather, Thomson proposes 'a specifically theological engagement with the notion of culture that seeks to properly recognize and account for the religious character of this world.'[101] Or, to put it another way, 'Religion is, once more, haunting the imagination of the West.'[102] Thomson goes so far as to suggest that the Church 'embodies the exemplary form of human community ... [and] the consummate expression of human living, or what may be called culture.'[103] At the heart of Thomson's thesis is John Milbank's notion of poetic theology.[104] Thus, we approach God not only ontologically and epistemologically but also culturally, through the poetry of God's 'utterance and reciprocity.'[105] In this participation in the '*poesis*' or creative and open interactionality of God, two 'divine transcendentals' become crucial: word (*verbum* – denoting God's creative impulse and the human creative response) and gift (*donum* – human participation in gift exchange with the divine).[106] Artistic endeavour, therefore, is naturally bound up with the idea of response to God's free and creative *verbum* and *donum*.[107]

In this context, the arts and culture cannot be understood as separate from theology, Christology, theological anthropology and ecclesiology.[108]

While Christian believers and theologians may nod their heads at these encouraging ideas, it is nevertheless the case that the creative Christian vocabulary for engagement with the *poesis* of God may no longer be part of our postmodern culture, or at least not in the same traditional form of biblical knowledge. The poet Michael Symmons Roberts has noted:

> Writing in 1951 [David Jones] had seen the early stages of what Seamus Heaney has since called 'the big lightening, the emptying out' of our religious language, but even he may have been shocked by its pace. He saw the English language littered with dying signs and symbols, specifically the signs and symbols associated with our Judaeo-Christian past. The resultant impoverishment hasn't just affected poets, but readers too, and this has been borne out by the now common struggles of English teachers in schools and universities to provide the biblical and historical literacy necessary to make sense of Milton, Donne, Herbert, T.S. Eliot, and others.[109]

What David Jones meant by 'The Break,' as he called it, was the end of religious ideology in culture and the dispensability of the arts in an age of technology: 'The priest and the artist are already in the catacombs,' he wrote, 'but *separate* catacombs, for the technician divides to rule.'[110] But just as this 'emptying out' of our religious and biblical vocabulary took hold of Western Europe in the late twentieth century, so now there has been a revival of the search for the spiritual life, perhaps not as expressed in institutional religion but in other ways:

> The Enlightenment project was meant to see off religion by now, but instead, many sociologists argue that it is secularism that's in retreat. Worldwide, the case is clear-cut. Christianity and Islam are growing very rapidly throughout the developing world, and a recent report placed the numbers of atheists worldwide at 3 per cent and falling. In Western Europe, it's more complicated. Most of our churches are as empty as ever, but in the last few years, a number of philosophers and sociologists (led by German philosopher Jürgen Habermas) have coined the term 'post-secular' to describe our current condition. People in the West may not be returning to organized religion, but they seem to be losing faith in organized secularism too.[111]

Philip Blond, in his work *Post-Secular Philosophy*, suggests that 'secular minds are only now beginning to perceive that all is not as it should be, that what was promised to them – self-liberation through the limitation of the world to human faculties – might after all be a form of self-mutilation.'[112] For the post-secular believer, nevertheless, being a committed Christian is just as countercultural as ever – requiring, as it does, commitment to every aspect of the Christian story, the darkness as well as the light. This applies to Christian endeavours in all art forms and especially in music, as Symmons Roberts has rightly suggested:

> The Scottish composer James MacMillan – with whom I have been working as a librettist and collaborator for the last ten years – has written about the current dominance of 'spiritual' music on the classical scene. He is often grouped with John Tavener, Henryk Gorecki, and Arvo Pärt – all overtly Christian composers, all commissioned and performed by orchestras across the world, all at the height of their reputation. Does this mean that music is less hostile to the 'religious' than poetry? Less parched even? Well, it doesn't take much listening to John Tavener's music to realize that his central vision, the icon of his music, if you like, is that of Christ risen, ascended, glorified. A Russian Orthodox convert, he dislikes Western Christianity's focus (as he sees it) on the Cross. Tavener, like Pärt and Gorecki, has in his music explicitly turned his back on conflict, drama, suffering, on fallen-ness. One of the most striking aspects of James MacMillan's music is that the whole story is there, the whole drama. Christ could not have risen if he had not been crucified first. The battle is ultimately won, but it continues all around us. Truly religious art, truly Christian art – whether music or poetry – must surely live and draw creative breath from that tension, that struggle, that completeness in the midst of incompleteness. Spiritual music, like spiritual poetry, has come to mean a kind of one-dimensional heightened or transcendent experience without any sense of sacrifice or conflict. Even though it is often very accomplished and very beautiful, it has come to mean a flight from reality, an escape from the darkness. Spiritual poetry is a term almost entirely stripped of meaning.[113]

Thus, for Symmons Roberts, '[David Jones's] image of the free-spirited and uncommitted artist is, and always has been, an illusion. Freedom is not absence.' This is the paradox of being bound in order to make one free and is evident in musicians such as Olivier Messiaen, 'whose technical and imaginative virtuosity underlie much of contemporary classical music – inspiring pupils such as Pierre Boulez.'[114]

But the music of Olivier Messiaen was problematic for secularists, such as Boulez, because of the derivation of Messiaen's creative passion, a devout and traditional Catholic Christian faith:

> Postmodernist music critics try to cope with Messiaen by separating his music from his faith, which they regard as a bizarre personal idiosyncrasy ... With Messiaen, it was a radical freedom won through constraint, a 'binding to make free'.[115]

One cannot extract the faith content from Messiaen's music any more than you can from MacMillan's work. For both composers the faith element does not represent an escape from the difficulties of the world but a binding of the divine to our broken world. It is incarnational.

MUSIC AND SPIRITUALITY: IMPLICIT AND EXPLICIT RELIGION, NATURAL AND APOPHATIC THEOLOGY

If we equate explicit religion with that which has its basis in the words of scripture, doctrine and tradition, and implicit religion as that which is based upon experience, encounter and relationship, then, I argue, there is a place and a need for both. However, Ellis, and to a large extent Brown and Hopps, do away with the need for explicit religion, heavily emphasising the experiential. Begbie and others, on the other hand, prefer to place all experience within the framework of explicit traditional doctrine. Therefore, our assessment of how these elements of religion, faith or belief should be balanced has been a matter for much consideration and debate. Added to this complexity is the recent work, by Iain McGilchrist and others, on the roles of the right and left hemispheres of the brain and how they function in different ways.[116] Depending on which hemisphere is dominant, our approach to religious knowledge and experience may be either more cognitive and logocentric (left hemisphere dominance) or more intuitive and experiential (right hemisphere dominance). For me, we cannot dispense with doctrine simply because we have an ecstatic or numinous experience. One does not replace the other. Nor does the spiritual experience take us beyond words and therefore make them redundant. But there is a paradox to grasp. Music, along with other experiences, can take us both beyond *and* more deeply into doctrine, scripture and tradition. It can both transcend *and* illuminate the written word, as we apprehend the divine not only cognitively but also intuitively. I will explore the notions of explicit and implicit religion in more detail now.

EXPLICIT RELIGION

As I have discussed above, the different modes or meanings inherent in the word faith (personal trust, lived-out reliance and so on) are contained in a single Greek word (*pistis*) because they are ultimately inseparable from one another. Any action, especially within the context of a religious ritual or service, has a kind of implicit proposition behind it, even if those involved in the action (like some of those interviewed in this book) also have intellectual problems with its explicit articulation. In our post-secular society, not all those who attend churches, chapels or cathedrals, and engage with the music and aesthetics therein, necessarily connect with the propositions of the Christian faith. However, if we come to the central questions of the Christian life, like the issue of salvation, does not a faithful Christian need to accept the Godhead of Christ? Contact with the numinous, through music or any other means, may be a gateway to the Christian life, but it is not the entirety of it. Therefore, something more explicit is necessary.

As I have mentioned, Durkheim considered religion to be 'a unified system of beliefs,' but I have also argued that a life or experience of 'faith' might be seen as more complex, nuanced and experiential. Jeremy Begbie has most recently emphasised the importance of a unified system of Trinitarian beliefs if one is to understand or encounter God through music. In this sense his theology is 'explicit': scriptural revelation, for Begbie, 'means that we know something of the pattern and colour of other senses of epiphany – music has this capacity, and it is highly effective and affective in doing so, unashamedly, being God's creation and key to his purposes for humanity.'[117] Yet, for Begbie, 'all implicit meanings in musical and artistic expression can be measured against the explicit fact of that which has already decisively been revealed in Christ.'[118] Any experience of the arts must be interpreted through the lens of Trinitarian doctrine.[119] Thus, he writes that talk of transcendence has lost its true meaning of the Christian Gospel. Begbie is concerned with 'the transcendence of the God of Israel testified in Scripture and made known in Jesus Christ.'[120] Nothing could be more explicit than that. Begbie is also critical of notions, such as that of Vladimir Jankélévitch, of a 'sublime other' (which might be God) in the arts that can be found at the limits of our speech: 'But if the "other" is merely the unknowable,' Begbie protests, 'it is nothing but emptiness and void.'[121]

There are four false assumptions, Begbie argues, to be found in contemporary scholarship on theology and the arts. The first is that the nature of the divine is discovered by experience and interpretation of our limits; second, that God is generally related to the world with no specific active role (that is, that we find God through the arts rather than Him finding us); third, that humans possess an 'innate and intact capacity to apprehend God', that is, to discern how God might be 'transcendent'; and fourth, that the arts can enable an encounter with a unitarian deity, onto which a 'Trinitarian God can be grafted onto a preelaborated unitarian theology without disruption.'[122] For Begbie, the story of God's salvation through Jesus Christ is a disturbing and disruptive transcendence. God *acts* by both creating the world and redeeming it, and he goes on acting by his self-giving love which sustains creation, including the arts.

Critics of Begbie's argument, such as David Brown, suggest that Begbie ignores other ways in which musicians or listeners might relate their art to the divine, such as 'peace, joy, presence, spirit, grace in our natural God-given world.' One might argue that such encounters are complementary to explicit scriptural and traditional Christian doctrines. But some think that encounter with the divine is possible without explicit beliefs at all, and thus I turn to the implicit.

IMPLICIT RELIGION

One place to start exploring the implicit divine is to focus on the notion of 'spirit' and 'spiritual', words that are often closely associated with the realms of music, the arts and faith. In today's post-secular world, in which new vocabulary is being explored, the word spiritual has come to mean anything from a heightened state of emotion to inner calm or from the neuropsychological condition of trance induced by ritual music and dance to a supernatural encounter with something beyond the world. It is sometimes seen as a state of being disembodied or taken out of our physical human state into another realm. However, the stories told in this book suggest another use for the word in which our bodies and minds are engaged in the spiritual process by our participation. In biblical terms this involves the movement of the Holy Spirit working within and through us, making us more fully human, physically, mentally and spiritually, as we are transformed into being more like the divine. As Jeremy Begbie puts it: 'We are re-humanized by the Spirit, not de-humanized.'[123]

Steven Guthrie has suggested various ways in which the spiritual and the aesthetic are closely related: as mystery and ineffability, where the arts help us to go beyond words and concepts; as expression and emotion, because art expresses the depths of our beings as the counterpart to worship and religious practice, and because music in particular has, since the birth of religion, shared in the action of communal ritual; as inspiration, in which the artist has a divinely instigated spirit-filled impetus for creativity; and as eschatological (relating to the end times), as artists are those who can glimpse a foretaste of the heavenly kingdom to come.[124] When the words spirit or spirituality are mentioned during the conversations in this book, one or more of these definitions may be implied. Guthrie makes it clear that these connections are all theological in nature because each one offers a certain understanding of (the Holy) Spirit, 'in other words, a pneumatology.'[125] But Guthrie proposes one reason why there has traditionally been such a close relationship between aesthetics and spirituality, which is deeply rooted in the biblical narratives of God's Holy Spirit, such as the Pauline notion that a spiritual person is one who lives in the Holy Spirit, the work of which, through 'creation, incarnation and redemption ... is *the humanizing Spirit*.'[126] The breath, or Spirit, of God רוּחַ (the Hebrew *Ruach*) creates life and humanity, the Spirit empowers the incarnation and humanity of Jesus, and the Spirit re-humanises us by the work of redemption and consummation.[127]

Others take a much broader and diverse view of spirituality. Using Crowe's term to describe music as soul-making, June Boyce-Tillman, working with Sarah Morgan's doctoral material on community choirs, defines spirituality in psychosocial terms of communal experiences that nourish the mind, body, emotion and the spirit.[128] Thus, the Spirit works not only upon the individual but also, and arguably even more so, when a community is gathered to make music. Following the secularisation of the arts in the twentieth century there became, Boyce-Tillman argues, a 'marginalization of the sacred' and 'a deep sense of loss.'[129] Morgan and Boyce-Tillman see the rise of the community choir as deeply connected with human nourishment and fulfilment, in which deep human needs are met by communal singing,[130] predicated on Robert Wuthnow's argument that 'Spirituality is not just the creation of individuals; it is shaped by larger social circumstances and by the beliefs and values present in the wide culture.'[131] In the post-secular West, spirituality is seen by some as increasingly diverse, relating to 'the experience of connectedness, relationship or oneness with ... a higher power ... nature and appreciation of personal growth and inner awareness of one's life journey.'[132]

Whatever our definition of spiritual and spirituality, art, whether it be music, poetry, painting, sculpture or any other art form, takes us, paradoxically, both beyond *and* deeper into doctrinal concepts, propositions and analyses. If it did not, then there would be no need for the art form in the first place. It is precisely because art can take us beyond the constraints of theological prose to the ineffable that makes it so necessary. Therefore I shall not be over-theologising references to spirit and spirituality in this volume.

As Karl Barth wrote, '*Exactly because of its lack of concepts,* music is the true and legitimate bearer of the message of Christmas, the adequate expression for the highest and final dialectical level, a level attainable by singing, by playing on flute and piano.'[133] Others agree, as Guthrie has noted, such as the theologian Friedrich Schleiermacher (1768–1834) and the philosopher John Caputo who, along with the artists L'Engle and Ellsworth, relate art and the spiritual with the unsayable in religion and the unknowable in God: 'The one who stands closest to the kingdom is not the lawyer, the philosopher, the dialectician – but the musician. This is the case, not *despite* the absence of words and concepts in instrumental music, but *because* of it.'[134] This aspect of not-knowing does not leave music in the category of self-referential absoluteness, but alludes to something greater by means of the expression of the music and the active perception and participation of the listener, which makes the allusive subject become real as experience.[135] Or, as Roger Scruton has argued: 'The expressive and the ineffable go together, therefore, not only in music but in poetry too. And if all art aspires to the condition of music ... it is because music achieves the greatest possible distance from the explicit statement, while still inviting us to "enter into" its expressive content.'[136] In the arena of faith, which, as the opening quotation of this chapter from Joseph Ratzinger suggests, is characterised by the lived experience of 'love' and 'joy', what we call God is not knowable in any conventional sense, but through a reflective mirroring of the divine action of love, as Richard Rohr has expressed:

> You cannot know God the way you know anything else; you only know God or the soul of anything subject to subject, center to center, by a process of 'mirroring' where like knows like and love knows love 'deep calling unto deep' (Psalm 42:7). The Divine Spirit planted deep inside each of us yearns for and responds to God – and vice versa (see James 4:5). The contemplative is deeply attuned and surrendered to this process.[137]

It is in this context that implicit theology helps us understand our world of faith rather than doctrinal belief. In asking 'How does faith feel?', Martyn Percy makes an eloquent distinction between implicit and explicit theology:

> The theology that ultimately shapes and informs faith is both implicit and explicit. The explicit is, perhaps, obvious: the creeds, the articles and the tradition. But ... we gain considerably richer understandings of faith traditions when we attend to the implicit – the apparently 'background' material of music, for example – that not only supports

> the tradition, but also actually contributes to its shape and eventual reception.[138]

Thus, implicit theology is about praxis, performance, embodiment of faith through what we do as well as what we say we believe – about the relational aspects of faith as well as rational aspects of belief. Or, as Percy puts it, the 'realization of a relationship between the gentle framing of faith ... through structures and practices allows us [to] ponder the significance of many things we might take for granted, and their theological weight.'[139] Percy recognises, therefore, that in an ecclesiological context there is a job for implicit theology to do: the texts which supply the belief systems of religions in the Christian tradition need interpretation, just as much through the performative and worldly means of 'music, ... dress codes, manners, the moderation of the collective emotional temperature' as through explicit doctrinal interpretation. 'This is because the shape of the church is partly brought about by the subliminal as much as by the liminal; and by the implicit as much as by the explicit.'[140] But more than that, whether people wish to acknowledge it or not, the belief systems and traditions of the Church are not fixed and immutable; they change over time.[141]

In this work, the conversations I have had concerning music and faith are with believers and non-believers. Some 'belong' to the Church in a formal sense, some do not, and some are on the edge. A sense of commitment to a prescribed set of beliefs varies in each case, but in all cases explicit belief (or explicit non-belief) is complemented by engagement with implicit theology through practice, performance, behaviour, relationship, historical and cultural context and aesthetics, to name but a few aspects of the implicit theological experience. Within the context of a religious institution, such as the Church, Percy makes a compelling case for the role of implicit theology: 'Attention to the role and vitality of the implicit is therefore vital if one wishes to comprehend the depth, density, identity and shaping of faith communities.'[142] Thus, the performative and embodied nature of creating, participating in and listening to music is an essential element to the ecclesial body and wider society as a whole. I will briefly explain how natural and apophatic theologies may be relevant to the realm of music and to the conversations undertaken for this book.

NATURAL THEOLOGY AND MUSIC

Traditionally natural theology has been seen as a way of seeking to prove the existence of God through observation and experience of nature, as opposed to a 'revealed' God by use of human reason. Classic texts on this subject have been by Thomas Aquinas (1224–74), Immanuel Kant (1724–1804), William Paley (1743–1805) and David Hume (1711–76), who was suspicious of natural theology, claiming that a revealed God, through Jesus, must be believed in through 'blind faith.' But in the late medieval period, Raymonde of Sabunde's (1385–1436) *Natural Theology* drew upon the ideas of fourth-century Christian apologists, who considered that 'deliberations concerning the essence and existence of God ... forego premises drawn from Scripture.'[143] They believed that knowledge of God required divine illumination, that nature contained divine essence, and that articles of faith are fallible.[144] Not surprisingly, in the logocentric era of early modern Europe, natural theologies became limited in their success and were often controversial. Nevertheless, the idea that God, and his will for the world, might be known apart from scriptural revelation manages to persist.[145]

Since the Reformation, natural theology has developed in many ways:

> A more modern view of natural theology suggests that reason does not so much seek to supply a proof for the existence of God as to provide a coherent form drawn from the insights of religion to pull together the best of human knowledge from all areas of human activity. In this understanding natural theology attempts to relate science, history, morality and the arts in an integrating vision of the place of humanity in the universe. This vision ... is religious to the extent it refers to an encompassing reality that is transcendent in power and value. Natural theology is thus not a prelude to faith but a general worldview within which faith can have an intelligible place.[146]

This is where music comes in. As a phenomenon of the natural world, developed through science, history and human creativity with moral, mental, physical and spiritual influence, music encapsulates the 'vision' of a modern natural theology that does not seek to prove the existence of a divine being but allows for a post-secular Western world where faith has a reasonable place. Thus Karl Barth's assertion that 'even if we only lend our little finger to natural theology, there necessarily follows the denial of the revelation of God in Jesus Christ'[147] can be countered with James Barr's acknowledgement that 'God has left evidence of himself in the natural world ... the scriptures must then include natural theology as part of revelation.'[148] and Emile Brunner's assertion that 'there is an Anknüpfungspunkt – a point of contact in human nature for God's grace to latch on to.'[149] Moreover, Brunner argues that both Old and New Testaments contain evidence of natural theology. In the Old Testament, God's glory is revealed through nature and complemented by his revelation in the law.[150] In the New Testament, St Paul speaks to the Greeks at the Areopagus, in the Acts of the Apostles, chapter seventeen, who do not know a Christian God, but although 'their natural knowledge of God is inadequate for salvation' it does still point to God.[151] Thus, as Holder suggests, natural theology arguments today are often inductive rather than deductive. That is, they use evidence to find the 'best and most likely explanation for that evidence, rather than aim for demonstrative proof'.[152]

Likewise, this book uses interviews to find evidence of how faith and music might relate to each other, for certain individuals, in the twenty-first century West but does not, thereby, seek to prove, or otherwise, the existence of God. This is not because I subscribe to Western philosophical notions of negation, which deny rational affirmations about God. Rather, the conversations in this book lead me to reflect on the true nature of the knowledge of God through experience. So I must talk briefly about apophatic theology.

APOPHATIC THEOLOGY AND MUSIC

The philosophy of rational negation (as mentioned above) and apophatic theology,[153] at a casual glance, seem to be the same. They might both seem to be concerned with what we *cannot* say about God. But, whereas the notion of rational negation leads to a void, apophatic theology is based upon experience. Real apophasis is an act of God by which those who desire to experience God do so, but in such a mysterious or transcendent way that it cannot be expressed in words. For Begbie, authentic Christian Apophaticism 'arises first and foremost from our participation (which includes spoken participation) in the risen life of the One who has become a speaking agent "for us and for our salvation"'.[154] For others, such as Schopenhauer, music is a kind of surrogate religion that leads to a place beyond this world to the ineffable. For others still, such as Schleiermacher and Philip Pullman, there is an awe and wonder to the universe that is equally captivating for theist and atheist alike. Brown, citing Peter Bannister, has suggested that the works of the 'holy minimalists' Arvo Pärt (b. 1935) and John Tavener (1944–2013) are examples of apophatic musical style, which demonstrates a kind of Christian *kenosis* (a self-emptying that relates to God's own self-emptying in his love for, and redemption of, creation through the sacrifice of Christ).[155] Likewise, the music of Olivier Messiaen (1908–92), to quote Sander van Maas, is possibly apophatic in nature, for it both 'dazzles' us and evokes 'negative forms of representation' of 'that which cannot be presented in positive form ... through shattered or shattering forms (e.g. faltering speech, a fractured language of the ineffable) or by falling silent altogether'.[156] I will return to the themes of natural, apophatic and implicit theology as we progress.

METHOD

My approach is theologically reflective and from a faith perspective. I hope that, as such, it will be complementary to more objective sociological treatments of the relationship between religion and faith, some of which have treated the subject rather sparsely. For instance, *The Routledge Reader on The Sociology of Music* ignores the thought of Plato, Aristotle, Augustine and Boethius and begins with nineteenth-century thought. Nowhere in the collection is there a mention of God, faith, sacred music or theology. There is one passing reference to religion.[157] Likewise, in the 1046 pages of *The Oxford Handbook of the Sociology of Religion*, music is mentioned on only six pages.[158] My emphasis, therefore, is theistic and religious. I have already argued for the importance of an implicit theological outlook and I will also venture into the areas of apophatic and natural theology. But my main methodological purpose is to explore how we can better understand faith through music; how we can better know the divine through actions of faith; and how faith, in this context, differs from belief. I make no claims about salvation, or what is necessary for it. I make no assessments of whether those interviewed for this book are 'saved' or what it would mean for them to be so. I merely present their experiences of how they connect with the Christian faith (through music or the word) and reflect upon the significance of those experiences for our post-secular society.

CHOICE OF INTERVIEWEES

The criteria for choosing these particular people to interview is, firstly, because of their personal interest in the Christian faith, whether that interest includes a personal faith or belief system or not; secondly, because they all have an interest in music and its connection with faith, whether that interest be artistic, religious, scientific, ecclesiastical, etc.; thirdly, I have chosen them because of their diversity in regard to gender, age, race, experience, denomination, belief, national background (including East and West) and musical preferences (from pop, rock, worship bands to classical music of all kinds), although I do not claim in any way to have chosen a group representative of twenty-first-century Western society, nor a group that represents every possible connection between music and faith; fourthly, I have chosen interviewees who I knew had the ability and will to express their opinions concerning music and faith, which has allowed me to draw out certain emerging themes as I thought appropriate. I hope that the, necessarily limited, range of people chosen demonstrates something of how post-secularism works today with a coexistence of diverse opinion and practice.

SCOPE AND OUTLINE

This book is not about what divides people through what they do, or do not, believe. It is about how people *do* faith; how they find it, live it, inhabit it, embody it and what it does to them. I will explore some examples of how the Christian story is still expressed in music and art and how it is received by those who experience those art forms, whether in church or not. In addition to the interviews, I have included an opening chapter on Western sacred music from ancient Greece through medieval and early modern Europe in order to draw comparisons between the state of late medieval music and devotion and today's post-secular struggles with biblical narratives and religious expression. There are also two short 'interludes' outlining examples of how sacred music has been employed today, namely the new girl choristers' choir Frideswide Voices and their involvement in medieval religious drama, and the enduring appeal of sacred music in the 300-year-old Three Choirs Festival. Ideas flow between the chapters, especially within each of the three main parts of the book, but each can be read alone.

Part one of the book focuses on some aspects of music, faith and aesthetic encounter. Following the first chapter, which draws a line of continuity between late medieval implicit theology and the contemporary search for spiritual experiences, the second chapter explores how faith has been expressed through music's relationship with literature, and especially the poetry of hymns, psalms and songs. I use interview and printed material from Anglican novelist, writer and broadcaster Ronald Blythe, as well as the medieval historian, English scholar and theatre director Professor Elisabeth Dutton. Chapter three continues the theme of aesthetic spirituality by examining the work of the artist Janet Boulton, whose 'Eye Music' incorporates visual art with religious experience and musical notation. This fascinating and interdisciplinary art form reveals much about the connections between faith and the arts.

The first interlude, which forms a short diversion between parts one and two, is a tribute to one of Britain's most enduring festivals celebrating faith and music: The Three Choirs Festival of Gloucester, Hereford and Worcester.

Part two of the book is entitled 'The Human Mind and Society' and takes us into the realms of science and social study. Chapter four comprises an interview with Professor Robin Dunbar on the benefits of singing, both for evolutionary purposes of social cohesion and in post-secular society for feelings of well-being and human flourishing. The following chapter examines how the human brain reacts to certain musical and religious experiences. My conversation with Professor Quinton Deeley reveals how our brain activity is deeply affected by music within religious ritual. The final chapter in this part broadens the discussion to consider a decisive change within human society, namely the communist revolution, by related conversations with people who lived through it and were closely involved with sacred music. Canon Michael Bourdeaux explains his experience in the Soviet Union and Balázs Déri how he continued to promote sacred music throughout the communist era in Hungary. Both tales reveal the powerful and dynamic spirit of humanity to declare faith through music, despite persecution and oppression.

The second interlude traces one example of the growth of choirs performing sacred music in post-secular society, by examining the work of Frideswide Voices, a new girl choristers' liturgical choir, and how they experienced late medieval religion and spirituality themselves when they performed in a fifteenth-century convent drama directed by Professor Elisabeth Dutton.

Part three concerns belief and belonging and relates to the experiences of believers and non-believers alike to music and faith. Chapter seven considers how atheism is no barrier to encountering the transcendent through sacred music, how un-belief is no barrier to church membership, and how music and art form a central aesthetic and spiritual bond between the so-called sacred and the secular. The final two chapters consist of conversations with those who both have belief and attend church: laity and clergy. Chapter eight comprises conversations with a Roman Catholic ethnically Sri Lankan musician, Shanika Ranasinghe, and a non-denominational half-Iranian charismatic evangelical, Firoozeh Willans. Their contrasting stories reveal how, from one point of view, the numinous and unknowable divine can be expressed and represented through music and, from another, how music can be a conduit for the Word of God through scripture, which leads to an encounter with a creator God, a personal Jesus and an inspiring Holy Spirit.

The result, I hope, is a rich and varied snapshot of some twenty-first-century viewpoints concerning faith and music. The journey of faith is not simply about arriving at a destination where a list of propositions are assented to and belief is cemented in certainty. Faith is an act, a process, a verb that takes place on the journey, not at the end of it. Whether we 'believe' in God or not, we are all 'faithing' our way through life, putting our trust in uncertain and unpredictable hopes and values, such as kindness, mercy, love, joy and compassion, while sometimes feeling disappointment, pain and despair. Music is the perfect means to express this journey, for it embodies, in sound, the process of our exploration to find meaning through encounter, experience and relationship, through which we find our nourishment and inspiration as human beings.

This book is for, and by, those who encounter, experience and value music and who make a connection, however loosely, with the lived-out life of faith. At its heart is a deep interest in, and love for, God, and how the divine might be found through the gift of music. Or, as Nick Baines would put it, how we discover that God has found us.

PART I

MEDIEVALISM TO POST-SECULARISM

CHAPTER ONE

MUSIC, MORALITY AND MEANING: OUR MEDIEVAL HERITAGE

Listen and attend with the ear of your heart.[1]

And hark! I hear a singing: yet in sooth
    I cannot of that music rightly say
Whether I hear, or touch, or taste the tones,
    Oh, what a heart-subduing melody![2]

If we are to understand the place of sacred music in the post-secular West we need to know a little about its place in history and what ideas and values we have inherited. In order to do that, we need to begin in ancient Greece.

Our 'ancestral' heritage of musical theological thought can be divided into two, overlapping, categories or narratives through history. Firstly, the Pythagorean tradition, which is closely allied to 'disclosive' modes of musical significance (that is, where God is disclosed to us through the cosmological, rational, material nature of the universe) and the Orphic tradition, which is more akin to 'affective' modes of significance (that carry us outside of ourselves, change our attitude or lead us to contemplation or a new state of being).[3]

The Greek mathematician Pythagoras (sixth century BC) and his notion of the harmony of the spheres was based upon his observations of the mathematical purities of musical ratios. Therefore his view was that the divine is disclosed through the created order and is, as Begbie puts it, essentially '*ratio*nal';[4] it is a reflection of the cosmic harmony. The disclosive tradition continued with Plato (427–347 BC), for whom 'Music gives us not only a model of harmonious balance, unity, and integrity, it actually implants cosmic harmony into the soul of humans.'[5] Plato's views were essentially dichotic or dualist, dividing the material from the ideal, the temporal from the eternal. But Plato also stood within the Orphic tradition, where music has the power to affect human emotions and soul. It could enhance virtue and it could be a 'means to correct any discord that may have arisen in the courses of the soul ... our ally in bringing it into harmony and agreement with herself.'[6] Listening attentively, therefore, was of crucial importance, for 'heard music for Plato has a positive ethical, political, and social potential.'[7] But music could also be damaging if unfettered by analytical language and philosophy: 'In this light we can understand Plato's strong desire to subordinate music to words ... something that is taken up by countless Christian writers in the centuries to come.'[8] Aristotle (384–322 BC) also acknowledged music's power to delight, relax or excite the inner being. He focused on music's educational benefits for the 'decorum' of both individual and society. For Aristotle, music could be used for pleasure, but it was also beneficial for civic service as well as contemplation.[9]

Centuries later, Plato's follower Plotinus (c. 205–270 AD) used Plato's distinction between ideals and material and created the 'Neoplatonic' scheme where the essence of the 'One', or the Supreme Being, emanates through the created order in a series of hierarchies, down to the lowest material. At the top of this hierarchy is intellect, or mind (*Nous*). Therefore intellectual reason continued to dominate music theory. For instance, Aristides Quintilianus's (c. third century AD?) important treatise *De Musica* considered music to be a science and an art,[10] which could elevate the soul beyond this world:[11] 'the object of music is the love of the beautiful.'[12] He drew upon Platonic and Pythagorean ideas that, in turn, informed early Christian thinking on music, such as Augustine of Hippo's (350–430 AD) own *De Musica* (387–91).[13]

The North African Bishop Augustine shared Plato's ambivalence towards music's emotive power, but also echoed his disclosive ideas. *De Musica* contained a 'vocabulary that would be mined for the next one and a half millennia.'[14] Augustine followed the Platonic notion that the cosmos was ordered by ratios and proportions. Music was a science of '*bene modulandi*', of a 'good measuring' of the world, involved in its numerical ratios, such as 'identifying, classifying, and creating relations between sounds – most often the written or spoken sound of words in poetic rhythm, meter, and verse.'[15] However, in the sixth volume of *De Musica* Augustine argued that although God, the supreme musician, created the cosmos from nothing and, in so doing, gave it form or music, fallen humanity, imprisoned by its love of inferior beauty, cannot fully hear or perceive beyond the corporeal and temporal to the incorporeal sounds of heaven.[16] Nevertheless, in his more positive moments, Augustine was able to perceive that there were times of overflowing joy in wordless singing, which he called 'jubilation,' where the experience went beyond words towards an ineffable God. Such singers 'are filled with such joy that they cannot express it in words,' and it 'signifies that the heart labors [*sic*] for what it cannot utter. And whom does this jubilation befit but the ineffable God? For he is ineffable [of] whom you cannot speak.'[17] For Augustine, every part of creation reflects the creator. Creation praises the *Deus Creator Omnium* and is, by so doing, sanctified by the source of all harmony and music.[18] Music binds performer and listener in divine cosmic order.[19]

But Augustine, like Plato, also belongs to the Orphic tradition, where music affects the senses, emotions and spirit, and, like Plato, Augustine was suspicious of the sensuality of music:

> How I wept during your hymns and songs! I was deeply moved by the music of the sweet hymns of your Church. The sounds flowed into my ears and the truth was distilled into my heart. This caused the feelings of devotion to overflow. Tears ran, and it was good for me to have that experience.[20]

Music can bring us to tears, to anger, to ecstasy or to stillness and silence. But it must be sung well: 'Many know what the choir signifies. [...] A choir is a band of singers. If we sing in a choir, we sing with our heart. In the choir of singers, whoever is unharmonious in voice perturbs what is heard ...'[21] But if the performance is good, then music has a power and a force that troubled Augustine: 'I fluctuate between the danger of pleasure and the experience of the beneficent effect [of music].'[22] He was desperate to move beyond the temporal distraction of beautiful, sensual sound,[23] towards God:

> I feel that when the sacred words are chanted well, our souls are moved and are more religiously and with a warmer devotion kindled to piety than if they are not so sung. All the diverse emotions of our spirit have their various modes in voice and chant appropriate in each case, and are stirred by a mysterious inner kinship. But my physical delight, which has to be checked from enervating the mind, often deceives me when the perception of the senses is unaccompanied by reason, and is not patiently content to be in subordinate place. It tries to be first and in

> the leading role, though it deserves to be allowed only as secondary to reason. So in these matters I sin unawares, and only afterwards become aware of it.[24]

Platonic and Augustinian themes were taken up in Boethius's (c. 480–525) *De Institutione Musica*. For Boethius, music was divided into three levels: the cosmic music (*musica mundana*), music of our human bodies and souls (*musica humana*), and the music we hear (*musica instrumentalis*):

> The goal of learning *musica* is to ascend to the level of reason. The fundamental principle motivating Platonic music theory is *knowing*, the acquisition of pure knowledge, and Boethius' threefold division of music and three classes of musicians resonate consistently with this principle.[25]

Boethius' music theory was assimilated into the Neoplatonic mystical thought of Pseudo-Dionysius (Syrian, sixth century), who modified the idea of the harmony of the spheres into the harmony of the angels, as well as the scholastic thought of Johannes Scotus Erigena (810–886), who amalgamated *music mundana* and *musica humana* in a single music heard sung in Church worship, and into Dante's fourteenth-century *Divine Comedy*, who employed Boethius's numerology.[26]

One interpretation of the above traditions is this: 'Simply put: music is being grounded firmly in a universal God-Given order, and thus it is seen as a means through which we are enabled to live more fully in the world that God has made and with the God who made it.'[27]

The medieval world combined a Scriptural and patristic vision of the cosmos that was coloured by classical heritage.[28] Both Pythagorean and Orphic traditions, disclosive and affective, continued throughout the period. Notions concerning music often developed through experience of, and reflection upon, the liturgy. An important figure in this phenomenon was Amalarius (c. 775–c. 852), Archbishop of Lyon. On cantors, for instance, Amalarius emphasised the importance of morality, manners and meaning in worship, so that even a deaf person would be able to perceive that the music offered was performed with dignity, integrity and sincerity of heart:

> David founded [the cantors. He] was a man [...] who loved musical harmony not with vulgar delight, but with faithful will, and who served his God – who is the true God – through a mystical symbol of great meaning. [...] Let the cantors here consider the meaning of their symphony. Through it, they urge the people to persist in the unity of

> the worship of a single God. And even if a deaf person were present, the cantors would make the very same point through their arrangement in the well-ordered choir [...] To the degree that the heart is greater than the body, what comes from the heart is offered to God more piously than what comes from the body. The cantors are themselves the trumpet, they are the psaltery ...[29]

If the cantor does his job well, then the text of the reading that is sung will both feed and lead the listener into a deeper, and more cheerful, appreciation of the Gospel, and bring both them and the singer himself to a tearful confession as the inner truths of the human heart are revealed and laid bare:

> During the reading the listener is led, in a certain sense, like an ox ... And the cantor is like the ploughman who calls out to the oxen to drag the plough more cheerfully ... The earth is furrowed as the oxen drag the plough when the cantors, drawing their innermost breath, drag forth a sweet voice and present it to the people. Through this voice they goad their own heart, as well as the hearts of others, to tears and to the confession of sins, as if laying bare the hidden parts of the earth.[30]

So important and elevated is the role of music, for Amalarius, within the liturgy that the musicians become likened to the angelic orders of heaven who continually praise God in song. Through singing, human beings become the tenth order of the angels: 'To [the] nine aforementioned orders [of angels] is joined a tenth order of human creation, in whose voice the priest says, "We ask that you permit that our voices also be received with theirs."'[31]

Through the later medieval monastic tradition, ideas concerning music continued to develop through liturgical practice. The French bishop Guillaume Durand (c. 1230–96), also known as Durandus, wrote an important medieval treatise on the symbolism of rituals of worship: *Rationale Divinorum Officiorum*. It was one of the most often copied texts in medieval Christianity and was a textbook for liturgists. In the work he drew parallels between the singing of the monastic day and night offices and the story of our redemption: 'The night Office [Matins] represents a time of misery in which the human race was kept under siege by the Devil; the day Office designates the time of our redemption and liberation through Christ, the sun of justice ...'[32]

Durandus also expressed the numinous, incomprehensible and inexpressible nature of divine experience through the spirit of worship and music, especially through the 'neuma' – an extended wordless vocalisation given to the final letter of an antiphon, which expressed the ineffability, eternity and joy that cannot be intellectually understood nor verbally described:

> The neuma or iubilus is the ineffable joy or exultation of the mind dwelling in the midst of things eternal. ... And the neuma is done on the one and final letter of the antiphon to note that the praise of the ineffable God is incomprehensible. For the joy is incomprehensible, which is signified by the neuma, which here, while being tasted, can neither be wholly expressed nor wholly passed over in silence, which is why the Church – with the words omitted – suddenly moves, with good cause, to explaining joyfully with a neuma, as if She is in a state of wonder, and if She were saying, 'What voice, what tongue may here declare ...' Here, words do not suffice, nor does the intellect grasp, nor also can love allow it to be expressed. For who can fully recount what the eye has not seen nor the ear heard, which has not entered in to the heart of man (cf 1 Cor 2.9)? Therefore, neumatizing (neumatizando) is a more expressive manner by which one speaks without words, about what can only be implied by words, where that heavenly joy is such that words will cease and everyone will know all things.[33]

Thus, for Durandus, such liturgical sound could bring humanity to touch, and even taste, an experience of the divine that goes beyond words, intellect and even human love. He is concerned with a knowledge, or rather an unknowing, that is apophatic in the sense that it points to those truths about God which cannot be known in this world through sight or sound, but which lie beyond, in a heavenly realm where, one day, all things will be known. Thus, we can see how developments of medieval musical thought put significant emphasis on the experiential, aesthetic encounter. Put within the wider context of European medieval aesthetics more generally, we can perceive that there was a disunity and contradiction in their religious, spiritual and aesthetic outlook. They were 'unable to reconcile, within a single orthodoxy, Héloise and the characters in Chaucer, Boccaccio and Gilles de Rais.'[34]

> But the Medievals tended to stress the points of convergence and unity, overcoming the contradictions by faith and hope. Their aesthetics, like all their thinking, expressed an optimum synthesis. They saw the world with the eyes of God.[35]

I shall now explore how this continued in the later medieval and early modern periods.

LATE MEDIEVAL RELIGION, LITERACY AND THE AESTHETIC

As Eamon Duffy acknowledged, in his groundbreaking work of revisionism, *The Stripping of the Altars*,

> Late medieval Catholicism exerted an enormously strong, diverse, and vigorous hold over the imagination and the loyalty of the people up to the very moment of Reformation. Traditional religion had about it no particular marks of exhaustion or decay, and indeed in a whole host of ways, from the multiplication of vernacular religious books to adaptations within the national and regional cult of saints, was showing itself well able to meet the new needs and new conditions.[36]

There are many examples of how the arts – visual, aural and theatrical – were an intrinsic part of religious experience.[37] For instance, Roger Martin's Elizabethan list of pre-Reformation religious observances, at the wealthy parish of Long Melford in Suffolk, intended 'to evoke the richness and beauty of the immemorial observances of late medieval piety before the deluge of reform and iconoclasm.' His list included images, furnishings, iconography, which alluded to 'a piety which seems rooted in stillness and looking, to ritual activity and a piety which seems geared to movement and elaborate communal celebration.'[38] Much of this piety revolved around the liturgical calendar and the regular round of feast days to celebrate the saints, with the result that, 'For townsmen and countrymen alike, the rhythms of the liturgy on the eve of the Reformation remained the rhythms of life itself.'[39]

One of the hallmarks of late medieval devotional practice was the connection of personal piety with financial wealth. As Richardson has observed, profit and piety were not unrelated goals in late medieval devotional life; religion and economics were closely connected at both local and national levels:

> Money played a major role in late-medieval Christianity. Salvation was for sale. Prayers had prices. Priests prayed for payments. Piety had pecuniary costs. Religious doctrine required people to pay significant sums for the salvation of their souls.[40]

But this connection of money with devotion can hardly be seen as a sign of corruption within the late medieval Church. The paraphernalia that accompanied the 'drama' of the Mass, such as vestments, chalices, images, colour, architecture, smell, and the consumption of the host itself, all contributed to the multi-sensory experience of religion, which people both rich and poor were willing to contribute towards in financial terms. As R.N. Swanson has pointed out, 'It may be debated how far the liturgy of the medieval Church (in particular the Mass) can be considered as "drama". But its theatrical impact and organization are undeniable.'[41] Of course, even beyond the Mass there were liturgical dramas where biblical stories and canticles could be learned or rehearsed through the drama of theatre and music. We cannot fully comprehend what the impact of medieval liturgical performance may have been upon a congregation or audience: 'Paintings give some indication, but their static nature precludes the emotionalism of presence which would have generated the response.'[42]

The visual and aural nature of both liturgical services and biblical dramas was essential to their power of communication. Theatrical liturgy had both its props and 'soundtrack', as it were. 'Throughout the country ... lists of plate, vestments, and books which served as aids to worship can be culled from a variety of sources.'[43] For instance, the Lichfield Cathedral lists of treasures used in procession in 1345 include 'One gold chalice, having in the foot an image of the crucifix, and also decorated with sixty-four precious stones'[44] and 'One precious gold cope, having images woven in on the gold ....'[45] The images depicted various biblical narratives which could have been viewed as the priest processed through the church or cathedral. How people reacted to this kind of aesthetic stimulation is very difficult to assess, of course, 'but some indications, and illustrations, can be extracted from the Lichfield material, especially fifteenth-century lists ... most of the vestments, books and plate were received from individual donors. Some benefactors made massive gifts: the collection of vestments and ornaments given by Bishop Walter Langton is outstanding ... Others include chantry priests and lesser clerics.'[46] Thus, the 'paraphernalia', as Swanson calls it, was not merely bought by the Dean and Chapter of a cathedral in order to glorify themselves, but often bought by pious individuals. Thereafter, vestments, plate and books were maintained by the church or cathedral, and often lent out to other less wealthy churches. 'A notable feature of the treatment of their treasures by the Lichfield Dean and Chapter is their willingness to lend them out. Several loans are documented in the 1345 list.'[47] The aesthetic element to worship was important for the late medieval believer:

> the investment of wealth, workmanship, and emotion in ornaments for liturgical purposes was functional, in a double sense: they decorated the house of God in an appropriate manner, provided for the proper celebration of the divine Office, and encouraged devotion by offering a route to contemplation and instruction.[48]

Thus, through the visual and sensory, both laity and clergy attempted to contribute to beauty of holiness in worship. Likewise, music played its own part in the beatification of holiness, as Professor Elisabeth Dutton, who works on medieval liturgical drama, has suggested:

> Music enhances drama in four ways. Firstly, music creates a setting, especially in medieval drama. Secondly, music can serve a practical purpose to cover the action. Thirdly, music can also create a pause, a moment when you want to highlight something or to provoke a reflection in an audience. For instance, particularly in medieval mystery cycles, if you've created a strong visual image and you want people to look at it for a moment, playing some music is a good way of achieving that. Fourthly, and perhaps the most obvious point, is that music moves people emotionally.[49]

However, the role of music, painting, sculpture, metalwork, jewellery, needlework and many other art forms to the service of holiness, were eventually 'considered superfluous and removed ... The destruction of England's pre-Reformation ecclesiastical ornaments is almost total.'[50]

Sacred music likewise came under criticism for the manner in which it was performed, especially by humanists. The term 'Humanism' is not a term from the Renaissance, but was developed in the nineteenth century from the Latin *humanitas*, as used by Cicero (106–43 BC) in classical times, and those *humanista*, of the fifteenth century, who studied and taught the *humanae litterae* (liberal arts) in universities. This new Graeco-Roman-inspired culture involved the *studia humanitatis*, which tended to involve the study of classical literature and languages, the rhetorical arts, such as debating skills, philology and the development of eloquent use of language. Almost every university in the world has a discipline called the *humanities*. Christian humanists applied humanist philological technique to the scriptures, seeking to achieve a more reliable text and to make from it a more accurate Latin translation than that provided in the Vulgate. Typically, they wish to base their religion, as far as possible, on the gospels and to investigate the practices of the primitive church where this can be deduced from the Acts of the Apostles and the writings of the early Church fathers. Conservative clerics, such as Stephen Gardiner (1483–1555), Bishop of Winchester, observed:

> the boys in the choir sang *Magnificat* in Latin, as loud as they could cry, each one uttering his own breast to the loudest, without regard to how he agreed with his fellows. I doubt not but God understood them, but of

> the number that sang I dare say a great many understood not what they sang; and we could much less mark their words, other than [when they] began the verse and ended it.[51]

These extreme accusations against late medieval polyphony and its importance had significant consequences for early modern reform. For instance, the 1549 *Book of Common Prayer* encouraged singing by 'clerks' or 'singing-men usually in minor orders'.[52] However, the 1552 Book contained 'very few references to singing and the clerks are nowhere mentioned. The only direction for singing any part of the order for Holy Communion is found at the end, when "Glory be to God on high" may be said or sung.'[53] Likewise, in Germany Thomas Müntzer modified the role of music within religion:

> [Müntzer] ... provided simplified, reformed German services for the people ... For the sake of the weak in conscience [to use Carleton's words], he retained the plainsong melodies familiar to his flock, adapting them to suit his vernacular texts ... The 1523 *Deautzsch Kirchenampt* service book kept hymns and godly psalms 'for the edification and growth of the Christian people' but 'destroying the bombastic ceremonies of the godless'.[54]

Carleton's notion of the 'weak in conscience' is typical of a pejorative view of late medieval lay devotional practice. Müntzer simply used the old chant of the medieval liturgy and added German words in order that they might be more easily understood. What was lost in the process was an artistic form that encouraged the believer to encounter the numinous and the unknowable transcendence of the divine: 'Choral music of the type beloved of the late Middle Ages, in which the text is almost completely lost to the ear through elaborate polyphony, is here eliminated',[55] Carleton writes, concerning the clinical erasure of the polyphonic musical art form. Syllabic music came to dominate in the Reformation era:

> Anything which gets in the way of the clear understanding of what is sung is anathema to the majority of reformers. The ideal musical setting consists of a single note to each syllable of text for perfect clarity.[56]

Thus, syllabic musical composition in England was exemplified by John Marbeck's *The Book of Common Praier Noted* of 1550, which provided 'so muche of the Order of Common prayer as is to be song in Churches'.[57] Marbeck wrote that the

> style of singing commended in Scripture is an inwards melody of the heart, praising the Lord in mind rather than in voice. Prick-song (singing in parts) and descant (adding a counter-melody to a given tune) were brought into the Church by Pope Vitalian (657–72) 'to delight the vain, foolish, and the idle ears of fond and fantasticall men.'[58]

Thus, Marbeck was taking a similar stand to Calvin's position that 'only unaccompanied monophony was acceptable for Christian worship.'[59]

Marbeck was part of the humanist tradition that emphasised text, rhetoric and poetry above all else, as Kim has demonstrated. But in other parts of Europe, humanism had resulted in a much more extreme cull of the musical voice in church, especially in Ulrich Zwingli's (d. 1531) Zürich. The humanist battle cry of *Ad Fontes* (back to the 'fount' or [biblical in this case] source) and Zwingli's love of Erasmus's critique of the late medieval Church led him towards an uncompromising stance regarding the authority and truth of scripture. There he found no evidence that singing or music was specifically commanded by God, but many examples of direct divine dictates demanding the adherence to the Word of God. In Zurich, Zwingli demonstrated a contempt for outward and empty ceremony, with the kind of sound, colour, smell, imagery and pomp that characterised much of the late medieval ecclesiastical liturgy:

> I will confess frankly that I wish to see a considerable portion of the ceremonies and prescriptions abolished ... I demonstrated that simple people could be led to recognition of the truth by means other than ceremonies, namely, so far as I was able to learn from Scripture, by those with which Christ and the apostles had led them without ceremonies.[60]

The spoken word and genuine private and public devotional prayer would, for Zwingli, replace the inane murmurings of repeated Latin prayers:

> Farewell, my temple murmurings! I am not sorry for you ... Welcome, O pious, private prayer that is awakened in the hearts of believing men through the Word of God ... Greetings to you, common prayer that all Christians do together ... I know that you are the sort of prayer to which God will give that which He promised.[61]

Zwingli was not suspicious of music for its sensuous pleasure or ability to excite the emotions: 'The heart of his argument is simply that God has not authorized music in worship, and Christ's command is that worship is to be an essentially inwards, individual, and private matter.'[62] In addition, Zwingli inherited a Platonic dualism in his thought, where he extolled the non-material and eternal God and denigrated the material, physical world:

> Since God himself is spirit: mind: not body, it is obvious that ... He is above all to be worshipped by purity of mind. And today the mass of Christians worship God through certain corporeal ceremonies: whereas the piety of the mind is the most pleasing worship. For the father seeks such worshippers as will worship him in spirit, since he is spirit.[63]

Thus, 'the creator is utterly free from the created world'[64] and music becomes entirely detached from any theological thought. It is completely secular: 'No men are so stupid that they are not captivated by [music] ... There are none, on the other hand, who are not offended by the confusion and discord of voices.'[65] Zwingli separates out the theological and musical in himself and sought also to do so in his Church. Music and singing were completely banned in Zürich churches from 1525 and only returned in 1598, long after Zwingli's death.

Zwingli's dualistic views on music are the product of the Pythagorean-Platonist tradition as transmitted through the Church fathers and Renaissance humanism. The logocentric primacy of the Word of Scripture, the separation of spirit, or mind, from the body, and the rejection of music as of any theological worth, are simply the extreme logical conclusion of taking the idea of *Ad Fontes* seriously and literally. Such an outcome could surely never have been imagined by ancient Greek, patristic, medieval or Renaissance humanist scholars, and the fact that the Zürich ban on sacred music was relatively short-lived, in historical terms, is testament to the church congregations' need to acknowledge music as part of God's divinely created cosmic order and their desire to come closer to God through participation in the music which God created.

Other magisterial reformers, of course, were not quite so drastic as Zwingli in his excising of music from the churches. For Luther, music was the greatest of God's gifts, next to theology, and was one that could work on both disclosive and affective levels.[66] On the disclosive plane, earthly music was a poor reflection, but gave a glimpse, of the beauty and perfection of celestial music. In Augustinian terms, we must hear *through* the inferior music of this world in order to hear the perfect music of the world beyond. But Luther also found that, according to the Orphic tradition, music was affective to the human emotions and spirit. Combined with the Word of God in Scripture, it could enable a powerful transformation: 'music combines the emotional power of sound with the spiritual power of God's Word in such a way as to affect the soul.'[67]

For Calvin, humanity's perception of the divine through the natural world was made almost impossible by the Fall, at which point there was 'noetic damage,' where our intrinsic knowledge of God through creation became distorted, marred and blurred. We are now, he suggested, like an old man with poor eyesight who is given a book to read. He cannot see it but, as he holds it in his hands, he knows it is a book. He can feel it but he cannot read it. The book in the metaphor is the world, creation. In order to understand and interpret it, the old man must put on his spectacles, that is, the glasses of Scripture. Through the lens of Scripture he may see and understand, perceive and interpret. Thus, although Calvin did not reject music, he did not give it the elevated status of Luther, nor did he banish it like Zwingli, but rather subdued it to the Word, especially in his use of metrical tunes to set the Psalms, which became so popular in the *Genevan Psalter* and spread so far through the Reformed world. The advantage of the musical setting, for Calvin and generations of followers, was that the music could enable the participant to learn, digest and meditate upon the word of the Psalms. This was its primary purpose. Today, however, it is not universally admired:

> The strictly unaccompanied, unison singing that Calvin approved for Psalms in public worship (which shaped Reformed worship long after) could scarcely be said to encompass fully the heights and depths of human emotion.[68]

MODERN AND POSTMODERN BIBLICAL ILLITERACY AND EXPERIENTIALISM

Despite Zwingli's concerted efforts to bring a Scripture-centred, Bible-based faith to his land, he and the Magisterial Reformers of the sixteenth century would have been shocked by the statistics concerning biblical literacy, or illiteracy, in the United Kingdom (and by implication many other countries in post-secular Europe) today. The marked fall in biblical literacy in Britain through the generations has been demonstrated by research released by the Bible Society:

> 30% of secondary school children (those aged 12 to 15) did not choose The Nativity when asked which stories they thought were in the Bible. Among 15 year olds, the figure rises to more than a third (35%). The

> number of 15 year olds that indicated they had not read, seen or heard The Nativity is similarly around 1 in 3 (34%).[69]
>
> By contrast, over a third thought that storylines featured in the Hunger Games (54%) and Harry Potter (34%) were or might be from the Bible. More than one in four (27%) thought the storyline of Superman was or could be in the Bible; while (46%) thought the same for the Dan Brown novel *The Da Vinci Code*.
>
> Parents themselves find it hard to distinguish the plot lines of well-known Bible stories from the latest Hollywood blockbusters. Asked to decide whether a series of plot lines appeared in the Bible, almost half of parents (46%) failed to recognise the plot of Noah's Ark as a Bible story; around a third were unsure or did not recognise the stories of David & Goliath (31%) and Adam & Eve (30%) as being from the Bible; a quarter (27%) failed to identify the Bible with the plot of the Good Samaritan.[70]
>
> Religion isn't always a factor. Almost a third (30%) of Christian parents say that they never read Bible stories to their children. Furthermore, 7% do not think that their child, aged over 3, has ever read, seen or heard any Bible stories. In stark contrast, 86% of parents read, listened to or watched Bible stories themselves as a child aged 3 to 16. But the picture isn't all bleak. Today, a significant 16% of our children are reading Bible stories by themselves once a week or more, with little age variation at 19% for primary and 13% for secondary school aged children.[71]

So why, in a new age of biblical illiteracy, is sacred music so appealing, both within the liturgy as well as in the concert hall? The most performed and most popular piece of classical music in British concert halls is, and has been for many years, Handel's *Messiah*.[72] 42% of those attending such a concert are likely to be aged 41–60; 37% likely to be aged over 61; and 7% likely to be aged under 31.[73] So what has happened to our reception of sacred music between the medieval and Reformation periods and the present day?

The disclosive, rational, Pythagorean tradition thrived from ancient Greek theory, through Hildegaard von Bingen (1098–1179) and many others who considered music to be an echo of the glory of heaven,[74] and continued well into the sixteenth century and indeed into the Baroque. As John Butt has acknowledged, the Pythagorean tradition of natural theology is evident in the music of J.S. Bach, who considered that 'the more perfectly the task of composition (and, indeed, performance) is realized, the more God is immanent in music ... that the very substance of music both reflects and embodies the ultimate reality of God and the Universe'.[75] But the Pythagorean tradition tended to fade out towards the end of the eighteenth century in Europe, along with the growth of the Enlightenment and the emergence of Romanticism. Music broke free of all liturgical function and became enthroned in itself as 'the medium of the ultimately boundless and utterly infinite, outstripping all earthly limitations'.[76] Thus the elevated metaphysical nature of music was seen as the means of encountering the epiphanic mystery of the sublime, concepts appealing to philosophers and musicians such as Arthur Schopenhauer (1788–1860) and Richard Wagner (1813–83), and indeed to theologians such as Friedrich Schleiermacher (1768–1834), for whom music was 'speech without words, the most definite, most understandable expression of what is innermost' contained in something that is 'exhaled which definite speech can no longer comprehend'.[77]

Such ideas have permeated Europe since the eighteenth century. For E.T.A. Hoffman, music transports one to the spiritual realm; for Wagner, to the eternal and infinite; for George Steiner, music transcends the sayable.[78] But has this move towards the sublime unsayable been partly responsible for a societal emigration away from the Word of Scripture also? In our post-secular society, non-theistic expressions of personal spirituality and transcendence, without allegiance to doctrinal religion, are apparently ubiquitous, alongside which sit 'Bible-centred' churches teaching the fundamentals of biblical orthodoxy, and yet more groups who search for meaning through the natural world and encounter the divine mystery both in and out of church. If biblical literacy is waning, what does that mean for our familiarity with our traditional belief and Christian heritage? What does it mean for those who may not have traditional Christian beliefs but who try to live out a life of faith? Are we returning to a period of medievalism, where non-literary sources of epiphany, encounter and enlightenment are the main access points to God for people in a postmodern, post-secular world? And what does the future hold? I do not seek to have the answers to any of these problems or questions. They arise naturally from the subject matter and from even the most casual observation of the twenty-first-century West. I hope that the conversations below, and the appended reflections, will help provoke continuing conversations about the role of faith in our world today.

CHAPTER TWO

PSALMS AND HYMNS AND SPIRITUAL SONGS

> Sing psalms and hymns and spiritual songs among yourselves, singing and making melody to the Lord in your hearts.[1]

One of the most obvious connections between music and faith is literature – the writings of those whose words are set to music in hymns, songs, plays, operas, oratorios, anthems and canticles. Words *about* music can be obtuse and meaningless in their analysis, compared with words *within* music, where poetry or prose is transformed into musical sound and the colour of each word is enhanced by musical painting. Think of a Schubert song, where even ordinary poetry can be transported into profound significance by the skilful use of melody and harmonic scoring, economically composed for a pianist and singer to interpret.

Writers have long made a close connection between the created order and divinity, from the garden of Eden in the book of Genesis, to the Hellenic world of Pythagoras, Plato and Plotinus, to Christ's incarnation itself. Many a poet has perceived God in nature and none more so than Thomas Traherne (1636/7–74), the seventeenth-century English Metaphysical poet, priest and theologian, in his beloved Herefordshire. For him the beauty of God was directly connected to the beauty of nature:

> My Love's the mountain range,
> The valleys each with solitary grove,
> The islands far and strange,
> The streams with sounds that change,
> The whistling of the lovesick winds that rove.

For Traherne, nature *was* Christ to him and he wanted nothing more than to be in the natural world and therefore dwell within Christ himself. The creativity that this 'natural' faith inspired spilled over into his poetry, which in turn has inspired composers such as Gerald Finzi to craft musical settings and responses to Traherne's words of faith. Both music and poetry have now inspired a third art form in Thomas Denny's visual tributes to both Traherne and Finzi in his Hereford and Gloucester cathedrals stained glass. Of the windows in Hereford Cathedral's Audley Chapel [Figure 1], Christopher Gibbs writes:

> In his glorious windows ... Natural wonders abound. He evokes the Herefordshire landscape, the wooded hill that hangs above the church at Credenhill and its distant prospects. We glimpse the city of Hereford, made celestial. We see our own wonderful world bathed in the light and wonder that streams from the Cross ... In this quiet, secret, holy space we rest before these wonders stilled, calmed, drawn towards 'Felicity'. For a precious moment raised Heavenwards, refreshed.[2]

Another artist, Nicholas Mynheer, has also been inspired by the work of Traherne and Finzi. Listening to Finzi's setting of Traherne's poem *The Salutation* affected how Mynheer worked as a sculptor.[3] The sculpture that emerged is dedicated to a little boy murdered in Thetford Forest, where the sculpture resides, with another version in Newcastle Cathedral [Figure 2].

Nature inspires faith. But as Ronald Blythe, himself a writer about faith and the natural world, points out, there is an inherent theological problem for Traherne, which was that he 'found himself born into paradise, and not to have to wait until he died into it. Angels and other citizens of heaven wander through his Welsh borders and his home counties, unable to tell the difference.' Ronald labels Traherne a 'landscape-ecstatic'.[4]

Martin Luther had no such theological problem. Although for him music was second only to theology as the greatest of all God's natural gifts to his people, this created order in which we live is no paradise, but a corrupted and decayed imitation of the paradise that is to come. Luther's 'Theology of the Cross' puts us firmly outside of heaven and at the foot of a cross, in which we see a suffering and pained God who is crucified for our sin. Our role in this world is to repent and believe, and thus be assured of our salvation through faith and by our total reliance upon the grace of God. But whether for Augustine or Traherne, whatever imperfections this world has, the connection between creation, creativity and experience of the divine is a close one.

When I visited Ronald at his home, Bottengoms, in Wormingford, Suffolk, I understood the close connection he had between the natural world, the arts and faith. Of the landscape and social history he has written much, being most famous for his classic study of English life, *Akenfield*, which was made into a film by Sir Peter Hall. But Ronald's work has included poetry, fiction, essays, short stories, history and literary criticism. His literary career is entwined with music, for he began his life as a writer in the Suffolk coastal town of Aldeburgh, as he assisted Benjamin Britten, Peter Pears and Imogen Holst in establishing the Aldeburgh Festival, before he was persuaded to leave Aldeburgh in search of a more independent literary life. He inherited the remote Bottengoms from John and Christine Nash, and the house is full of John Nash's beautiful paintings. The house is both part of its natural landscape, entwined into the countryside with trees, plants and streams surrounding it, and cut off from modern civilisation, with no mains water or modern conveniences of heating. Two black-and-white cats gracefully patrol the tiled floors and rugs, and tables hold stores of fruit, vegetables, bottles, books and memorabilia, forming still-life scenes around the rooms. We sit by the fire and talk of music, art and faith. Ronald has written about his life with musicians, such as Britten and Imogen Holst, and declared that it was these early explorations at Aldeburgh that taught him not only to 'see' the world around him and observe, but also to 'listen'. 'Listening,' he wrote, 'has been a large part of my craft ... Listening in the strict sense of the word means to hear attentively.'[5] It is in listening to the sound of life around us, and especially music, that we learn how to be with God. That may mean listening to the music of nature in the countryside or to the created human sound of composed music. Either way, the *musica mundana* of this world, as Luther would have it, points towards the *musica caelestia* of the heavens. We hear the imperfect music of a fallen world and, like seeing through an icon to the divinity beyond, we listen through the imperfection to perceive the perfect music yet to come.

Ronald worked closely with Imogen Holst preparing the 1956 Festival while Britten and Pears were away in Bali, and he oversaw the production of the Festival Programme Book, including the articles, photographs, printing and line drawings (by John Nash).[6] On a visit he lent me a copy of the brochure to take home. He was justly proud of the production, which became a catalyst for further editorial work and for his eventual departure from Aldeburgh. Imogen became a firm friend and ally of Ronald as well as an influence. Regarding the importance of hymnody, she once opined of J.S. Bach that 'It would be fairly safe to guess that the first tune he ever heard was a hymn tune.'[7]

The language, or literature we might say, of hymns is perhaps the most obvious expression of faith in words and music, and perhaps the most accessible and enduring characteristic of the Christian religion, as Ronald asserts:

> When (and if) the longest-lasting residual popular element of Britain's religion has to be named, it won't be the Bible or this or that liturgy, or some sacrament-turned-folk-rite, such as a christening or a 'church' wedding, but the hymn. In churches and chapels up and down the land it has become the most enjoyed part of the service and certain hymns are now the summaries of such convincing beliefs and images as an individual is likely to hold to any depth.[8]

What Ronald accurately observes here is that the combination of words and music becomes an enjoyable and engaging way in which to express what one believes. This is more captivating than dogma, liturgy or preaching and is thus likely to be the most powerful means by which people can vocalise their faith. He also acknowledges that the modern and enduring popularity of televised hymn-singing, and other worship songs, taps into our fascination with private devotion displayed as public worship and music-making, as well as the deeper notion of humanity's innate desire to sing about, and to, divine beings:

> If the success of televised hymn-singing was analysed, we would see that it derives from staring into a great range of faces made privately devout while engaged in public song. From the beginning men have sung to, and of, their gods, and the splendid anthology known as the Book of Psalms is the oldest collection of such God-addressed songs still in general use all over the world.[9]

The connection between psalms and hymns is ancient and enduring. All human emotion and experience is contained within the psalms and would have been expressed in musical form from the earliest times. The story of God's people through triumph and tragedy is mapped out in heart-felt expression from exaltation to desolation, and musicians have used the words of the psalms in music to demonstrate their own life experience. During the European Reformation both music and the psalms became useful tools, even weapons, for expressing theological conviction and identity. The words of the Psalms were employed polemically in the turmoil between Catholic and Protestant believers. In the sacred choral music of the early modern period, psalm settings could denote secretive, or not-so-secretive, allegiances, and the manner of psalm word-setting became an important factor in how religious fervour was expressed.

THE PSALMS: FROM MEDIEVAL TO MODERNITY

The Psalms were central to medieval Christian devotion and learning. They were at the heart of the Divine Office for monks and nuns, clergy and laity. They were also the basis for infant literary education. The language of the Psalms enabled prayer and praise, as well as confession, and encouraged meditation upon even New Testament themes, such as incarnation and resurrection. The principal method of singing the Psalms was, of course, chant. In English cathedrals, both monastic and secular, they were sung by the clerks of the choir, or vicars-choral. At St Paul's Cathedral, for instance, the original number of vicars-choral was the same as the number of canons, which was thirty, so that each canon had a deputy to sing the offices for him, should he be non-resident or incapable of singing.[10] In practice, the canons probably left all singing duties to the minor ranks. The vicars-choral, as well as singing the offices instead of the canons, assisted at the altar during Mass.[11] Although all minor clergy had singing duties, the vicars-choral bore the brunt of the daily choral routine and were answerable, in the first instance, to the minor canons for their standards of behaviour.[12] On special occasions, such as large services, the vicars-choral would join forces with the chantry priests and minor canons to form the full choir, along with twelve boy trebles.[13] Similar in status to the poor clerks of Lincoln, they were sometimes referred to as '*Pauperes clerici*'.[14] At Salisbury, most vicars-choral lived with the residentiary canons and were treated as household members. At York, the precentor was chief cantor, or singer, while the chancellor instructed choristers and vicars-choral on divinity and Church history and examined the vicars-choral in psalms and histories at the end of their first year.[15] However, standards of singing the Psalms varied. One Richard Smith failed to achieve the required standard in his one-year probation at Salisbury:

> [Smith] Hath no fitt voyce to singe the tenor for that it is to small, neither the countertenor for that it is not tunable therunto, neither the bass for that itt is utterly unfitt for that parte.[16]

Standards of behaviour were also expected to be high for the vicars-choral serving in other English secular cathedrals (that is, clerical but non-monastic establishments). According to their adopted Norman rule of Chrodegang, Minster officials at York were expected to show humility, moderation, diligence, piety, dignity, seriousness of purpose, charity, chastity and urbanity. The succentor drew up a 'single-table', or rota, for their canting duties: there were to be the correct number of vicars-choral on each side of the choir; if a vicar-choral was to be paid, then he had to be in place by the *Gloria Patri* at the end of the first psalm. Scholarship suggests that the minor clergy of English secular cathedrals were badly in need of behavioural discipline on the eve of the Reformation:

> Drastic reform was certainly necessary at this [junior] level of the clergy, whose idleness and immorality provoked much of the satirical and sermonising literature against clerical misconduct.[17]

While this assertion rather overstates the case – good behaviour was naturally not documented – there is evidence of occasional misbehaviour among minor clergy as well as vehement criticisms of the standards of chant and polyphonic musical performances, especially from humanists. What the 'prince of humanists', Erasmus, heard in church was a great deal of incomprehensible singing performed badly:

> nowadays, the clamorous voices are observed not only in many churches but also in monasteries, with thundering and raucous yelling, so that the sounds obscure everything and nothing can be understood. I call their prayers uttered without the mind murmuring; this is indeed more to murmur than to pray.[18]

Likewise, the Italian humanist who resided in England for most of his adult life, Polydore Vergil (1470–1555), gave a less than glowing account of English musicians:

> our cantors shriek to such an extent in our churches that nothing ... can be distinguished other than the sound of their voices ... in short, they are convinced that they are the only decorations in God's house.[19]

The Elizabethan settlement of 1559, which included an Act of Uniformity and Injunctions, sought to bring clarity of text back to music with this dictate:

> The Queen's Majesty ... willeth and commandeth, that first no alteration be made of such assignments of living, as here to fore have been appointed to the use of singing or music in the Church, but that the same so remain. And that there be a modest distinct song, so used in all parts of the common prayers in the Church, that the same may be as plainly understood, as if it were read without singing ...[20]

An interesting example of syllabic psalm-setting can be found in 1567, when Thomas Tallis contributed nine tunes for Archbishop Parker's *Psalter*, a collection of vernacular psalm settings intended for publication in a metrical psalter then being compiled by the Archbishop of Canterbury, Matthew Parker. The eight psalm tunes as printed in Parker's *Psalter* appear to have become obscure for some centuries following the death of Tallis, but the set includes some of his most famous melodies, including 'Why fum'th in fight', in the third or phrygian mode. Meanwhile, the recusant Catholic composer William Byrd was pre-eminent among a growing number of proficient and often excellent composers and musicians in England. His motet *Infelix Ego*, which takes its text from a meditation upon Psalm 51 by the Florentine reformer Girolamo Savonarola (d. 1496), presented a public witness to a personal faith and a message of hope to a persecuted Catholic audience. Catholic recusant composers used the psalm themes of Babylonian exile and of the return of Jerusalem to denote Catholic isolation and persecution as well as the desire for a return of the true faith and one true Catholic Church. This is most clearly demonstrated in the compositional exchange in two pieces with words taken from Psalm 137: *Super Flumina Babylonis* (By the rivers of Babylon we sat down and wept) by de Monte and *Quomodo Cantabimus* (How shall we sing the Lord's song in a strange land?) by Byrd. De Monte's knowledge of how English Catholics were being treated seems to have been his motivation for sending Byrd a setting of the first four verses (in the Vulgate numbering) of Psalm 137 (136 in the Vulgate). However, the verses are rearranged so as to emphasise the plight of Catholics.

The rhetorical nature of the exchange between de Monte and Byrd, the historical, theological and political contexts in which it was made, and the manner in which the text was chosen, manipulated and set, is more than enough evidence to demonstrate that these two pieces of music are more than art, they are more than sacred music even, for they are polemical critique and theological statements of purpose and hope.

To the West Country organist Thomas Tomkins (1572–1656), Byrd was a revered master. Byrd's verse anthems, as well as the domestic version of the consort song, became an inspiration to Tomkins and he became an expert composer of the vernacular form, with solo and chorus alternating. Ritual use of this form was opposed by the puritan divines. A comment by Robert Browne in *A True and Short Declaration* of 1583 derided 'the tossing to and fro of psalms and sentences ... like tenisse plaie whereto God is called a Judge who can do best and be most gallant in his worship'.[21] This comment criticises not only the performance but also the echoing acoustic of cathedrals where, like rallies in a game of real tennis, the musical phrases bounce off the walls like tennis balls. Fundamentally, this is the same critique as the fifteenth-century and early sixteenth-century criticisms of psalm-singing, namely incomprehensibility of words. Tomkins's verse anthems demonstrate elegant comprehensibility but also some popish tendencies. The anthem *Rejoice, rejoice and singe*, for the Annunciation or Lady Day, was written for a feast that had been banned since 1548, except under Mary Tudor. Somehow it was acceptable to perform such an anthem in the Chapel Royal, in Elizabethan and Stuart England. It ends with an eight-fold benediction of the Virgin Mary, which is unique in English music of the time. If this piece is a clue to Tomkins's religious leanings, then what interpretation do we give to his 1622 setting of Psalm 120, verse five: 'Woe is me, that I am constrained to dwell with Mesech [that is, foreigners or barbarians] and to have my habitation among the tents of Kedar [like the nomadic Arab tribes cut off from the true God]'?

In all the turbulence of the religious conflicts of early modern England, music became both an expression of true religious sentiment and a source of devotional solace, as well as a way of reaching out to believers of similar allegiance. Psalm settings were a powerful way of asserting religious practice, especially in the communal and 'common prayer' singing of metrical psalms in the vernacular, whereby believers were taught the scriptures in their own language and conformed to a unified liturgical practice. But psalm settings could also be used in both private and public devotional ways to express rebellion against such Reformation conformity, whether in Latin or English. Composers, performers and listeners always found a way to express their true feelings, whatever the religious authorities dictated. In music and the Psalms, Christians found an outlet to express their innermost beliefs.

HYMNS

Hymns are the siblings of psalms, and our modern-day way of declaring faith within our cultural context. Whether we adhere to the *Book of Common Prayer*, from Cranmer's day, or worship in the style of the rock concert, what we sing with our lips we believe in our hearts. That is why the doctrine contained within hymns is so important. Early Christian hymns made much use of scriptural images, so that one might call them exegetical in nature, interpreting scripture, even preaching the Word of God.[22] The definition of a hymn was set out sixteen centuries ago by St Augustine:

> A hymn is the praise of God by singing. A hymn is a song embodying the praise of God. If there be merely praise but not praise of God it is

> not a hymn. If there be praise, and praise of God, but not sung, it is not a hymn. For it to be a hymn, it is needful, therefore, for it to have three things – praise, praise of God, and these sung.[23]

Ronald has added a fourth characteristic definition of a hymn, namely 'that a hymn is the singing of praise of God by a congregation of people'.[24] Thus it is not a solitary exercise but a communal activity, a notable characteristic often, but not exclusively, of music, whether in its composition, performance or reception. C.S. Lewis connected communal singing with medieval ideas of angelic heavenly music. In *The Screwtape Letters* (letters from a senior Demon to a junior one), the laughter of joy is mocked by the senior Demon as being like 'that detestable art which the humans call Music, and something like it occurs in Heaven – a meaningless acceleration in the rhythm of celestial experience, quite opaque to us'.[25] For Dimitri Conomos and Bishop Kallistos Ware, Lewis's thinking and theological orientation 'is profoundly in harmony with the patristic and Orthodox standpoint'.[26] Conomos explains:

> The description of heavenly music is a case in point: it demonstrates Lewis's intuitive affinity with at least two medieval Neo-Platonists. In his *The Celestial Hierarchy*, Dionysius the Pseudo-Areopagite (c. 500) makes reference to the ranks of angels who in heaven are united in song. Each choir sings hymns, the music of which is passed from the highest and nearest to the throne of God down the ranks of the angelic choirs to the lowest before finally being transmitted to the praying congregations of the church militant.[27] In the medieval West, an opposite point of view was expressed by Remigius of Auxerre (c. 841–c. 908): 'True music is always in the heavens ...'.[28] Accordingly, Screwtape's 'detestable art' is in fact the human imitation of divine song whose music is comparable to 'the laughter of joy'.[29]

Despite this angelic elevation of hymns, Lewis, like Erasmus in the Middle Ages, was heavily critical of some hymns and those who sing them, describing them as 'one long roar'[30] and 'fifth-rate poems set to sixth-rate music'[31] with 'confused or erroneous sentiment'.[32] When he was asked, in 1946, to judge contributions to a new hymnal, Lewis declined, stating that 'hymns are mostly the dead wood of the service'.[33] Erik Routley, who had invited Lewis to judge the hymns, was incensed by Lewis's snobbery. Hymns, he insisted, 'were never meant to be a garnishment to the service – never a medium for community singing, or for aesthetic, non-spiritual indulgence – but a vital part of the liturgy itself'.[34]

But Lewis maintained his view of most hymns as emotional low-brow culture, to which church-goers must submit in humility: 'The door is low and one must stoop to enter.'[35] His 1949 essay, 'On Church Music',[36] argued that church services may have a cultural value but this is not the purpose of their existence. Church music is to be praised as long as it 'edifies the faithful,' otherwise it is pointless.[37] 'Popular hymns,' therefore, may provide an emotional uplift but not religious edification: 'I do not yet seem to have found any evidence that the physical and emotional exhilaration which it produces is necessarily, or often, of any religious relevance.'[38] But, as Conomos has pointed out, 'By limiting his range of focus on Victorian hymn compositions, his conclusions eschew such genres as psalmody, biblical tropes, antiphonal and responsorial compositions, liturgical responses, choral motets, plainchant, and many more.'[39] However, even when considering 'high-brow' musical excellence, Lewis is doubtful as to its spiritual worth:

> I must insist that no degree of excellence in the music, simply as music, can assure us that ... [a] ... paradisal state has been achieved. The excellence proves 'keenness'; but men can be 'keen' for natural, even wicked, motives. The absence of keenness would prove that they lacked the right spirit; its presence does not prove that they have it. We must beware of the naïve idea that our music can 'please' God as it would please a cultivated human hearer.[40]

Thus Lewis warned of the danger of an 'aesthetic religion of "flowers and music"',[41] leading Conomos to suggest that, 'It is a fact that, today, in their frequenting concert halls or listening to CDs, people have discovered a substitute sacrament.'[42]

Thus the hymn, of whatever quality, brings us back from the realms of the concert hall 'substitute sacrament' to the communal worship of a gathered faithful. Because for a hymn to be a hymn, and indeed effective as such, it must be sung together. The congregational aspect is essential for, as Wesley asserted, one cannot be a solitary Christian. Indeed, hymns have been used throughout the centuries, including those of the Wesley brothers in the eighteenth century, to revive a flagging Church:

> It is no coincidence that the times of the great awakenings of a periodically dozing-off Church produced fresh and often superb hymns. Ambrose, Luther, Charles Wesley, and John Mason Neale understood how to create the collective affirmation of their centuries by means of the hymn. They altered and re-presented old hymns, ancient country songs even, as well as inventing new ones. They fashioned a veritable

> indestructible pattern of tune and language, knowing that for most people their hymns would be the least complicated path to religious experience. Others rhymed the Psalms, occasionally modishly.[43]

Not only was the composition of new hymns and tunes a feature of Church revival, but the manner in which they were taught to new audiences and congregations enabled their reception, and the reception of the Gospel of which they sang, to be more easily assimilated and welcomed:

> Wesley's hymns were often taught by 'throwing' their lines, one by one, to the congregation, a method used later by music-hall artists – Gracie Fields did it with 'Sally' – except that what Wesley's audiences caught was a rich mixture of contemplative and social Christianity so exultantly set to music that it made them both prayerful and activist.[44]

But these times of revival become historical events. In today's British society, Wesley's Methodism is on the wane and a new evangelical revival has a musical sound and language of its own, which is more suited to the guitar and keyboard than the organ or harmonium, although the technique of learning new worship songs through 'throwing the line', with call and response, still thrives. And yet, even archaic and dated language in hymnody can endure if the theological import behind the words still makes an impact: 'Hymns are heavily dated yet during the singing of them they become timeless, their archaisms no obstacle.'[45] One composer who, although agnostic himself, was a great champion of the British hymn and compiler of many, was Ralph Vaughan Williams. It was he who 'said that the hymns of Christendom show more clearly than anything else that a unity of spirit actually exists in the Church,'[46] although, at times in the Christian history, congregational singing has been suppressed. We have already seen how Ulrich Zwingli did so in early sixteenth-century Zürich, when he banned music from the churches and removed the organ pipes. A talented musician himself, he was nevertheless suspicious of music's ability to charm the senses and to distract the believer from the Word of God by its sensuous and mysterious ways. Ronald is a little despondent about clerical education in the ways of hymnody: 'even now there are many priests who know little about it as an act of collective worship for which there still remains a hunger.'[47] I find this a little too downhearted, for in our cathedrals, churches and chapels hymns remain the most reliable source of theological expression for the gathered people in worship, and there has been little musical or poetic progress that has threatened to usurp the hymn from its elevated position in artistic expression of faith. But Ronald becomes more positive when reflecting upon hymnody's credentials:

> Among all the outpourings of religious analysis it would be hard to find an intelligent and inspired account of what occurs to the individual worshipper of Christ as he takes up the tune and words of a fine and loved hymn. This singing of encapsulated spiritual thought of every age provides for the ordinary Christian the best historical understanding of his faith that he is ever likely to receive. Hymns, like secular songs, are firmly dated but, because they deal with the eternal, the best of them cannot become obsolete. They are religion's most enduring popular art.[48]

Examples of how hymns remain an enduring conduit for religion, even in the hearts and minds of non-believers, are not difficult to find. June Boyce-Tillman's notion of a 'Missing God' in today's society, which reflects a 'memory of a former belief system, perhaps associated with childhood or a particular culture',[49] is perhaps evident in a comment in the Alister Hardy Archive: 'At the age of 88 years I am practically religionless except that most days I am obsessed with Moody and Sankey hymns.'[50] Likewise, Theresa May chose 'When I survey the Wondrous Cross' for her Radio 4 Desert Island Discs because 'it reminded her of the togetherness of a church congregation.'[51] Boyce-Tillman also quoted some beautiful words by Alan Bennett that express how singing hymns can help a sense of belonging:

> I am one of those boys state educated in the 40s and 50s who came by the words of *Ancient and Modern* through singing them day in and day out at school every morning in assembly. It's a dwindling band, old fashioned and of a certain age. You can pick us out at funerals and memorial services because we can sing the hymns without the books ... I have never found it easy to belong. So much repels. Hymns help, they blur.[52]

The comforting role of hymns in easing a sense of belonging is also extended to their healing and palliative property in critical care with the sick and dying, as Robin Knowles-Wallace has observed: 'I work with dying people and often hymns are among the last things they forget ... Hymn singing at the very end of life is incredibly reassuring.'[53]

While many hymns offer an explicit doctrinal framework in the text, they so often work on an implicit level. As Boyce-Tillman observes, an atheist may sing 'How great thou art' with joy because of the cultural connection to

Wales, and members of cathedral choirs can be deeply moved by the music they sing without believing the words.[54] As I have argued before, the divide between sacred and secular is not as rigid as some people would have it,[55] and music helps to penetrate through dogmatic hymnody and produce, in the listener and the singer alike, a complex and rich experience of implicit religion. As Kathryn Jenkins has written:

> Reason demands that the text of the hymn is of primary importance in all contexts and the music is secondary. But long practice, experience and human nature decree otherwise. The success, the memorability and the popularity of the hymn ... are almost invariably due to its music.[56]

Moreover, Linda Clark has asserted that it is not just the sound of the music that becomes so meaningful, it is the embodiment of the musical and linguistic experience through performance that makes a hymn so powerful: 'A hymn does not tell *of* the faith, it *tells* it, declares it, bodies it forth.'[57] As such, for Boyce-Tillman, congregational singing is 'embodied theology'.[58]

For Don Saliers, the music and text of a hymn combine to become what he calls 'lyrical theology', which should be 'placed alongside dogmatic, philosophical and systematic theology' so that 'more formal notions of giving an ordered account of the doctrine of the Christian faith depend upon what is prayed and sung and proclaimed'.[59] What Saliers calls 'The formal language of reasoned reflection on Christian doctrine', which 'requires the primary theological "language" of sound',[60] equates to what I have described as cognitive belief systems. Saliers' idea of 'lyrical theology' seems to be part of the 'implicit theology' that we have explored. Not only does the music in hymns provide an accompaniment to the language of belief but it also enables the participants, whether singing or listening, to access a deeper and more durable relationship of faith, so that 'when the music itself is strong ... it becomes part of the body's memory of words, thus creating permanent access to lyrical theology. It is the musical setting that accumulates to itself associations of time, place, persons, and encounters which ever after are contained in the singing.'[61]

In a post-secular society, hymns and psalms provide us with a direct connection with our Judeo-Christian cultural past. They are the remarkable vehicles of meaning and history that carry theological insights accessible to all feeling human beings. They have proved, and continue to prove, to be enduring conduits of faith and implicit experience of the divine, or at least an imagined deity. Whether sung in a church, a school assembly or a football ground, they help us to embody an incarnate sense of the mystery of our past and future, of creation and the transcendent, of memory and meaning. A few notes of a single hymn, perhaps containing a brief paraphrase of a line of a psalm, can evoke thousands of years of Judeo-Christian history in a moment of time, while concurrently revitalising intense experiences, associations and relationships in the personal life of the participant. Hymns have a remarkable ability to evoke cultural and personal memory and, in their relative simplicity, to take us into the rich and complex world of the numinous, transcendent and unknowable mystery beyond us.

CHAPTER THREE

EYE MUSIC

Painting is the grandchild of nature. It is related to God.[1]

There are many responses to the music of faith in our society today. Music has the power to move us deeply and to inspire us. Some responses to powerful and inspirational music are eloquent, beautiful and artistic expressions in their own right. One example is the work of the Wiltshire-born artist Janet Boulton who, in recent years, has been working on an artistic project known as 'Eye Music.' It is Janet's motivation, faith and inspiration that form the focus of this chapter. For me, Janet's 'Eye Music' project beautifully captures the relationship between music and faith. The artistic connection between the sung notes within Christian liturgy, particularly in the service of *Tenebrae* in Holy Week, is explored in a personal way, recognising the movement, both within the liturgy and within the heart of the believer, from darkness to light, from despair to hope. My research into this interconnectedness between sacred music, its impact on a congregation or audience, and the subsequent artistic expression of that experience in visual art has been hugely advanced by knowing Janet and her work, and learning of the fascinating motivation and meaning of this important project.

The 'Eye-Music' series of watercolour/collage and paper-pulp reliefs are inspired by the idea of graphic musical notation. Janet writes that she

> has combined observations of a still life installed in a window (comprising five plate glass shelves and rows of jam jars) with the forms of musical notation used in early medieval plainchant. In a process of deconstruction and re-invention, with music strongly in mind, she has made images which are intended to be seen independently as well as being a source of musical inspiration. Although there are no

> specifications for instrument/s or interpretation she became increasingly conscious whilst making the pictures of the spatial and tonal potential of sound.[2]

Joe Scarffe writes of her work:

> Janet Boulton refers to her collection as 'Eye-Music,' but it is important to recognize that she is using the term in a special way. Technically speaking 'Augenmusik' (eye music) is the 'practice of utilizing graphics to embellish staff notation, with a largely graphic or typographic function, in order to reinforce the affective meaning of the music.' Janet, on the other hand, is using the term to describe the visual impact of the works and the significance of their autonomy.[3]

Scarffe sees Boulton's work not only as a visual art form but as a stimulus for musical improvisation:

> [Medieval] Augenmusik or Eye Music adds visual interest to their scores to enhance the expressive impact of the music.[4] ... As Boulton is primarily an artist and the Eye Music Series has not included performance notes, these works can also be appropriately described as autonomous. By this, I mean that the works are intended to be enjoyed both purely as visual art and as a stimulus to improvise from.[5]

This dual intention for the works is a distinctive feature of Boulton's work. But where did the idea for Eye Music come from?

> Janet's work originates from a still life installed in a window, comprising five glass shelves and rows of jam jars. She has said to me that she became increasingly aware of the co-relation of music and tone, so much so that sometimes it was as if sounds were playing back to her while she was painting. Through the process of creating the Eye Music Series, she began to understand the importance of the spatial aspect of music. [Figure 3][6]

Moreover, Janet's childhood was infused with psalms, hymns and the music of the Church, as she relates:

> As so often when tracing the beginnings of ideas I find myself in our village church attending Sunday School or being in the choir. Hymns and psalms were sung to the sound of an organ, whilst following the musical notation in an old leather-bound hymnal. During piano lessons, a highpoint of the year was being given the new music

> required for the next examination. On opening the book for the first time, reading the title and seeing the shapes of the notation rising and falling effortlessly among the horizontal staves, the light and dark notes, curves and parallel lines. The manuscript as a whole, with its foreign words and Arabic numerals seemed a graceful expressive thing in its own right, without the necessity of being realized in sound. Thus, in the course of everyday life we absorb the existence of other non-verbal means of communicating and are introduced to the wider world of semiotics.[7]

Janet's relationship with institutional religion has been an interesting one and will be explored later in this chapter, but the religious or theological essence of her work is clear, as she explains:

> St Bernard of Clairvaux (1090–1153) once said, 'Hearing leads to sight.' Conversely, in these Eye Music pictures it could be said 'Sight led to hearing,' since the long process that led to making them came initially through considering the purely visual possibilities of the still life in the window.[8]

Thus Janet's still-life paintings of clear jam jars on five glass shelves (echoing the five lines of the musical stave) led her to explore this relationship between sight and hearing, but the paintings also connected her with an artistic tradition:

> The jam jar has a number of attributes. Being simply a cylinder made up of vertical, horizontal and elliptical elements it contains the all-important 'cube, cone and sphere' defined by Paul Cézanne (1839–1906) as fundamental in his researches into the universal nature of form. The black and gold label 'Chinese Stem Ginger in Syrup' represents to me a connection with those early twentieth-century followers of Cézanne – the Cubist painters: Braque, Picasso and Gris. These artists incorporated many graphic devices along with the naming of people and things in common usage into their still life pictures: for instance, 'Vin' on a bottle of wine or 'J.S. Bach' on a sheet of music beside a violin, or the name of a loved-one.[9]

The connection between that tradition, her work, music and religion came together in a single time and place:

> Thinking further along these lines I eventually (while attending the pre-Easter celebration of the *Tenebrae* at Blackfriars in Oxford) saw a connection between the jar with its label and the early medieval

> musical notation used for plainchant. The idea of strong black squares, rectangles and lozenges, grouped within the framework of vertical (the window) and horizontal staves (the shelves) seemed to reinforce and substantiate the musical content of the pictures, giving me a wider, more relevant vocabulary ... Another discovery, early on, was finding that when making the support to contain the still life, it inadvertently formed a construction which bore similarities to the pages of a conventional musical manuscript. Namely, the five plate glass horizontal shelves enclosed in parallel vertical lines with a shallow perspective.
>
> The basic shape gave me an appropriate and meaningful format on which to base all the works in this Eye Music Series. Added to which, the static and rather flat, repetitious nature of the glass still life arrangement is offset, indeed liberated, by the contrasting freedom and movement inherent in the view of the garden as well as to be found in musical composition. Moreover, by appropriating the simple graphic shapes of early musical notation I gained the tools and the language, whereby in a process of deconstruction and re-invention I could make pictures which embraced the formal and random languages of both painterly and musical traditions and ideas. It is as if an *abstract* occurrence is taking place in a *real* space.[10]

Moreover, the relationship between colour and music is an important feature of Janet's work. There is a kind of synaesthetic element to the paintings in which music is evoked by the use of colour:

> The idea that colour and musical notes are intrinsically related has been in existence since Isaac Newton (1642–1727) split the optical spectrum into seven colours and linked them to the seven notes of the musical scale. Since that time there have been innumerable important treatises and theories about the relation of colours to sound and emotion as well as to each other.[11]
>
> In twentieth century European painting, artists such as Kandinsky, Kupka, Klee, Van Doesburg, and Itten all turned to colour theory alongside musical values as prime sources in their researches into abstraction.
>
> The choice and the arrangement of the colour, the tones and the graphic elements in this Eye Music Series of paintings and the relief works is purely subjective, being personal and random. These paintings are neither a blueprint nor a musical score. They are not prescriptive of any instrumentation or performance and have no starting or ending point – but I do have music in mind.[12]

Janet's Eye Music project has been further developed in very recent times by her work for an exhibition at Magdalen College, Oxford entitled 'Fragments of note: the afterlives of medieval manuscripts,' held between November 2017 and April 2018, which examined the numerous medieval manuscript fragments held at Magdalen, largely medieval books dismantled in the early modern period and re-used as binding waste or covers. The main exhibition took a particular focus on fragments featuring musical notation which were complemented by a selection of contemporary watercolour, collage and paper-pulp relief works by Janet. The exhibition was co-curated by Dr Giovanni Varelli (Prize Fellow in Music at Magdalen) and Daryl Green (Librarian).[13] Further discussions with Janet have led to an initiative for 2019 in which a selection of *Tenebrae* pictures will be exhibited in Magdalen College Chapel to coincide with Lent and Holy Week (14–21 April) and with the publication of this volume.

I first visited Janet in Abingdon in 2016 and walked through her garden, which is celebrated for its design and numerous inscriptions. I saw a depiction in slate and stone of the word 'Faith,' and further on Epicurus's injunction to 'Live Unknown' cut into a piece of cherrywood. Both were placed in the borders beside the path leading to Janet's studio. In this way I was alerted to the importance of the inclusion of words and signs, sometimes of a religious or moral nature, in her art. In the studio I was intrigued by the use of medieval notation within her compositions. Janet is a convert to Catholicism and one of her most important liturgical experiences has been attending the *Tenebrae* service on Maundy Thursday at Blackfriars in Oxford. The service is distinguished for the ritual of gradually extinguishing candles, while psalms are sung to plainchant or polyphony (such as the setting by the Renaissance Spanish composer Tomàs Luis da Victoria). *Tenebrae* literally means 'darkness,' so I asked Janet what this service of darkness meant to her and how the liturgy and the music inspired her recent work.

JB: After I started at art school in 1953 I lost interest in religion and church-going. It was a conscious decision. I didn't just drift away since it involved me resigning from the choir and teaching in Sunday School. All this was because my new interests and way of thinking conflicted with the teachings of the Christian faith – at least as a rather simplistic seventeen-year-old understood it. It was an era that witnessed the emergence of a youth culture. Typical of student life in those days, I was introduced to an eclectic mix of folk and skiffle along with jazz and blues coming from America and a way of dancing quite different from the staid attempts we had at ballroom dancing – shuffling around at a Hunt Ball. At the same time I heard my first recordings of Russian Gregorian chant. My Protestant upbringing was challenged and overturned by debates about existentialism, atheism, communism and conscientious objection (an alternative to National Service which was still obligatory for young men in the 1950s). Pubs and cafés were the convivial places where most exchanges of new ideas took place and thinking back it must have been at about this time that my susceptibility to alcohol first showed up and marked the beginning of my dependency on drink.

JA: I know that you don't drink now. What was it that influenced you to recognise that you had a problem?

JB: Really, I shall never completely understand how it was, seemingly out of the blue, that a crack appeared in the armour of my denial and that I was lucky enough to face the reality of my illness. The loss of confidence and sense of isolation I experienced in those early months of abstinence was balanced by having the great good fortune to meet, quite by chance, a mature recovering alcoholic. It was she who introduced me to a group of people in the same position who maintained their sobriety by meeting regularly, supporting each other and sharing their feelings truthfully. It was by being welcomed and encouraged to participate in this that I have learnt to follow a programme of recovery, thus living a happier, more fulfilling life free from all mind-altering dependencies. As you will understand all this involved some radical changes in my thinking and general approach to almost everything. In fact, it has become the most valuable means towards practising my spirituality.

JA: So why, after twenty years, and relatively late in life, did you decide to go back to the Church and, further still, to go as far as committing to Roman Catholicism?

JB: Learning to live a life of sobriety was a slow progression but it was not without a sense of being led by some kind of benign higher power. The relevance of relating these details about my early life is that it led to me, albeit in a circuitous way, eventually returning to the church. To answer your question; the decision to commit to Roman Catholicism must in retrospect have involved quite a number of different influences. For many years between making paintings of gardens in Italy I spent hours in churches, drawing, photographing and generally looking around. On occasion I would sit at the back of the church during a service and depict the ongoing scene. Somehow I began to feel left out, an intruder and something of a voyeur. A favourite place was the church of Sant' Ambrogio in Florence, where the market people came, lit votive candles and prayed before a polychrome figure of the Virgin Mary standing on a side altar, surrounded by masses of flowers. I began to seek out similar sculptures, and to recognize that in the local life of these churches, full of great art and tourists, it was around these, often modest, figures that the most vital, meaningful activity took place. Also, I have a number of Catholic friends and was attracted by their varied and open approach and the willingness to discuss their faith freely. Added to this, there may be some truth in a friend's comment that my conversion was an attempt 'at recapturing a sentimental view of my happy village childhood experience'. It goes without saying that the aesthetic and cultural influence was strong. Anyhow, all this led me to Blackfriars Priory in Oxford, finding an interest in medieval plainchant notation and inspiring the 'Eye Music Series' of pictures.

JA: You might have gone on thinking about this forever!

JB: Yes, indeed! But whatever the sources and reasons, and in spite of certain misgivings, rather than sit on the edge looking in, I decided to 'obey my instinct', take the risk, and get into the middle of the boat, aware of the possibility of finding myself all too soon landing among the lapsed. I couldn't aspire to being 'a good Catholic' but I did think that my strength lay in the experience of, and belief in, the power of prayer while, at the same time, wanting to re-engage as fully as possible with the origins of the culture to which I belong.

JA: It must be almost another twenty years now since you went back to the Church. Has your experience during that time been a happy one?

JB: Mostly, yes! I am glad for no longer being an outsider and for having the sensation of arriving full circle. I'm free of that troublesome equivocation, which often comes across as sounding like 'Don't get me wrong, I'm not religious but I am spiritual'. It's not that I think that my life of faith is in any way at all perfect but that I accept the existence of religion as still being relevant today. I know now just how unpopular this viewpoint is in much of the world, but for me there is something about an entirely secular approach to life and art which seems sterile.

JA: So how do the most recent developments in the 'Eye Music' pictures relate to all this, especially, for instance, in the works that we are showing in the Antechapel at Magdalen College during Holy Week 2019?

JB: It was in the first paintings of *Tenebrae*, started in 2015, that I stopped making paintings in which the elements of musical notation were unrelated to any known written music. This was the outcome of attending Blackfriars during Holy Week and being inspired by that particular place on a particular occasion; being one of the congregation, standing in a part of the church where I could see the altar, and the candles being gradually extinguished as the service progressed, ending in the dramatic moment when some of the Dominican Brotherhood fall simultaneously, full length, onto the black and white marble paving. It was here that I first made a connection between faith and music. Since then I have made a number of paintings of this subject, trying to get nearer to a way of expressing this powerful and moving service. The falling from light to darkness is something, I would guess, most of us have experienced. So even without the Christian story it would resonate one way or another. However, no amount of circumstantial or narrative detail is going to make a satisfactory painting. There has to be a strong pictorial integrity for it to stand in its own right. These pictures have been about controlling the extremities of tone in order to depict the descent from serenity to chaos – trying to express the sense of the music in that space while, at the bottom of the image, the picture culminates in a bleak, jagged landscape, formed by the letters of the word *Tenebrae*, and a gleam of hope [Figure 4]. The red lozenges represent not only an element in the notation for plainchant but also drops of blood – the colour red being essential to the subject and the composition.

JA: The work you made last year in response to the collection of manuscript fragments held in the Old Library at Magdalen College seemed to break new ground. Can you say something about this and your experience of working in the college?

JB: In some ways it was new ground but in other ways not. I had already established the idea of making pictures that tried to express the sensation of hearing sacred music as an integral part of a specific religious service. It is crucial for me that my pictures express the experience of sacred music heard in the environment for which it was intended. At Magdalen I was given the perfect opportunity to work from original medieval manuscripts containing musical notation written for the liturgy, but also I was immersed in an environment with a centuries-old thriving life of worship and music. So I just carried on with the *Tenebrae* at Blackfriars idea. The intensity and focus of the story of Holy Week as it unfolds towards Easter is a very human one. Listening to the music and looking at the art made over the centuries, variously describes or enacts, for example, the words and meaning of the Lamentations of Jeremiah or Mary's suffering at the foot of the crucified Christ in the *Stabat Mater*.[14] I have found it increasingly easy to relate to them in a personal way.

JA: Why do you think this is? I know you attended our Good Friday Liturgy in the Chapel at Magdalen in 2017, in which the choir sang Thomas Tallis's *Lamentations of Jeremiah* (I) and (II).

JB: Age and experience must help! I sat in the Antechapel during this service because I felt it necessary to be distanced from the intensity of the chapel. In this way I hoped to be able to be more focused and objective. The picture I have made is nevertheless set in the chapel with its powerful altarpiece and steep rows of choir stalls – dramatic and inward-looking [Figure 5]. I have used the medieval plainchant notation, taken from a fragment in the library, albeit deconstructed, and adapted it in an attempt to make some kind of equivalent to the content and experience, you might say, of being in the presence of the 'Lamentations'.

JA: The last of your trilogy of paintings for Holy Week is a *Stabat Mater*. Why does it mean so much to you?

JB: Since my experience in the Church of Sant' Ambrogio in Florence, wherever I have been I have sought out depictions of the Virgin Mary and have incorporated the idea of a woman as mother goddess in a number of pictures. The central importance given to Mary and Marian culture was a big factor in attracting me to Catholicism. Recently I have made some pictures of the stained-glass window in the Chapel at Magdalen devoted to a *Madonna and Child* associating it with neumes, an early form of musical notation, in an attempt to acknowledge and include an earlier, even archaic, association with a mother goddess [Figure 6]. Years ago I met the composer Gabriel Jackson fleetingly at a function at Tate Modern and have followed his music ever since. When I heard that the premiere of his *Stabat Mater* was to take place at Merton College I knew I had to be there. Once again, I sat in the Antechapel with a central view towards the altar. Subsequently I made the preparatory drawings, obtained a copy of the score and the recording,[15] and studied a small medieval window high above the altar depicting the Crucifixion. I am working on a version of this picture at the moment and seem to vacillate between a state of terror and one of bravado. The inspiration and the intention are there, but a lot of what goes towards making a picture involves more head than heart. I am only at the beginning of getting anywhere near finding an adequate equivalent to the electrifying experience of being in the presence of this profound and tragic music in the chapel for which it was written.

JA: Now that you have a made substantial body of work devoted to the music written for Holy Week, has it influenced your view of being a Christian?

JB: Where to begin ... my subject matter has always been intertwined with my life but it's a very nice surprise to find at this late stage a new source of inspiration which also relates to so much of my past. The process of making these pictures has given me a better insight into church history and brought me closer to its associated rituals, liturgy and music. Furthermore, from the beginning I've met all kinds of new people who have been more than generous in sharing their expertise and understanding my aims.

Janet's theological outlook is both incarnational and akin to realised eschatology, in which the Kingdom of God is a present reality; there is no heaven or hell where future justice will be meted out, nor rewards dispensed. For Janet, any sorrow or joy is to be experienced in this life. She is aware of those on the margins of society, perhaps a little like herself, a countercultural believer, artist and recovering alcoholic, but she is also well aware of the Church's failings as well as its artistic treasures.

Further evidence of Janet's views on faith were revealed in a public interview about her work on the manuscript fragments with Magdalen College librarian Daryl Green, which was musically illustrated by the lutenist Linda Sayce. During the conversation Janet talked about her first encounter with the musical notation of lute tablature, which she responded to with an image, painted while she was working in the Old Library at Magdalen and which was executed quite quickly by lineating the notation with masking fluid and watercolour. Janet mentioned that she was struck by how the tablature 'looks the way it sounds' [Figure 7]. Her artistic response to the tablature captures the essence of 'visual sound', and her works in response to the liturgy of Blackfriars or Magdalen Chapel capture the multi-sensory experience of light, darkness, movement and sound. This connection between music and faith is not fanciful or romantic, but practical and grounded. Janet is under no illusions about the human potential for self-destruction and sorrow. God is to be found here and now, with little regard for a future paradise. Fulfilment, peace and joy, if they are to be found, are in the immediacy of now. This is beautifully portrayed in Janet's work, which is vibrant and alive, with the essence of the present moment in time and space frozen, as it were, for us to see as paint on paper. For Janet, there is great joy to be found in the creativity of the interrelationship between the art of music, the movement and sound of the liturgy, which sweep through the time and space of the architectural tones of a chapel, and the faith of the participants and listeners. Janet's art teaches us lessons, in today's post-secular society, of how to live with the tension of powerlessness and struggles for existence alongside the joyous fruitfulness of faith and creative endeavour, especially when engaged in interdisciplinary collaboration. The mixture of manuscript notation, penned by anonymous monastics long ago, sung by clerics and clerks in churches and chapels as part of devotional worship, and Janet's modern-day artworks, links together centuries of traditions in Western Christianity, including artists, musicians, theologians and priests, and brings them together in the life of one human being and her response of faith.

INTERLUDE I

'O SISTERS TOO': REVIVING THE MEDIEVAL IN POST-SECULAR BRITAIN

'That woman ... is a woman!' So declares the shocked Sir Edmund Tilney at the sight of a woman playing a female role in a Shakespeare play (*Shakespeare in Love*). We may be familiar with the idea that men or boys played women's roles in Elizabethan drama and one might assume that this was also the case in previous centuries – especially, you might think, in the Middle Ages. But not so. Recent research has discovered that women, particularly nuns, were involved in the production and performance of medieval drama of many kinds.[1]

This short chapter is the story of how a collaboration between a new medieval drama project and Frideswide Voices, the first girl-choristers' choir to be founded in Oxford since the university's medieval beginnings, might help us to rethink how we use our churches and chapels in a post-secular society. A recent production of a medieval liturgical drama, in New College Chapel, Oxford, attempted to give us a better understanding of the sights and sounds of late medieval drama and even, perhaps, an opportunity to learn from our medieval ancestors the many and varied, colourful and stimulating ways by which this kind of experience might help us to engage with the Gospel.

A new project on Medieval Convent Drama has found a surprisingly large and detailed amount of evidence for female involvement in drama from convents in what is now France and Belgium.[2] Although the Dissolution destroyed many monastic and conventual documents, there is even reference to convent drama in England, notably at Barking Abbey. As most of the dramatised stories were biblical, the project aims to discover how women in these communities approached the stories, what manner of productions were laid on, what the devotional or educational aspirations were for the plays, who the audience may have been, and whether the nature of liturgy and music within the drama had any specific impact or aims. In some cases male roles were taken by women too, giving a complete reversal of the Shakespearean norm many years later.

References also survive of female performance outside the convent, including women singing in the *Coventry Innocents Play* (c. 1500), and the singing and dancing of a group of 'Virgins' in the Digby Manuscript (c. 1512) *Candlemas* and *Killing of the Children* plays. These 'Digby Plays,' although not convent dramas in themselves, were staged in an exciting production in New College Chapel, Oxford, in February 2017, shortly after the feast of Candlemas, and brought to life the biblical, liturgical and musical drama of late medieval England. It was the intention of the director of the play (and project leader of the Convent Drama Project), Professor Elisabeth Dutton of Fribourg University, Switzerland, to use young female performers as the singing and dancing virgins of the medieval script and also to have some older girls playing some of the speaking and dancing roles. These female parts were taken by members of the recently formed Frideswide Voices, the first liturgical girl-choristers' choir to be founded in Oxford. Established in 2014, the choir promotes opportunities for girls aged between 7 and 14 to sing within the liturgy in Oxford college chapels. Through weekly rehearsals and services, girls gain a rounded choral education singing Anglican repertoire.

Each year Frideswide Voices are 'in residence' at Christ Church Cathedral (for the Michaelmas Term before Christmas), New College (for the Hilary Term before Easter) and at Magdalen College (for the Trinity Term in the summer), and have also sung at Exeter, Jesus, Oriel, Queen's and Worcester colleges, as well as at St George's Chapel, Windsor Castle, Salisbury Cathedral and St Paul's Cathedral. In co-founding the choir, Tanya Simpson sought to address the imbalance of opportunities for boy choristers with those for girls: 'There was no opportunity for girls to experience singing within the liturgy, to gain all that boys could from the training experiences of choristership.' Likewise, director Will Dawes sees room for more equality: 'In this day and age it seems only fair that there is an opportunity for girls in a city of great choral foundations to have a go themselves. We're not trying to break the system, but we are trying to re-shape it slightly.'

So how were these modern-day choristers, in the Anglican tradition, incorporated into the pre-Reformation medieval liturgical drama? The Digby manuscript of the play contains a reference to 'virgins who shall sing and dance,' although the biggest roles are male: Herod, as well as a non-biblical role for a clown called Watkin, who is Herod's messenger, and is sent by

Herod to obtain the soldiers to go and kill the children. But, as Professor Dutton explains, the male characters in the play are subject to ridicule, especially by women: 'The adult men are idiots who are exposed as being cowardly and pathetic. The contrast between them and the innocent singing and dancing virgins will hopefully create an interesting dynamic in the play ... Because *Frideswide Voices* choristers are aged between 7 and 14, some of the older girls play the mothers, who have two or three little speeches each.'

The original play is in English, rather than Latin (the language normally used for biblical narrative and liturgy in the Middle Ages), which begs questions concerning the audience, if indeed we can use that term at all, and purpose of the play. Professor Dutton explains that medieval liturgical drama and the mystery and morality plays that incorporated scriptural and liturgical material were not all performed in the same way: 'We don't know entirely about the audiences, but we do know that they weren't all performed in the same spaces. The York [Mystery Plays] we know used wagons, moving around the town. Some of the other plays, for example at Wakefield, seem to have been performed on different stages, but rather than moving the wagons around, the audience moved around. But then you also have plays like the N-town Mary Play [where N stands for the Latin *nomen*, or name, so that, wherever it was performed, they could insert the name of the town as appropriate], which I'm pretty certain was written to be performed in a church. It makes much more sense in a church space than it does in the outdoors and it's also clearly written to teach the liturgy, such as the *Magnificat* in Latin and English.'

So these dramatic portrayals of biblical narrative were educational tools for teaching, by means of the spoken word, liturgy and scripture, but they were also aids to moral improvement, as Professor Dutton suggests, perhaps portraying the values of Mary's *Magnificat* itself, with the wisdom of the wise overthrowing the powerful: 'Because you have the purification in the Temple [Candlemas] and the killing of the children together in this play, you have two events, both of which have to do with children.' Thus the humble children and women making grown male tyrants look foolish depict a world where traditional power balances are overturned. There is more theological and historical evidence for why these two stories were joined into one play: 'In Bethlehem,' Professor Dutton explains, 'the location that was marked out as the site of the slaughter of the innocents, a place reverenced by medieval pilgrims as they walked around the holy sites in Bethlehem, was also considered to be the site of the circumcision of Christ. So there was a connection, iconographically, between the idea of the first shedding of

Christ's blood, in his circumcision at the presentation in the temple, and the blood of the innocents. For pilgrims, both events were commemorated at the same place.' Even for those who could not travel to the holy land, members of religious orders were encouraged to make metaphorical pilgrimages at home: 'We know that nuns were encouraged to make imaginative pilgrimages around the space of a convent, mapped out as visiting the holy places of Jerusalem.' So, although the 'Digby Play' is not a convent drama, the connection between the biblical events would have made sense to a medieval religious audience and, as 'those two biblical stories are often treated together in convent drama that does survive from the continent, it seems plausible that something like this would have existed for a convent drama in English.'

A lay audience, then, would be invited to make the same biblical and devotional connections: 'The plays were, in many cases, used to teach people who either couldn't read or, more likely, could read a little bit, but couldn't read Latin,' Professor Dutton suggests. 'Even if they could read Latin, most would have had very limited access to books. So their learning was done in this way, with a dramatic form, which combined the visual, the auditory, and even smells – incense could have been used, for example – that can help fix ideas in the mind and in the memory. There are clear lessons that can be learnt.'

There were also several clear functions for music within the drama. Chant settings of Latin hymns, such as the *Te Deum* [We praise Thee, O God], would often be indicated in the manuscripts, thus giving an opportunity for the listeners to learn, or re-learn, the music and perhaps join in. On 8 February, Frideswide Voices sang chant settings appropriate to the period and the audience were encouraged to participate. Professor Dutton also included the Coventry Carol from the *Coventry Innocents Play* 'because the carol also exists specified for performance by the mourning mothers in the killing of the children.' They sang:

O sisters too, how may we do
For to preserve this day
This poor youngling for whom we sing,
'Bye bye, lully, lullay'?

Herod the king, in his raging,
Chargèd he hath this day
His men of might in his own sight
All young children to slay.

There is a wider brief for music within these kinds of production too: 'Music has such an extraordinary capacity to move people,' argues Professor Dutton. Music can create a setting, it can cover action, and it can create a pause, but it also moves people:

> All medieval drama is to some extent religious in whatever way, and for a modern audience of people who don't necessarily have faith, the fact that they will still respond to the music is extraordinary. I find it completely fascinating how uniformly people will respond to, for example, a really beautiful piece of church music, even if they have absolutely no faith at all.[3]

The combination of drama, story, teaching, music, liturgy, movement and dance seems to encourage us to break down the barriers between ideas of congregation, audience members, catechumens or devotional pilgrims. For, in medieval liturgical drama, we cannot easily categorise those who attended, any more than it is easy to categorise the performances, which emphasised auditory, visual, even aromatic experience, and combined teaching with entertainment, liturgy with music and devotion with humour.

So what do a modern-day audience take away with them from the performance and should they suspend ideas of being an audience, or a congregation, or a group of bystanders, or pupils, or participants? Professor Dutton thinks yes: 'I think so. We have such a problem with the way people behave in church today. Obviously a chapel was, and remains, a sacred space, but I don't think people understood that as meaning you always had to whisper or that they were not allowed to laugh in there. I wish to find a way of bringing home to people that churches were not a separate part of your life – places that you went to for a couple of hours on Sunday only – but were spaces where all sorts of aspects of life took place.'

This medieval liturgical drama can help us to see that, in today's post-secular society, just as in medieval Europe, our churches and chapels are not just for Sundays but for every part of the rich tapestry of our lives. The young singers of Frideswide Voices and the ancient text of the 'Digby Play' created a vivid encounter with two gospel stories in a new and dynamic way.

Figure 1 'The Thomas Traherne Windows' by Thomas Denny in The Audley Chapel, Hereford Cathedral

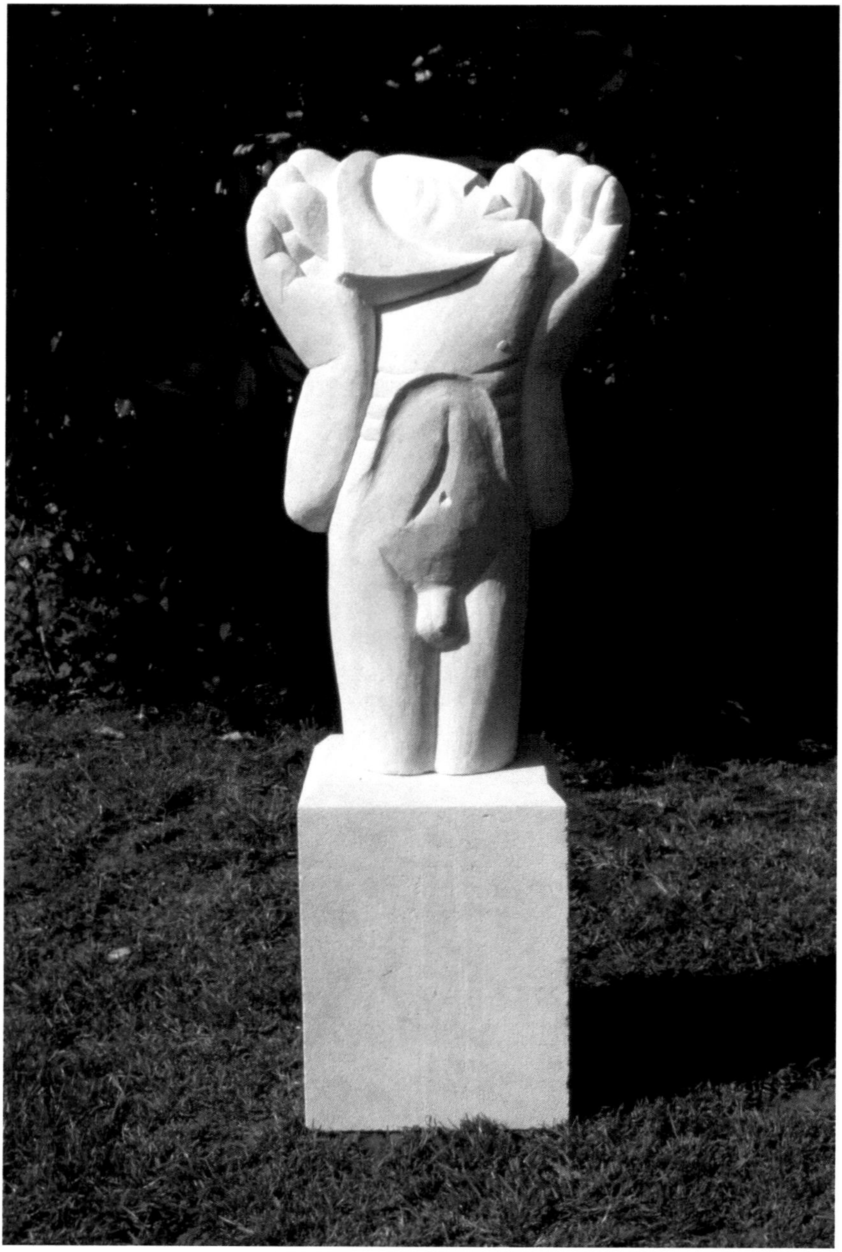

Figure 2 'Salutation' sculpture by Nicholas Mynheer

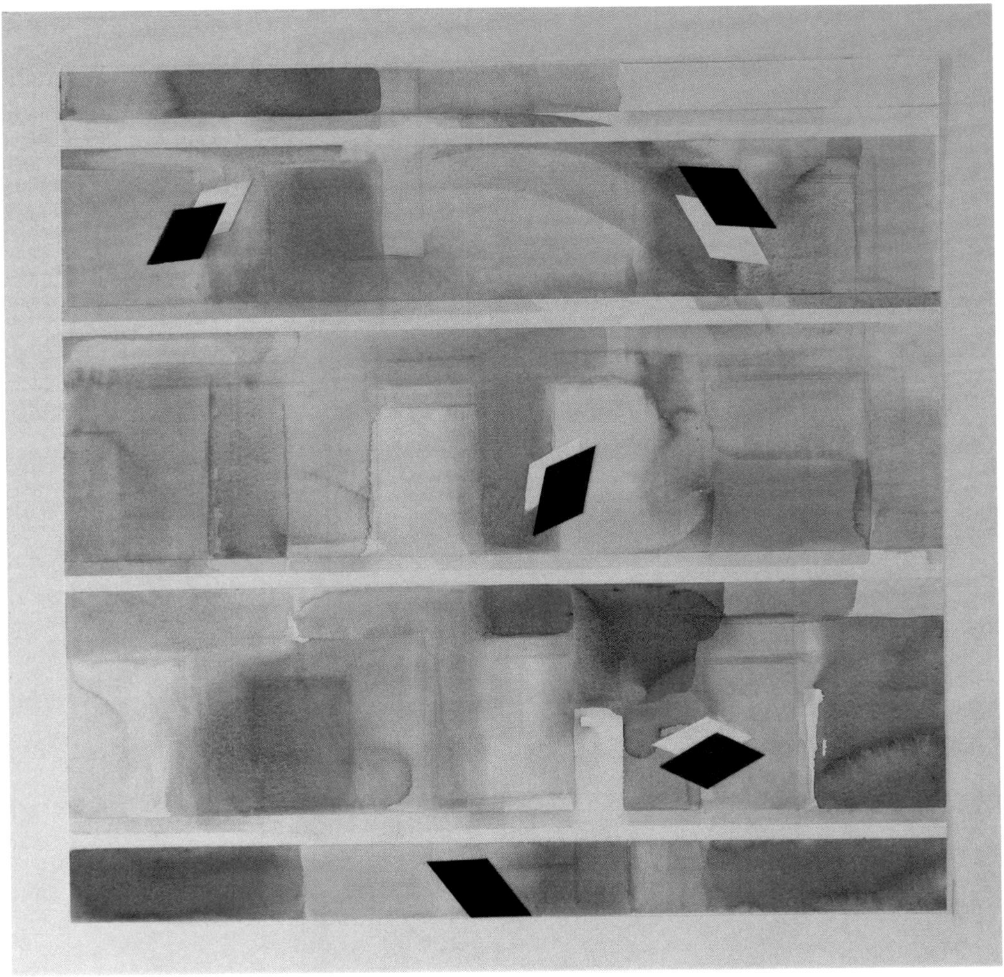

Figure 3 'Jam Jars in a Window: Green and Terracotta II', 2011 by Janet Boulton

Figure 4 'Tenebrae: Blackfriars Oxford II', 2016 by Janet Boulton

Figure 5 'Plain Chant, Choral Evensong', 2017 by Janet Boulton

Figure 6 'Neumes, Virgin and Child, Study III', 2017 by Janet Boulton

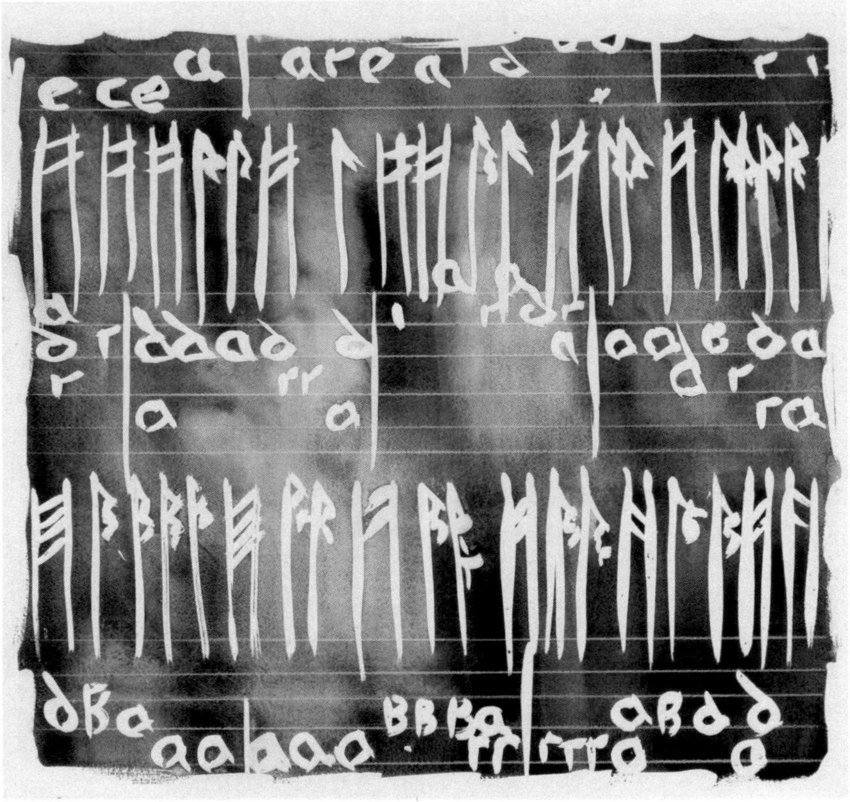

Figure 7 'Music for Lute, Cloister (Night)', 2017 by Janet Boulton

Figure 8 Labyrinth

PART II

THE HUMAN MIND AND SOCIETY

CHAPTER FOUR

SINGING IN SYNCHRONY: MUSIC, BONDING AND HUMAN EVOLUTION

> I am convinced that music really is the universal language of beauty which can bring together all people of good will on earth.[1]

'Humans are a cultural species.'[2] We inherit and acquire a plethora of cultural practices, which fundamentally affect our behaviour. We may agree with Mesoudi that culture changes and evolves but, with regard to music, we may also agree with Davidson that, throughout human history, the creation and performance of music has had a constant and unchanging characteristic and aim – it has almost always involved a level of social communication.[3] The 'real or implied presence of others', even when music is practised alone, points to the human need for social interaction. We have seen, in our brief exploration of the powerful social effects of psalms and hymns in the Judeo-Christian story, how music's social purpose has been a constant feature of Christian faith communities throughout history. Outside of any religious context, music, and especially singing, implies interaction: 'singing a lullaby, a work song, a hunting song, or a school song; chanting as a member of a football crowd ...' and so on.[4] A wide spectrum of research techniques in the psychology of music has developed in order to examine music as social behaviour,[5] but in the realms of psychological or anthropological evolution, one scholar in particular has developed experimental techniques and analyses which help us to understand the fundamental importance of communal singing for our social cohesion and well-being.

Robin Dunbar is Professor Emeritus of Evolutionary Psychology at the University of Oxford. He describes his work as being 'concerned with trying to understand the behavioral, cognitive and neuro-endocrinological mechanisms that underpin social bonding in primates (in general) and humans (in particular). Understanding these mechanisms, and the functions that relationships serve,' he says, 'will give us insights into how humans have managed to create large scale societies using a form of psychological mechanism that is evolutionarily adapted to very small scale societies, and why these mechanisms are less than perfect in the modern world. This has implications for the design of social networking sites as well as mobile technology.' He is well known for the 'Dunbar Number,' which is 150 – the maximum number of people with whom we can meaningfully have a stable relationship at any time. An important feature of his studies 'has been the constraints that time places on an individual's ability to manage their relationships, and the cognitive tricks used to overcome these.'[6] Music, Robin suggests, and particularly choral singing, plays an important role in social bonding and how we relate to others to help create cohesive societies.

When I met with Robin to discuss his work, I asked him if he could explain, for a lay person, why social cohesion is so important, evolutionarily speaking.

RD: This goes back to the nature of primate sociality. Primate sociality is essentially a form of implicit social contract. Living in groups provides a functional benefit, which the individual alone can't provide. And that functional benefit is usually defence against predators, and it's by grouping together that they keep predators at bay. Basically, predators won't attack groups. So their problem is how to trade off immediate selfish interest with long-term selfish interest, because individuals have to be willing to forego some of their immediate interests in order that everybody else gets something close to a reasonable share – I avoid using the word 'a fair share', because it isn't necessarily so – of the benefits of living together. Otherwise, those who don't get a fair share will leave and the benefits everyone else derives from the group will diminish proportionately. In part, this is a coordination problem as much as anything: each member of the group has to be willing to go along with the whole group, otherwise the group will disperse – it's as simple as that. So primates produce these groups by means of a bonding mechanism that involves social grooming. The problem with human evolution in this context then is that we clearly have evolved much bigger groups, and these are consequently much harder to bond.

In terms of group sizes, I asked Robin about his research that led to his famous 'numbers'.

RD: One picks these grouping layers up in the distribution of primate group sizes. So five, fifteen and fifty are natural grouping numbers for primates, and it's only humans that group in sizes of 150. So these group sizes are like layers: some species can only achieve one layer, because they're not very complex, socially or cognitively. Some species can achieve two layers. But to get from one layer to the next, a species needs to develop or evolve some new cognitive and behavioural mechanisms to support that. And at each step you're hitting up against time budgets. Time is really the big constraint, because this social bonding is extremely time costly. So grooming, and we still do grooming, works exactly the same way. It works at the intimate level just as it does in monkeys and apes, but the problem is that grooming will only allow you to bond groups of about fifty, the upper limit in primates on average. That's not to say they don't live, from time to time, in bigger groups than that, but those groups are often very unstable.

The key question, then, is how we got from groups of fifty (the size of group you expect to see in social great apes like chimpanzees, and which seem likely to have been typical of Australopithecines) to the 150 typically found in modern humans. But with this larger group size we have a social bonding problem: how do you keep these groups together when you don't have the time to do it by grooming? You need some other mechanism. We came to the conclusion quite early in our research that one mechanism was singing and dancing. These practices long pre-date language and so initially involved singing without words.

Once you have language, of course, you can put words in too, and that gives you a new dimension, which possibly becomes much more important with bigger grouping levels than 150. So once groupings grow to the sizes of villages, towns or cities, cultural icons start to play an important role in creating a sense of belonging to a group. And that has to be done through language – it can't be done any other way. But singing clearly kicks in very early, in evolutionary terms, and seems to work through the pharmacological mechanism of the endorphin system in the brain. Social singing triggers the release of endorphins in the brain.

JA: So what made these additional mechanisms?

RD: We think they evolved in three steps. The first step is laughter, which probably dates to around two million years ago, so it's probably the oldest characteristic we share with the great apes. Laughter has an involuntary visceral quality to it, which doesn't rely on language. In other words, if somebody else laughs, it's very difficult not to laugh with them: it's extremely contagious. So it seems likely that laughter existed very early on and then was followed by singing and dancing. Again, singing and dancing don't require language: you just do them by imitation. Once language evolved, it facilitated the telling of stories of various kinds, such as origin stories, about who we are and where we came from; or they might be religious stories, or theology, concerning our beliefs about why the world works the way it does; but equally, they can be fictional stories. Fictional stories produce the same release of endorphins as all these other mechanisms, it turns out.

JA: So endorphins make you feel good?

RD: Yes, and it makes you feel very bonded to those with whom you're doing that activity.

Evolutionary psychologists Dunbar, Weinstein, Launay, Pearce and Stewart have attempted to demonstrate how humans create and maintain social bonds in large groups, and have argued that 'evidence from historical and anthropological records suggests that group music-making might act as a mechanism by which this large-scale social bonding could occur'.[7] In an experiment, individuals from a community choir that met in both small and large groups

> gave self-report measures of social bonding and had pain threshold measurements taken (as a proxy for endorphin release) before and after 90 min of singing. Results showed that feelings of inclusion, connectivity, positive affect, and measures of endorphin release all increased across singing rehearsals and that the influence of group singing was comparable for pain thresholds in the large versus small group context. Levels of social closeness were found to be greater at pre- and post-levels for the small choir condition. However, the large choir condition experienced a greater change in social closeness as compared to the small condition. The finding that singing together fosters social closeness – even in large group contexts where individuals are not known to each other – is consistent with evolutionary accounts that emphasize the role of music in social bonding, particularly in the context of creating larger cohesive groups than other primates are able to manage.[8]

Overall, therefore, they discovered that the 'social bonding effects of singing are actually more substantial in larger group settings compared to smaller, more familiar groups'.[9] As Robin told me, the remarkable aspect of this phenomenon is that it doesn't matter whether the people you are singing with are friends or not. Even with complete strangers, the resulting rise in endorphin levels is still the same. Communal singing, especially in large groups, gives you a feeling of well-being and belonging to a very specific community of singers, as well as raising your pain threshold.

While Robin Dunbar is not a religious believer, his research points to a deep human need for meaning through experience, relationship and feeling, rather than rational cognition. For many, this connection between music and communal experience, offering a 'high' of endorphin release, is to be found within local community choirs. The most famous of these in recent times have focused around the work of Gareth Malone, who has inspired many new initiatives of community choirs throughout the United Kingdom. But the phenomenon existed long before. In the mid- to late twentieth century, community choirs such as Joan Taylor's Can't Sing Choir at Morley College in London, Polly Barton's Singing for the Terrified and Frankie Armstrong's 1988 Natural Voice Network, which seeks to build 'accepting, non-judgmental communities that sing together',[10] have all played an important part in introducing people to communal singing who don't necessarily have musical training or are unable to read music but who, through a process of aural and oral learning, gain a sense of the joy of inclusive, embodied, nourishing music-making through communal singing.[11] The Birmingham Wellbeing Choir, for instance, promotes itself thus: 'Attending a choir rehearsal is an uplifting and friendly experience.'[12]

A good example of the healing power of a community choir is the Manchester Survivors' Choir, who began to meet after the Manchester Arena terrorist bombing on 22 May 2017. On the first anniversary of the attack they performed and recorded a song, *I will Rise*, which gained national and international attention.[13] The *Manchester Evening News* reported it thus:

> It was a love of music that took them to the Arena on May 22 last year.
>
> And that same love has helped them through the dark days, weeks and months that followed. ... Every fortnight the choir, some of whom were badly injured in the blast which claimed 22 lives, come together at Sacred Trinity Church in Salford to share their experiences or simply lose themselves in singing.
>
> On May 22, their defiant voices will sing out when they take part in *Manchester Together – One Voice* memorial concert in Albert Square.

> And now, one year on from the atrocity, choir members have been sharing their incredible stories.[14]

One survivor explained one of the benefits of the choir: 'Singing together is really cathartic. It feels like a release.'[15]

In their work exploring the community choir, June Boyce-Tillman and Sarah Morgan have found that there has been an 'opening up' of the idea of 'choir' over the past fifty years and that the 'fragmented nature of contemporary society' has brought a need for 'creating communities based on the valuing of difference.'[16] Moreover:

> By concentrating on the experiencing of music and the processes involved in creating events rather than musical products, music has been seen as a way of enabling people to encounter and respect difference in order to create a unity based on encompassing diversity.[17]

Boyce-Tillman goes further still and suggests that 'it is in the community choir that some people are finding some answers to their spiritual search.'[18] It is into this context of the rise of the community choir that Robin's empirical research is situated, and he told me about another remarkable finding:

RD: What's interesting is that it's specific to the people you're doing the activity with at the time. It doesn't affect your sense of bonding to even your good friends who are not there on the day – it's very specific to the context. My sense is that, with early singing and dancing, once a certain point of physical exertion was reached, they slipped into trance. My guess is that, what was discovered very early on was that if you keep dancing round the circle, accompanied by a great deal of singing and clapping to provide musical accompaniment, then at some point the brain goes into a trance state. I have this slight suspicion this is probably related to a combination of the endorphin system with one of the other neuropeptide systems, which can be triggered after a relatively short amount of moderate exercise.

This phenomenon has been explored by scientific experimentation by Dunbar, Launay and Pearce, where, in a 'semi-naturalistic study,' they followed newly formed singing and non-singing (crafts or creative writing) adult education classes over seven months: 'Participants rated their closeness to their group and their affect, and were given a proxy measure of endorphin release, before and after their class, at three timepoints (months 1, 3 and 7).'[19] They were able to show that 'although singers and non-singers felt equally connected by timepoint 3, singers experienced much faster bonding: singers demonstrated a significantly greater increase in closeness at timepoint 1.' The conclusions relating to the 'ice-breaker effect were, therefore, that singing promoted a fast social cohesion between unfamiliar people, which did not require them to know each other. Thus, Dunbar, Launay and Pearce argue that 'singing may have evolved to quickly bond large human groups of relative strangers, potentially through encouraging willingness to coordinate by enhancing positive affect.'[20]

Likewise, regarding communal dance, Tarr, Launay, Dunbar and Cohen found, through experimentation, that the release of endorphins, which act as a reward-inducing analgesic, also helps fast social bonding. They examined the exertion brought about by dancing and a corresponding synchrony in social bonding: 'Both demonstrated significant independent positive effects on pain threshold (a proxy for endorphin activation) and in-group bonding. This suggests that dance which involves both exertive and synchronized movement may be an effective group bonding activity.'[21] Thus, I asked Robin whether the sensations experienced (via the release of endorphins) through the performance of communal music and dance have long had a place in religious or ritual activity, particularly in relation to trance states:

RD: Trance states and trance dancing is culturally almost universal in small-scale societies all around the world. All these societies employ essentially the same description of what happens when you go into trance, which is a tunnel with the light at the end. It doesn't matter if that's in Africa or Siberia or South America, it's the same description.

JA: Is that similar to the near-death experience of sensing that you are travelling down a dark tunnel towards a light?

RD: Yes, it's probably the same, and it's interesting that that's the case, because one of the things that terrifies all of these cultures that do this is that they believe that, when you go into trance and you go down the tunnel, you enter the spirit world, where a combination of good ancestors and wicked spirits, or ogres, exists.

JA: Such as in aboriginal cultures?

RD: Yes, that's right, such as shamanic religions, which used to be called animism, but I call them shamanic religions because they're all built around trance states. Once one is in the spirit world, they believe, the ogres and the wicked spirits endeavour to trap you and prevent you from finding your way back. Thus, they all are universally terrified of not being able to find the exit, because it's believed to be very small. In fact, very occasionally, people die in trance states, the interpretation of which, in these communities, is that they could not find the way back out. Thus, in this belief system, it is very important to have good spirits to meet you on the other side, which would normally be your ancestors, in order to guide you about, defend you against the ogres, and enable you to find the way out.

Thus, a shamanic trance is a kind of transcendental experience which, once language developed, needed to be explained to other people. If many people in the group undergo the same kind of religious trance, there emerges a commonality of experience. Music seems to have played such a major part in this experience. I'm not aware of anybody using laughter to get to trance states. Although you can exhaust yourself with laughter, somehow it doesn't quite hit the same buttons that music does. So my view of the evolution of religion, then, is one which begins with what used to be called animist religions, then doctrinal religions emerge, which become the world religions as we have them now.

The earliest religions probably began in the Neolithic settlement, where the chief problem to overcome was not the lack of agriculture, as cultivation occurred a couple of thousand years earlier. What was crucially important was protection against raids by neighbours. But if living together for protection is the solution, then the problem is how to prevent people living in close proximity from killing each other as a result of the accumulation of the stresses that we all experience. In hunter-gatherer societies, small-scale societies, which are based on fission-fusion, those stresses can be dissipated by individuals being able to leave the group. So a community of 150, let's say, who occupy usually a particular area, don't live all together; they live in smaller overnight camps of anything between thirty and fifty people. So your extended community will consist of three, maybe four, camp groups. And you can switch from one to another. If you get fed up with the people you live with because they're irritating you so much, you can just get up and go to another camp, while remaining within the same larger community – you don't have to go and live among strangers, you can go off and be among friends and live with them.

JA: So how does music help facilitate social cohesion? Is it by reducing stress?

RD: Yes. Stress, in the modern world, comes from a number of different sources but, in the archetypal ancestral context, this is just the same story as you see in primates.

JA: The problem of getting on with each other?

RD: Yes, and the stress is closely linked to fertility and group size. Stress levels are very specific to the number of females in the group. So the more females in the group, the lower the fertility. The negative relationship between the number of females in the group and female fertility is so steep that it limits group sizes dramatically, to fifteen, in which you might have five or six females. Now the only way that primates could solve this problem of stress within groups was to produce a buffer which reduced that stress. That buffer is creating complex multi-level societies based around these grooming cliques. The grooming clique protects its members from harassment by the other members of the group, particularly other females. So if a primate is attacked, their grooming buddy will come to their aid.

If a predator can see we're in a group, they're not going to come near us, it's not worth their while. And by the same token, if Jemima sees I have a grooming relationship with Alfreda, she won't bother me. Two against one. What it does is keep everybody off your back enough to reduce this pressure, and this allows the monkeys and apes that can do this to have bigger groups. For us humans, however, with our much bigger groups, something else was needed to keep the community bonded and working together. And it is here that what I call 'religions of experience' (meaning that you are immersed in the rituals) seem to become so important in binding groups together.

JA: Without creeds or doctrines?

RD: That's right. No creeds or moral codes, just experiences that are wonderful and exciting and engaging. I have a colleague who works on bushmen in south-west Africa, and he has said that these trance dances tend to occur when things are getting a bit tense in the community. The trance dance wipes the hard drive clean of all those niggling irritations, and they can start again.

JA: But then the tension slowly builds up again?

RD: The tensions build up until someone instigates another dance. They tend to be at quite longish intervals, like once a month. But with the move into closed settlements in the Neolithic, the pressure to keep these communities together suddenly got a lot worse and something really strong was needed to keep the peace. And at that point what seems to have come into play is effectively doctrinal religion. So rituals, theologies, hierarchies and temples appear for the first time – religious spaces where everybody can enact their religion. And at that point theology itself becomes very important as a way of justifying what rituals need to be done and how often. And with this the ritual arousal levels of the religious experience seem to get toned down. Thus, in the major world religions today, mystical trance experience is not common. By and large, the religious ritual experience today is of low intensity, with the consequence that, maybe, you have to have it more frequently.

JA: So, there's a lower-level fix, but you get it more often?

RD: You just need it more often.

JA: Like daily prayer?

RD: Exactly. And then, of course, it becomes very important to have moralising high gods to keep social order. It's the classic case of, 'we may not know what you're doing when we can't see you but God does'. So you can't escape, you've got to toe the line. The introduction of gods provides a framework that makes everybody conform. There's some very good work by the American anthropologist Rich Sosis,[22] showing that, among nineteenth-century American utopian cults, the more things one had to give up to join the cult, such as swearing, eating meat, alcohol, etc., the longer the cult lasted. This is interpreted as a sort of entry-cost problem – once you've joined, you've paid such a high price ...

JA: ... that it's not worth your while to leave?

RD: Well, you've got to have a very good reason for leaving, because of what you've actually had to sacrifice. I've been collaborating with Rich more recently, and what is interesting is that the effect doesn't apply to secular cults, but only to purely religious cults, for instance the Shakers, the Mormons, the Hutterites and so on. What we have demonstrated is that the optimal size, at foundation, for longevity in these cults is about fifty for secular cults, and about 150 for religious ones. There is something about a religious ethos that helps keep things from falling apart for longer.

JA: Is music an important component in both religious and secular cults?

RD: Of course, it's always involved, yes.

JA: But the religious communities can be larger because they have a bigger hold on the individual member?

RD: Yes, something makes people behave better. But there is also something special about these particular numbers, the fifty and the 150. We can see this in the fissions that Hutterite communities undergo when they get too big. The Hutterites are communalistic, where everything is done by common consent in the community. We have all their fissions, from two of their lineages, over a century, so it's a very large number of fissions, and we know what the sizes were at fission and what they fissioned into. The statistics show that if, after fission, they split into a group of fifty or 150, then the community is less likely to fission again for much longer than if they end up with a group of a hundred. In that case, they are much more likely to have to fission again soon, because a group size of 100 somehow doesn't work as well. They very explicitly split their communities once they get above 150, because you can't manage a community bigger than that by peer pressure alone – you have to have policemen and laws and hierarchies, and that's against their whole ethos. If you have a group up to about 200, the members have a choice of how they split it. One group can be fifty and the other can be 150, and that works, or you split it into two 100s, and it doesn't work. But what is critical here is the fact that the religious component somehow makes people behave better. So it allows them to diffuse something. But it's clear that it is religious rituals generally that are important, and this of course invariably involves singing in some form, even in the stricter religious cults.

JA: So singing is usually encouraged in all these groups?

RD: Well that and very long, boring sermons. I suspect that both trigger the endorphin system.

JA: So a forty-minute sermon might induce a trance-like state?

RD: Perhaps, but music clearly plays an extremely fundamental role, in my view. We can show, with singing, that it has an instantaneous community bonding effect. We called it the icebreaker effect, because it's so fast. Complete strangers and completely novice singers in a singing class, run by professional singing teachers, after a two-hour session, were all best buddies, and it was quite extraordinary how quickly that worked.[23]

JA: I noticed this at Worcester College when our music director, Thomas Allery, began a staff choir.

RD: Suddenly the Fellows were talking to each other!

JA: Yes. We had secretaries, computer technicians, cleaners, porters, junior and senior academics all singing together. It was absolutely tremendous.

In fact, it was something we put on in a 'health and wellness week', and it was by far and away the most successful event. After that it became a weekly event, and that regular 'fix' of communal music-making and social bonding was something that people really wanted.

RD: This is interesting. We came across the Sunday secular religion group, the Sunday Assembly.[24] It was started by two comedians who discovered that, although they had no religious beliefs, they missed school assemblies, chapel, singing hymns and church. Reflecting on this, they decided to start a secular church on the same principles. What's interesting about it is what they do. Like many churches, there is some kind of sermon or talk, there are readings, music and communal food.

JA: So it's liturgy?

RD: Yes, it is absolutely extraordinary. You're practically walking into an Anglican church, which is an interesting question for historians of liturgy. But, like the monastic hours, from which liturgy arises, there's an awful lot of singing. In the Abrahamic religions there have traditionally been liturgical activities that trigger the endorphin system, such as kneeling, because putting the body under stress, such as kneeling or standing for long periods, triggers the endorphin system. As well as counting rosary beads in Christianity. Islam has the same thing, counting the names of God on beads. Those kinds of little regular soft movements are extremely good at triggering the endorphin system. Then there is more extrovert liturgical behaviour, such as in the Coptic Church, where deacons dance before the Ark of the Covenant. Of course, in the Sufi tradition in Islam, dancing and singing is what they use for inducing a trance state.

JA: Whirling?

RD: Whirling Dervishes, yes. But I think the doctrinal religions, and particularly in the Abrahamic tradition (Christianity, Islam and Judaism), had so much trouble with mystical sects, because the superstructure aimed to maintain a kind of theological rectitude and discipline within the community, while natural religion bubbled up underneath, rather like house churches. As human beings, we want to be in these little communities, which are somehow much more intimate, and if you look at the origins of the Methodists, the Quakers and the Baptists, they all started as charismatic movements until they were corralled into institutions and some discipline was imposed. If you read Wesley's diary, he's constantly complaining about the fact that he can't control these communities.

He's trying to impose some discipline on them, and they're all resistant to conformity, as they prefer the mystical experience.

So if you look at the history of all the Abrahamic religions, you constantly see a bubbling up of charismatic sects. Some of them take off and become major churches or denominations in their own right. But always the centre, or the mainstream, is desperately trying to weed them out. Likewise, there are the Sufis in Islam, the Kabbalah in Judaism and the Cathars in Christianity. In the first few centuries AD in North Africa, there were lots of very charismatically mystical sects that caused much grief for the patriarchs in Jerusalem and Rome.

JA: So the mystical seems to be something which is instinctive and intrinsic to what humans want to experience. Ian McGilchrist's *Master and His Emissary*, about the right and left hemispheres of the brain, mentions that singing is an earlier evolutionary phenomenon than language.

RD: Yes, language is basically left hemisphere, and the right hemisphere deals with emotion and often responds much faster than the left hemisphere.

JA: Can I move on to ask you about your personal experience of music and singing? Do you enjoy listening to sacred music?

RD: I just love early Church music. It probably goes back to the fact that the prep school I went to in Africa, before I came to live in England, was run by a Catholic order, and so it was often the case that we all had to troop off to Mass, which was always a said service, but they always did Benediction on Sunday, and that was always sung by the priests. So I came to like that style of Gregorian chant, and I became very hooked on it when I was extremely young, and continued to like it – I still do. I think there's something absolutely magical about Gregorian chant. I've no idea what it is. In fact, we are just about to try some research on the differences, from an evolutionary psychology point of view, between singing in unison and polyphonic singing.

JA: That's very interesting because there's some movement, particularly in the Catholic Church, towards a return to chant, which was instigated by Pope Benedict XVI and various Catholic musicians like James MacMillan, the Scottish composer.[25]

RD: Indeed, and so my own musical journey began with chant and there was a phase where I didn't think there was any good music written after the seventeenth century.

JA: So you made it from chant to the Baroque and then stopped!

RD: With the death of Bach the Elder! But since then I've finally managed to get to the twentieth century. I'm not yet in the twenty-first century, I must say! But what's interesting is that I really do like music. I wish I could play but I know I can't do it because I've tried in my youth. And I know I really can't sing, and I'm not sure I'd even improve with the training!

In fact, Robin wrote an entertaining and rather passionate article about the need for more musical education in our schools in the *Times Higher Education* supplement. Entitled 'Together', in it Robin laments his lack of musical training, but now sees the potential benefits of learning music, which helps with virtually all other academic disciplines in some way. He ends, perhaps tongue in cheek, by arguing for a much greater place for music in the educational curriculum:

> So, my bottom line is that we should do away with the entire school curriculum and have one long music lesson instead (not forgetting the salsa class in the middle). That way, we would cover pretty much everything in the national curriculum, all within an overarching themed structure – and have a great deal more fun doing it. I sometimes wonder whether we haven't missed the point of education.[26]

Despite Robin's lack of early musical training, I ask him about his eclectic tastes and appreciation of a wide variety of music today:

RD: What I like from the later twentieth century is music by Arvo Pärt. The tintinnabulation is very appealing. I have even come to appreciate pop music. We've just been to see The Wailers.

JA: As in Bob Marley and the Wailers?

RD: Yes, this is The Wailers minus Bob, but there's two of the originals there, and then the rest are younger generation, and they performed the original Bob Marley music. Everybody was swaying to the music because it has a kind of rhythmicity to it, and it's very calming. There was an unbelievably friendly audience. My wife puts it down to the concert being in Liverpool, but I put it down to the music. Everybody was incredibly friendly, and casually talking to you as they walked past, which I've never ever seen anywhere else, not even at a Sixteen concert!

JA: Well, no. There's a certain amount of formality.

RD: Even in Liverpool, where we heard The Sixteen sing. But in that choral music there is a mesmeric component to it, which is also present in Gregorian, particularly in the really solemn style that popularised it back in the 1960s.

JA: Rowan Williams spoke to me about the lack of emotional manipulation involved in plainchant, perhaps similar to the later choral music of Arvo Pärt, whereas the nineteenth century saw the rise of music that was perhaps emotionally compelling, even manipulative, which gave more direction to how the listener might feel. Chant just allows you to *be*, to respond to the text in whichever way you want to. I don't know if that's true, or perhaps all music is emotionally manipulative?

RD: I'm sure it is emotionally manipulative in the sense that it is hitting something, if you like, on the right brain side, which is where emotion is mainly dealt with, but it is properly emotional because it's really subconscious, it's visceral, and it's not something we can consciously ponder afterwards. It's not something you can talk your way into in that sense. So, to me, that's an emotional response: it's just pressing a particular button that produces this effect. But given that it seems that music triggers the endorphin system, what's interesting about it is, if you do it in behavioural synchrony, *together*, it ramps up the endorphin hit by 100 per cent, for no extra effort.

We have demonstrated this with communal exercise, such as with rowers. If they rowed on the ergs on their own, they got an endorphin hit, because of the physical exercise and of course the rhythmicity of the rowing. If they did it linked together on the ergs so that they're rowing in unison in a virtual boat, as it were, then the endorphin release is massively increased.

We demonstrated this again with dancing. We compared those who danced in synchrony (with the same movements at the same time) and those who danced out of synchrony (either doing different movements or all doing the same set of movements but doing them in a different order). We found that you don't get anything like the endorphin hit (or sense of social bonding either) in the dancing that is out of synchrony. I am sure it is the synchrony from unison that gives Gregorian chant its special appeal.

Then there's the interesting question of whether gender makes any difference. When you have all men, or all women, singing together, there is a perfect match of same-sex synchrony of voice. However, even when men and women sing together, there is a matching of vocal sounds that are a certain pitch apart (for instance, an octave), which produces a different kind of synchrony again. So whether you match men's and women's voices, or with boy trebles' voices of a traditional cathedral choir, you're achieving that perfect social synchrony, but on two, or three, or four pitch levels, as in polyphony.

JA: So being part of a choir makes you feel good?

RD: Yes.

JA: And does the standard of singing make any difference? Whether it's an amateur or a professional choir? I wonder if there might be slightly different senses of enjoyment and bonding depending on the standard? Also, when you're a member of the audience or congregation, what kind of endorphin hit are you getting?

RD: The short answer is I have no idea. All I have is my impressions as a random member of the audience. However, I suspect that we in the congregation don't get such a big endorphin hit as the choir do, because they're putting in a great deal of physical exertion. An important feature of singing is obviously breath control and this creates work for the diaphragm and chest wall muscles that in and of itself will trigger the endorphin system.

JA: That diaphragmatic movement?

RD: Yes, it's movement of the diaphragm and the chest wall muscles that allow you to produce these long, controlled exhalations during singing. So it's different with laughter because the exertions tend to be very punchy. The way we laugh is different to the laughter you find in great apes. We tend not to breathe: it is exhalation, exhalation, exhalation in these forced punches, emptying the lungs, and it is exhausting in itself. Whereas the way great apes do it, and to a lesser extent monkeys, is basically a pant: so it is exhalation, inhalation, exhalation, inhalation, and humans have evolved to suppress the inhalation, partly in order to magnify this effect.

So singing and speech are slightly different in the sense that they're even more controlled. If you look at x-rays of people laughing and people singing or speaking, you can see the chest is doing something different, but still it's about breath control, and I think that's why breath control then becomes a major tool in trance induction in the Indian tradition. Very often the key to it is breath control, or breathing exercises to produce this light-headedness and so on. But that breath control in itself is dependent on having had this remodelled form of control over the diaphragm and chest wall muscles in the course of a long period of having laughter, which is a key form of chorusing. And this is where laughter and singing become intensely social. You are thirty times more likely to laugh at a comedy video if you watch it with three or four other people than on your own.

JA: Is that bond increased if you are in a theatre with 2,000 people?

RD: Yes, it's the contagion effect that seems to be very important in terms of copying. Imitation produces a sense of bonding. You're much more altruistic to someone if they imitate you.

JA: So, in terms of sacred music within a Christian religious service, if the choral music is largely non-participatory for the listener, unless you're singing a hymn or creed, does it make any difference to your experience whether you're vocally joining in?

RD: It doesn't to me Jonathan, because I'm in a trance state. I just sit back and allow the music to flow over me. For the singers, for the choir, every service probably produces an uplift, no matter what the music is. For the audience (and this is pure speculation on my part, but it's based on my experience) there are certain pieces of music that really press a button. For me, they probably tend to be older pieces rather than more recent ones. Some of the late Victorian, early twentieth-century pieces are very interesting to listen to, but if I hear music by Palestrina or Byrd, I wallow in it and it creates a magical effect. I also enjoy when the choir sings in unison, all on one note, for instance for the Lord's Prayer, because the mix of voices all converging and producing this unison sound is a magical moment. It's an interesting question as to what way of performing choral music produces the biggest effect for the congregation. Nonetheless, there are probably many paths to the top of the mountain, as they say.

JA: Well. When listening to the choir, presumably you get a bigger endorphin hit if the choir's good?

RD: Yes. I think that's right, and if you regularly attend a cathedral, church or chapel with an excellent choir you can forget how extraordinary the standard is when you listen to it every week. Well, you may not, but amateurs like me do.

JA: No, I agree, and when you see the amount of rehearsal, education and preparation that goes on behind the scenes of a really good choir, you realise what a remarkable achievement it is.

RD: This is really brought home to me by comparing listening to a village church choir and listening to a professional chapel or cathedral choir, which is in a different stratosphere.

My conversation with Robin affirmed, for me, the importance of music and dance in human evolution, from the beginnings of human communities, social interaction and ritual practice. It confirms the significance of music as a primary form of communication, even pre-dating speech and language itself, as Iain McGilchrist has shown: 'the control of voice and respiration needed for singing came into being long before they would ever have been required by language.'[27] Language came later: 'intonation, phrasing and rhythm develop first; syntax and vocabulary come only later.'[28] Therefore, 'our love of music reflects the ancestral ability of our mammalian brain to transmit and receive basic emotional sounds.'[29] This love of music, which developed largely in the right hemisphere of the brain, was concerned with communication, social cohesion and harmony, and helped bond people together in community. In the age of modernity, from the sixteenth to the twentieth centuries, language and the printed word have dominated society for generations. However, in the twenty-first century and an age of postmodernity and post-secularism, even when commitments to the life and doctrine of religious institutions are waning, the search for spiritual encounter and relationship is as strong as ever.

Robin's research and findings illustrate the fundamental nature of communal singing and ritual to human flourishing, and that, even when religious belief has been lost from society, the practice of coming together for regular ritualistic music-making is as strong as ever.

CHAPTER FIVE

'FEAR OF THE MYSTERY': MUSIC, FAITH AND THE BRAIN

Where words leave off, music begins.[1]

Music plays a crucial role in social bonding, and the continued importance of community in promoting mental health and well-being within a cohesive society. Robin Dunbar and others have demonstrated that music, and especially singing, is a fundamental part of who we are as human beings. Boethius asserted, many centuries ago: 'Music is so naturally united with us that we cannot be free from it even if we so desired.'[2] Likewise, as Anthony Storr declares today: 'No culture so far discovered lacks music. Making music appears to be one of the fundamental activities of mankind.'[3]

Music is one of the most effective means of bringing people together in order to encounter something numinous, immanent or mysterious (without trying to define these terms too rigidly). Such experience does not separate body and spirit (secular and sacred, corporeal and incorporeal), as in a dualist ideology, but combines the physical and the embodied with the communal. This experiential quality of music is both disclosive and affective, Pythagorean and Orphic, to use Brown and Hopps's terms: 'Music brings about similar physical responses in different people at the same time. This is why it is able to draw groups together and create a sense of unity.'[4] It is no surprise, then, that music also has a remarkable effect on brain activity, including the easing of symptoms of neurological diseases or, conversely, provoking epileptic fits ('musicogenic epilepsy'). Many scientists, psychiatrists and psychologists have charted music's effects on the brain.[5] Oliver Sacks, for instance, analysed how music can affect those who suffer with neurological problems, such as Parkinson's disease, aphasia, dementia, epilepsy or melancholia. He writes, 'Our auditory systems, our nervous systems, are indeed exquisitely tuned for music.' However, physiological reasons for such fine tuning have not yet been discovered:

> How much this is due to the intrinsic characteristics of music itself ... and how much to special resonances, synchronizations, oscillations, mutual excitations, or feedbacks in the immensely complex, multilevel neural circuitry that underlies musical perception and replay, we do not yet know.[6]

However, one explanation posited for the highly influential role of music on the brain has been the notion of possession. In attempting to demonstrate that music leads us from sound, to tone, to melody, to harmony, to rhythm, to composition, to performance, to listening, to understanding and, finally, to ecstasy, Robert Jourdain has argued:[7] 'Music seems to be the most immediate of all the arts, and so the most ecstatic.'[8] Drawing upon Sack's work with Parkinson's patients to demonstrate how music 'possesses' us,[9] Jourdain attempts to articulate the nature of this 'possession' by using the language of encounter, relationship and experience:

> By providing the brain with an artificial environment, and forcing it through that environment in controlled ways, music imparts the means of experiencing relations far deeper than we encounter in our everyday lives ... Thus, however briefly, we attain a greater grasp of the world ... It's for this reason that music can be transcendent. For a few moments it makes us larger than we really are, and the world more orderly than it really is.[10]

Such a definition of transcendence would not please many a reformed theologian, but this explanation places musical experience within the realm of deep relationship and expansive existence:

> We respond not just to the beauty of the sustained deep relations that are revealed, but also to the fact of our perceiving them. As our brains are thrown into overdrive, we feel our very existence expand and realize that we can be more than we normally are, and that the world is more than it seems. That is cause enough for ecstasy.[11]

Jourdain is not alone in giving a scientific basis to expansive transcendental experience. The neurologist Macdonald Critchley acknowledges that

'Music can bring about a veritable perceptual spectrum ranging from the simple reception of auditory sense-data to impressions which ... well-nigh baffle description. So evocative, overwhelming and transcendental may these be as to defy description.'[12]

This experiential approach to the power of music upon the brain, leading to the explanatory analyses of 'ecstasy', 'transcendence' and the revelation of 'deep relations', is the starting point for my own explorations into the relationship between music, faith, religious ritual and altered state. As David Aldridge has observed, 'Many religions identify the ideal state as an altered state of consciousness: losing one's body and one's self, uniting with some sort of Divine Being.'[13] Likewise, and in keeping with the thesis of this book, Aldridge argues that the experiential nature of musical performance within religious ritual brings an intuitive understanding of spirituality, which words alone cannot create: 'That is why many religious forms feel redundant or restrictive because they have achieved a verbal dogma that fails to encourage the intuitive wisdom of current performances.'[14] It is in this context that I wish to explore the nature of 'trance'. Again, we have heard the word being used by Robin Dunbar to describe the endorphin-induced sense of well-being when experiencing music, but let us now explore this phenomenon in more detail by considering scientific research on music and the brain. Firstly, we must concur with Rouget that 'trance' and 'ecstasy' (as mentioned by Jourdain) are not the same:

> Trance is always associated with a greater or lesser degree of sensory over-stimulation – noises, music, smells, agitation – ecstasy, on the contrary, is most often tied to sensorial deprivation – silence, fasting, darkness.[15]

Thus, trance-inducing music within a religious ritual such as shamanism, which uses the body to make contact with the divine, or spirit world, through singing and dancing, is specific to the multi-sensory experience of the communal activity. In this context, scholars have concluded that music must possess certain characteristics in order to induce a trance. As John Pilch has shown based upon Kartomi's research, music must be mesmeric if it is to induce a trance: 'Music that best assists in inducing trance has regular pulsation and repetitive tonal patterns based on a restricted number of pitch levels.'[16] However, such trance-inducing music need not be shamanic. The calm, meditative chanting of the French Taizé community may equally assist:

> Just as the Javanese in trance believe that they are in contact with their deities and spirits ... so too do modern devotees of Taizé prayer believe this music is most capable of bringing a person into the presence of the Deity.[17]

In either situation the resultant experience (of trance) is through both music *and* ritual: 'Music has become one with ritual and is not a separate aesthetic category.'[18] In wishing to explore this close relationship between music, trance and the brain, I met a neuropsychiatrist whose research is at the forefront of scientific explorations into how music and religious ritual interact: Quinton Deeley.

Quinton is a Consultant Psychiatrist and a Senior Lecturer in Developmental Neuropsychiatry at the Institute of Psychiatry, Psychology and Neuroscience at King's College London. He writes of himself: 'I conduct research into developmental psychiatry and related fields, and have ongoing research and publications on the relations between mind, brain and culture. This is an area that I have started pursuing since my dual qualifications, first in Theology and Religious Studies from Cambridge University, and later in medicine from Guy's and St Thomas' Medical School.'[19] When I met him at the Maudsley Hospital in London, I asked him to explain a little about his research.

QD: I'm a psychiatrist and senior lecturer in social behaviour and neuro-development. Before I started medical training I read theology and religious studies at Cambridge, where I was supervised very closely by John Bowker [Dean of Trinity College at the time].

JA: A great man.

QD: A great man. He had very broad-ranging interests, but had a particular interest in the relationship between genes, brain and culture, especially in its application to understanding religion. This encouraged my interest in this topic. I had an interest in Jungian theory of religion, within the broader context of psychological and anthropological accounts of religion. And, of course, Jung had this concept of archetypes of the collective unconscious. At one point I was set an essay question about the extent to which Jung's theory represented intuitive proposals about the structure of the mind which have been validated by subsequent discoveries. This pointed towards theories addressing the relationship between genes, brain, cognition and culture. So I went on and eventually wrote an undergraduate dissertation on the biogenetic structural theory of myth and ritual. Biogenetic structuralism was a theory in the 1970s and early 1980s predominantly, which sought to synthesise structuralist anthropology with what was known about the brain. It was part of the project of neuro-anthropology – in other words, the attempt to identify universal, or near-universal, aspects of human experience and behaviour; and to understand whether they were motivated by features of brain structure and function as part of our characteristic endowment as a species. After that dissertation, I considered doing a PhD in biological anthropology at the University of Pennsylvania in order to pursue these questions further. However, I decided to undertake medical training, because I felt that it would allow me, through neuropsychiatry and cross-cultural psychiatry, to approach many of the same sorts of questions. I retained those interests during medical training.

Now, of course, in the meantime neuroscience and the human sciences evolved, so that by 1999 or 2000, when I started to do psychiatric research, functional neuroimaging was available, which hadn't been available at all in the '80s except in extremely rudimentary forms. I became involved in two broad lines of research, both of which are relevant to understanding cultural behaviour and cognitive and neurocognitive constraints on culturally variable behaviour. One line of research was into disorders of social cognition and social understanding, such as neuroimaging research into autism and criminal psychopathy. Psychopaths in this sense are people who engage in persistently antisocial behaviour without guilt or empathy for victims. Research on psychopathy is important in that it provides insights into how moral socialisation and the development of empathy can go awry. People with autism have difficulties with social understanding and social imagination, which again provides insights into quite basic mechanisms supporting social behaviour.

That was one line of research. But there was another line of research which really came out of my interest in neuropsychiatry and the broad category of what are now called 'functional neurological disorders'. That is to say, there is a very wide range of common symptoms and conditions whereby people present with or experience neurological-type symptoms in the absence of any underlying organic abnormality. For example, people with so-called conversion paralysis, where they have the experience of being unable to voluntarily move a limb, but there is no underlying neurological abnormality. These symptoms and conditions show the influence of implicit beliefs and expectancies, and point towards what we might term the 'power of belief' in symptom formation.

In the nineteenth century, there had been a very considerable interest in this topic by neurologists and psychiatrists, the period when the whole field of neurology and psychiatry as we now understand it was forming. The dominant form of explanation inherited from that period was the 'lesion-deficit method': a very powerful and successful method of delineating organic causes of illnesses by correlating symptoms and signs of disease with an organic lesion. Modern neurology and other medical disciplines are founded on that model. But, at the same time, there was a recognition that 'morbid ideation' could affect symptom formation. There was a great French nineteenth-century neurologist, Charcot, who became very interested in what he called hystero-epilepsy – what we now call non-epileptic seizures (those occurring in the absence of epileptic brain activity) – and other so-called hysterical phenomena, what we now call functional disorders. Charcot applied the method of hypnotism and suggestion to treat these conditions, but also experimentally to investigate or model them. Suggestion in hypnosis was therefore recognised as both a therapeutic and experimental tool for producing alterations in experience and behaviour, which are essentially involuntary from the point of view of the subject. Charcot and others' recognition in the nineteenth century of the link between functional symptoms and the power of ideas conveyed through suggestion was revived towards the end of the twentieth century by psychologists and cognitive neuroscientists.

So I started research in this area with David Oakley, who was a professor of psychology at University College London; Peter Halligan, a professor of cognitive neuropsychiatry in Cardiff; and Brian Toone, a neuropsychiatrist at the Maudsley Hospital, and essentially we started to use 'suggestions' combined with functional magnetic resonance image scanning to produce an experimental model of 'dissociative limb paralysis'; in other words, what previously had been called 'conversion limb paralysis' or 'hysterical limb paralysis'. What we could now do, which was not available at the end of the nineteenth century, was measure brain activity during the formation of these symptoms, and therefore provide insight into how ideas, beliefs and expectancies can produce changes in experience *via* effects on brain function. Not only was this research opportunity novel, but it was also from a conceptual or philosophical point of view very important as an alternative way of understanding the contribution of the brain to changes in experience and behaviour – not only to disease processes, but also non-pathological processes. This might include ordinary everyday characteristics of human experience and behaviour, but also what are often called altered states of consciousness. 'Alterations' in this sense are departures from more typical modes of experience of the self or other components of experience.

This research is interesting in its own right, but I asked Quinton how it specifically relates to the brain's response to religious ritual, faith and musical expression.

QD: We have conducted a series of experiments in recent years also with my colleagues Mitul Mehta and Eamonn Walsh at the Institute of Psychiatry, Psychology and Neuroscience at King's College London, in which we have been using suggestion to model a range of alterations in experience that occur both in pathological settings, such as psychiatric and neurological symptoms, but also altered states of consciousness as they occur within religious and other kinds of cultural setting.

So, for example, we have had a particular interest in the control, ownership and awareness of different components of normal experience, especially regarding action or movement, but also thought. Within psychiatric phenomenology, for example, it is recognised that there is a class of experiences called 'alien control phenomena'. So, a patient with schizophrenia may have the delusional experience that their hand is being remotely controlled by a maleficent agent, such as the CIA in the building opposite. They feel somewhat like a puppet and not in control of themselves. It is a very distressing experience. Similarly, there exists the phenomenon of 'thought insertion', where a person is aware of thoughts coming into their mind, but they're not their thoughts, and they don't feel in control of them. The patient will interpret them, or experience them, as belonging to somebody else, a maleficent agent typically, who is inserting these thoughts into their mind. So thought insertion and alien control of movement are different kinds of 'alien control phenomena', but there are also others, which relate not just to thought and movement but to other components of experience, such as speech or emotion.

RITUAL, DISSOCIATION AND ALTERED STATES

QD: From a phenomenological point of view, experiential changes occurring in spirit possession and shamanism, as well as some modalities of mystical experience, are what we could describe as 'dissociations' or 'alterations' of the normal experience of selfhood. In such phenomena, people may experience their thought, speech or movement as being controlled by a supernatural force; for example, in experiences of revelation. Therefore, both in pathological and non-pathological settings, you can see a category of experiences or variations in experience which involve these dissociations of selfhood. In our research we were very interested in creating experimental models and measuring brain activity to provide insight into fundamental brain mechanisms underpinning these types of experience. Essentially, we did a series of experiments on highly suggestible individuals – people who respond well to suggestions. About 10 per cent of the population are highly hypnotically responsive. One of the experiments was like this: imagine yourself lying on a scanner. You have a joystick that you move with your right hand, and you receive instructions periodically. Every three seconds you receive an instruction to move, for thirty seconds in total: so ten commands in a row. Then there's a rest period for another thirty seconds, followed by more move instructions, then rest instructions, and they alternate. So you're lying in the scanner, you're in your normal alert state, and you're moving the joystick ...

JA: The commands are right, left, up, down?

QD: Move the joystick forwards and backwards, and it's just the right hand. After the initial experience of being in control of the joystick, we then perform an induction procedure for hypnosis (remember we are using highly suggestible people). So then we repeat the experiment: you still have the normal experience of moving the joystick, but you happen to be hypnotised, so you're in a very relaxed and focused state. Then we make a suggestion that when you hear a command, your hand will move by itself. It's not you moving your hand, it will move by itself. We measure brain activity during this experience of involuntary movement. Then we make another suggestion that the hand moves by itself but you're not aware of this movement. This is important because during non-epileptic seizures, people produce involuntary movement with reduced awareness – about half of those who have non-epileptic seizures lose awareness during the seizure. Also, in mediumship or other possession states some people have no recollection of their movements during these episodes. It's therefore important to understand brain systems that can be involved in mediating this loss of awareness. Then we go on to make a suggestion that an engineer is conducting the experiments, and that they're using a machine to remotely control your hand movements. This is modelling a delusion of control in the schizophrenic sense, but is also comparable to some religious or cultural phenomena where people might feel their actions are being remotely controlled by a spirit, for example.

The experiment continues (still with the volunteer under hypnosis) with the suggestion to the participant that the engineer has gone away and that the machine is now malfunctioning. So the movements become random, impersonal: there is no internal or external agent in control of the movements. Then we make a suggestion that the engineer has found a way to enter your mind and body from within. So you're aware of the thoughts and feelings of the engineer, but you're a hapless witness to the fact that your movements are being controlled by another agent. By that stage, we are modelling a type of spirit possession called 'lucid possession' in which you retain awareness of the possessing agent, as opposed to complete loss of awareness of the possessing agent. By contrasting brain activity during personal control (when the engineer is controlling hand movement either remotely or through possession) and impersonal control (the machine malfunctioning), we can identify brain regions which support representations of a controlling agent (in this case, the engineer).[20]

The key point about this experiment is that it provides insights into the type of brain changes that accompany different sorts of dissociation of control. More fundamentally, this perspective demonstrates how ideas can produce radical alterations in subjective experience through effects on brain function. Medical research has tended to examine the brain as an organ system that is somewhat extracted from social context. The change in behaviour (the symptom), it is assumed, arises from a physiological disturbance as the primary cause. That is a lesion-deficit model, and rests on a patho-physiological conception of disease. But what we're doing in this kind of research is re-embedding the brain within culture as an environment in which the exchange of meanings organises brain activity to influence experience and behaviour. In practice, communication occurs not only through language, but also through many non-verbal and non-linguistic communicative components within our culturally organised environments. What we're starting to experimentally demonstrate is how those processes modulate brain activity to produce changes in experience. That's very important, to understanding the huge burden of illness which has previously been off the radar of physiological explanation, but also to understand how human beings' subjectivity, agency and cognition more generally are culturally embedded. By virtue of that cultural embeddedness, the brain, located within this larger system of relationships, can be influenced and modulated in order to produce characteristic forms of experience. That, of course, has implications for anthropology and for understanding religion in general, and for understanding potential mechanisms through which religions and religious contexts can have such powerful effects on people. So we could say that this research has drawn attention to the power of belief and expectancy, the power of symbolic representation, as well as symbolic action in a broad sense.

HUMAN SUBJECTIVITY, CULTURAL CONTEXT AND MUSIC

QD: So far our experiments have been in people who are highly suggestible, and we're using verbal suggestions, whereas in practice, and particularly in cultural contexts, many constraints or cues within the environment are non-verbal. Of course, that would include musical content as well. The verbal suggestions we use in our experiments can be classed as 'cognitive-symbolic' – that is to say, verbally encoded in language, evoking attributions of meaning, memories or expectancies. Cognitive-symbolic communication is clearly important in differentiating experience into the forms which are typical of a particular culture and context, or indeed influencing symptom formation in illness. But there are many other ways in which cognition and brain function can be influenced by cultural practice or by the features of the environment. In addition to these cognitive-symbolic forms, which primarily involve attributions or meaningful representations of one kind or another, there are sensory and affective components of cultural forms and practices which are also cognitively and experientially very evocative and constraining. So a general analytic framework for thinking about cultural processes can point to components which we could understand as predominantly cognitive and symbolic, and those which are sensory and affective.

And we should bear in mind others which are primarily motoric or movement-based, when we're thinking about the place of the body in culture, and the effects that that can have on experience. But, of course, cultural practices and forms such as ceremonial ritual typically draw together all of these different modalities and components of experience.[21]

Quinton's research clearly contributes to our understanding of how cultural contexts, such as religious music or experience, might affect the brain, but he also points out that, in a real context, there are many aspects of a religious service, for instance, that might affect brain activity on multiple levels at the same time:

QD: One of the explanatory fallacies of the application of psychological or cognitive theories of human behaviour is that there is a tendency to a rather atomistic conception of the effects that particular components of the environment might have. Thus, you might ask what the effect of smell on cognition is, for instance, incense in a church? Or what's the effect of rhythm? Or what's the effect of repetitive movement? Or what is the effect of religious icons? But, of course, none of these phenomena typically occur in isolation. They're orchestrated together and work together. So the interactions are synergic: they work with one another to produce effects which are probably not simply additive, but multiplicative. Moreover, from the point of view of the experiencing subject, the effects occur pre-consciously. In other words, experience emerges as a kind of late product of processing, which is multiply constrained, and we don't in general have conscious insight into the many processes that precede the emergence of experience. So as sensing and moving subjects we experience the world as a kind of rich totality. I think that's very important as a general observation, providing insight into how cultural practices can be so profoundly affecting. But I also think it demonstrates the limitations of reductionist approaches of laboratory-based research, which simplify the world in order to explain it – in other words, experiments are carefully controlled to allow inferences about causal processes which are not hopelessly confounded. However, when you take those conclusions and try to apply them to a human subject embedded in the world, it requires different methods to understand how the processes that have been isolated in the laboratory context then contribute to sensibility in complex real-world situations.

From a scientific point of view, we are still confronted with this problem of so-called 'ecological validity'. That is why cultural neuroscience, social neuroscience or neuro-anthropology are still at a relatively preliminary stage. We are at the point where we are identifying processes that are involved in the formation of altered or exalted forms of experience of various kinds, but we must be careful that we don't over-interpret those findings: a certain humility at this point is required.

Thus, there arises the question of relevance and what the value of this kind of research is in terms of our self-understanding. Is it just to alleviate the suffering of those with mental illness, or are there wider implications for the understanding of human experiences, such as religious music?

QD: In the medical case, I think the relevance is fairly plain, because we want to understand what causes suffering and disability and distress, in order to do something about it. In the case of understanding religious or aesthetic experience, or attributions of ultimate meaning, this kind of research has a potential bearing upon the interpretation that one places upon experience, but the direct relevance is not always as obvious as it is in the medical case. The wider conclusions might be more in the realm of general anthropology, that is, our account of ourselves as human beings – what used to be called the doctrine of man in theology. The findings also raise philosophical and theological questions as to what sense we make of these essentially naturalistic accounts of forms of experience that have arisen, for example, within religious settings. But not just religious settings: similar challenges or questions arise concerning attributions of meaning and value that occur within secular settings as well. For example, does the value of aesthetic experience change if we know what evokes it at a mechanistic level? So I think that's a different category of questions or set of considerations.

At this point I am fascinated about what we can see happening in the brain during religious ritual, so I ask a lay question about the experimentation and what one is looking at in the neuro-imaging of the brain and what changes one observes.

QD: I can probably answer that question best by describing another experiment we conducted using automatic writing as a research paradigm. Automatic writing, where the hand writes 'by itself' without conscious direction by or in some cases even awareness of the person holding the pen, is a phenomenon that was of great interest, particularly in the nineteenth century, within the context of spiritualism and mediumship. From our point of view, it was interesting because when people write automatically, there is a motor component – the hand moves by itself when the writing occurs. But there can also be a component of thought insertion – the thoughts that you write down are not your own thoughts, they're introduced by an external agent. There are instances of automatic writing as being a religiously interpreted modality of revelation, but I think in broader terms it points to a class of dissociations of complex thought and movement which provide insights into revelatory experience as a category of psychological processes.

We conducted an automatic writing experiment in highly hypnotically responsive individuals who were required to think of a sentence ending to a prompt, and then write it down.[22] During the automatic writing experiment it was suggested that an engineer either i) inserted a thought of a sentence ending into the mind of the participant; or ii) remotely controlled hand movements when a sentence ending was written down; or iii) made the participant lose awareness for automatic writing in which both thought insertion and alien control of movement occurred (this latter condition modelled classic mediumship, in which the medium has no recollection of the message they have written down during control by a spirit). We measured brain activity during all of these conditions using functional magnetic resonance imaging (fMRI). During these experiments we measure something called BOLD signal. Essentially, we apply very strong magnetic fields to the brain, which allow differences in paramagnetic properties of oxygenated and deoxygenated blood to be detected. Regional brain activity creates a change in blood flow to that region to carry away deoxygenated blood and return oxygenated blood. The difference in the magnetic properties enables a proxy measure of brain activity, because blood flow is linked to brain activity. So we are not looking at the activity of individual neurons, we are looking at an indirect product of the net activity of many millions of neurons comprising brain tissue, and systems or networks of brain regions. Thus, in terms of the type of analysis that we do, we're interested in a measure of activation of these brain regions, but we can also tease out another property called 'functional connectivity'. This is a statistically derived measure of the functional coupling of different brain regions. In other words, brain regions which are distributed across the brain, but where their activity is correlated in time. This is important because it is never the case that some feature of cognition and behaviour is produced by a single brain region acting in isolation. There is always a network or a set, a kind of ensemble, of brain regions, cooperatively working together to enable a function to emerge. Therefore, functional connectivity gives us an insight into the extent to which different brain regions work together to produce a particular function. Changes in functional connectivity help us to understand the types of cognitive functions which are brought together, potentially, in order to achieve a particular task or some other component of experience we're interested in. In summary, we are measuring regional brain activity, and functional connectivity or functional coupling.

JA: In the experiments, do you see particular areas of the brain being much more active than others?

QD: Yes. So, for example, in the case of the automatic writing experiment, we found very extensive non-overlapping or distinct changes in brain activity during thought insertion compared to alien control of movement. This is to be expected, because thought is different from movement. Yet we were very interested to find that there was a brain region that was overlapping between the two conditions. So when the volunteers had the experience that their thoughts were being externally controlled, and when they had the experience that their movements were being externally controlled, there was a reduction of activity in the supplementary motor area.

The supplementary motor area is a well-studied brain region which is known to be involved in action preparation and the formation of intentions to move. So it's a brain region that becomes active immediately preceding the conscious awareness of the intention to move. During an experience of alien control of movement, the reduced activation in this region is likely to underpin the loss of the experience of self-control, or self-initiation of movement. The brain regions involved in the execution of movement are active, but a brain region involved in the formation of motor intention, and the initiation of control of movement, has reduced its activity. What's interesting, though, is that the same region showed reduced activity during thought insertion. This suggests that the supplementary motor area's role may not be restricted only to movement, but it may have a broader role in different types of control and ownership of mental content. This was a novel finding, because the experiment was the first experimental model of thought insertion. What would be interesting, from a cognitive neuroscience view, is to see whether other types of so-called 'passivity' or alien control phenomena equally involve a reduction in the activity of supplementary motor area, because that potentially provides insight into a fundamental brain mechanism by which components of experience that we normally experience as under our control and ownership can dissociate and be experienced as not belonging to the self, or not under self-control.

EXPERIMENTS WITH SUGGESTION AND RELIGIOUS GROUP ACTIVITY

These experiments have been conducted on particularly suggestible individuals. But religion and cultural practice is very often group activity. Thus, I wondered whether there is any research that would connect that suggestibility with collective behaviour. For instance, when I was young and attended an evangelical Baptist church, with very often large groups, some people would occasionally speak in tongues, and it seemed that there were particular settings in which they were apparently given this so-called gift, whereas if you met them individually they wouldn't speak in tongues. So is there any correlation between these things?

QD: There are a number of observations to make. In terms of conducting experiments using brain measurement techniques for people in groups, that's an extremely interesting question and difficult to achieve in practice. It's technically very difficult to do, but one approach is to measure brain activity in two people simultaneously while they're conducting a joint task or interacting with one another, and that potentially provides powerful new insights into the change in brain function by virtue of being embedded in a social context, an interaction or a relationship. Arguably, most brain-imaging experiments are extremely artificial, not just in terms of the way that the environment and tasks have to be simplified, but also the abstraction of the person from social interaction. So it would be very interesting, for example, to investigate how knowledge of oneself as interacting with somebody else alters brain activity, either in specific brain regions or more globally, and the extent to which the variation in the activity in one person's brain can be predicted or explained by the variation in the activity in another person's brain. Now that might sound a bit like telepathy or telekinesis, but it doesn't have to be viewed in those terms, because there's a huge amount of brain which is dedicated to social cognition and social representation, which, in a way, tunes us in and allows us to notice, represent, understand and respond to the social intentions of people around us quickly and automatically. This is partly what is sometimes called 'theory of mind', or mentalising, or perspective-taking, the brain networks of which are well characterised by now. This is the ability to make attributions of the content of the thought, understanding and perspective of somebody else. But there has been a great interest in so-called 'simulation' of other people's mental states, and mirror neuron systems, the core idea of which is that the brain regions which are involved in, for example, producing an action by yourself, are also active when viewing an action in somebody else. In this model, perception of others allows us to 'simulate' their internal state through the automatic activation of the brain regions they are using to generate their behaviour. Mentalising and simulation accounts of social cognition point to a fundamental orientation towards the social world grounded in brain structure and function.

If we think about the example you gave, of an evangelical service where people speak in tongues, I think that illustrates the point that lots of things are going on at the same time, all of which may influence or constrain the behaviour and experience of individuals in that setting. You can see that many different research disciplines have important things to say about what's going on. There's a body of social psychology research, for example, stemming from Erving Goffman, about the importance of frames of behaviour, or implicit scripts. These dramaturgical analyses of behaviour rest on the idea that, in social contexts, we can be viewed implicitly as actors with roles following implicit scripts which structure our behaviour, and that validates it and makes it meaningful. Now that is by no means opposed to a cognitive neuroscience perspective, which would ask how those implicit social schemata are represented in the brain and how they contribute to action formation and experience. We do have some understanding of the brain regions comprising these mentalising networks, including the memory systems in the brain involved in storing or representing social scripts or schemata.

We might also consider the infectious quality of emotion that can occur in social settings, and the power of observing group action. The notion of simulation, or the mirror neuron concept, provides a potential mechanism for understanding how our brain activity can automatically be hooked up, as it were, to what's going on around us. If people around you are behaving in a particular way and expressing certain kinds of emotions, then all the brain systems in yourself that would be involved in that kind of behaviour, or expressing those kinds of emotions, are at least partially activated by the mere observation of it. Thus, you're already creating an internal template in order to enact or reproduce the behaviour of people around you, just by virtue of perception. This may not be sufficient for you to behave as your peers, but it creates a potential to share their experience.

Understanding social context and social role is really important in understanding behaviour within religious settings, including in ritual settings. For example, Gilbert Rouget, a French ethnomusicologist, wrote a book, *Music and Trance*, which is a very wide survey of different types of possession cross-culturally and historically.[23] He observed that within the annual feasts for Shango among the Yoruba, at least several dozen adepts among a large crowd are capable of being possessed by Shango. However, only one of these adepts actually embodies the god. By contrast, among the neighbouring Fon and Gun peoples, Khevioso, a homologue of Shango, can be embodied by several dancers simultaneously.[24] These examples illustrate how the trance behaviour of adepts conforms to shared implicit conventions – what Rouget called ideologies of possession, which we would call schemata – implicit models of how to experience and behave in ritual settings.

Rouget also points out that the performers of music in possession cults don't become entranced, not only because they are concentrating on producing the music but also because it is not their role to become possessed. However, in the case of shamanism, where the shaman dances *and* produces music, the musician is the creator of his own trance. So these modalities of response are highly structured and organised by implicit models. Of course, there is an important question about how we learn these implicit models, which can be partly answered by the study of memory, social perception, social interaction and, very importantly, the study of non-verbal communication and social modelling. Then one must examine how the brain systems which are involved in that learning and representation interface with other brain systems involved with the organisation of action and emotions, as well as other components like attention, memory or awareness. The research on suggestion is relevant here, because we have demonstrated that phenomena such as involuntary movement can be accompanied by different causal attributions and experiences depending on the suggestions we administer (for example, whether the hand movement is remotely controlled by an engineer, or caused by a malfunctioning machine). In other words, whether or not a change to the usual sense of self-control occurs, as well as the *type* of broader experience within which that change occurs, is exquisitely sensitive to belief, expectancy and context. Similarly, even within a group of people in the same religious ceremonial setting, there are different forms of experience that can accompany the performance of music, listening to music, and other aspects of a ritual setting, including when and among whom altered states of consciousness or sensibility occur. These differences can be influenced by social role, expectancy and prior experience. Consequently, while cognitive processes such as mentalising or simulation may enable sharing of types of experience, cognitive processes relating to role, expectancy, prior experience and training also contribute to the responses of participant, performers and officiants.

RELIGIOUS RITUAL AND POSSESSION

QD: To switch to a cross-cultural perspective for a moment, there are many possession cults that are associated with amnesia, which is connected to the logic of possession, because, if a person is 'possessed' by a different identity or agent, why would they remember what that different agent is experiencing? Logically, one doesn't normally have access to the memories of somebody else. (There is an exception, however, to this experience, which Oesterreich called 'lucid possession',[25] where the 'possessed' does have awareness of the thoughts and feelings of the possessing agent.) In our research modelling possession states we have measured brain activity during reduced awareness of suggested involuntary movement. So, for example, we identified reduced activation in Brodmann Area Seven (BA 7, which is part of the parietal lobe) during reduced awareness which is part of the parietal lobe, which we know from other research is involved in awareness of the control of movement in immediate extra-personal space. We also noticed reduced activity of the insula, which is involved in the processing of afferent sensory information from the body. So these are plausible brain mechanisms for understanding how it's possible to have a loss of awareness of immediate surroundings, of movements and bodily sensations during possession states.

These experiments study relatively 'downstream' changes in brain activity, which accompany specific alterations in experience. There's a very important question about what happens more 'upstream' at a higher level of control. What are the processes, and when do they happen, that reorganise brain activity into the late changes that underpin ritual or other religiously evoked experience? The question of what happens more upstream is not well understood and very difficult to study, because it pushes us up against trying to unravel the very rapid and conceptually quite tricky alternations between different levels at which experience is organised. For example, the attributions and interpretations implied or expressed in our immediate social and physical environment; our underlying beliefs and expectations; and the way these 'higher level' processes are represented in the brain.

We bump up against not just the mind–body problem, but what we could describe as the mind–body–culture problem, as we try to create a causal model that can handle these complex and rapid adjustments or interactions between different levels at which we're organised.

JA: That's a very difficult challenge, absolutely. The areas of the brain that you were measuring, are they in any particular hemisphere, or predominantly in any particular hemisphere?

QD: There's a very long tradition of research about the role of different hemispheres in contributing to different forms of experience or styles of experience in cognition.

JA: So I'm thinking of McGilchrist's *The Master and his Emissary*.[26]

QD: Yes, among others going back some way (for example, Turner 1983).[27] In terms of our research using suggestions to model altered states of self-control and consciousness we're not making very strong global generalisations about the contributions of respective hemispheres, but some research does point to different routes into altered forms of experience or altered sensibility.[28] This is both at the individual level, where different cognitive styles relate to the predominance of functions that are more supported by one or other hemisphere. But different cultural forms also engage distinct types of information-processing and hemispheric activity.

So, for example, there's good evidence that a more poetic mode of language-processing, where there's a greater emphasis upon evoking remote or indirect associations between words, would enlist a relatively greater engagement of right-hemispheric processing.

Also in musical-processing, there is some work that points towards a relatively greater engagement of right hemisphere. So entering more emotionally exalted states, through say poetry or the use of certain kinds of mental imagery, or icons or other types of visual imagery, or music and so on, engages the right hemisphere relatively more.[29] Equally, heightened emotion and significance can be evoked by sensory-affective stimuli.[30] Again, this shows the range of elements that can be orchestrated in ritual or religious settings to evoke heightened experience.

There are different routes, then, into altered experience in ritual and religious settings, but also different forms of experience and sensibility. This returns us to a critical phenomenology as a starting point for religious studies. It is important to move away from the idea of generic altered states of consciousness, aesthetic or religious experience. Hopefully this is a qualified and nuanced approach, which does justice to the complexity of experience and behaviour, and how it becomes embedded within cultural processes, but also, critically, how the experience varies across time, across development: through childhood, teenage years and early adulthood experience evolves, sensibility evolves.

DEELEY'S RESEARCH AND PERSONAL VIEW ON FAITH

In Deeley's research, I wonder whether it has caused him to reconsider the nature of belief, and whether it has changed a philosophical or theological perspective for him.

QD: In a narrow scientific sense, it's changed my sense of belief, because it's made me think of belief, on the one hand, as a very important category of psychological phenomena, which has explanatory relevance, while at the same time prompting me to think about how belief is fractionated into different processes. In terms of my philosophical and theological orientation, it has strengthened my sense of the importance of culture. We use the term 'biography' as a way of embedding an individual within society, within relationships with other people, within context. I'm going against a grain, the trend of neuro-reductionism, which sees the brain as the first cause of experience. The explanation of a phenomenon, it says, begins with the brain. But the approach that I'm taking points towards the notion of reciprocal causation and a more systems-based approach. This involves thinking of human life as organised at different levels, in which there are complex interactions all the time, over different timescales, across development, prenatally, postnatally, from infancy throughout life. Thus, in order to understand any particular phenomena, you have to delimit the frame of explanation to pick out causes or constraints which are most immediately relevant. But what counts as immediately relevant partly depends on the question you're asking – if it's a question about development, for example, or if it's a question about immediate causation, or even if it's a question about evolution. But also it underscores the importance of environment broadly conceived to brain structure and function, as well as the importance of brain structure and function to the explanation of behaviour.

It is a scientific point that I'm making, but it's also a philosophical point, because it's about recognising the richness and complexity of human life and experience and sensibility, the primacy of relationship and social involvement in terms of what we are. It resists a kind of simplistic reductionism, which devalues experience and, if used as a basis for policy or medical treatment, can be very harmful to people. For the sake of argument, let's say that, in order for you to have a sense of greater connectedness with the world around you, there is an attenuation of the sense of oneself as being strongly separate from the rest of the world. Let's also say that that sense, when it occurs, can be experienced as inherently valuable. There may be, then, an ethical implication that you should love your neighbour, or you should help people, however you want to think about it. So if you say that, in order to have that experience, your parietal lobe, among other brain regions, has to function within certain parameters, does that diminish the value accorded to that experience? Now this is an important question, and I think the question here is answered not by whether or not a brain region or network has to be active to have a certain type of experience. I think how one evaluates those experiences involves broader considerations which aren't about whether or not a particular brain region is active, or indeed whether or not a certain type of brain behaviour is necessary for certain types of experience. In order to know that 'one plus one equals two' requires a certain type of brain behaviour, so the actual judgements about truth, even narrowly conceived, require certain types of brain behaviour in order to have the competence to make them. Yet the truth or value of a mathematical operation is given by the criteria for determining its truth, and is not based on the various ways it might be implemented in a brain – or even a machine. Judgements about other types of value, such as beauty, are not just conceptual, nor are they as easy to demonstrate in terms of the self-evidently correct application of a system of rules such as you get in logic or mathematics. Nevertheless, you can see within communities of people, who form judgements about the aesthetic value of something, that there are criteria applied. There are local consensuses that can be reached, and that extends to art or music: it may be a very general sense, but you do get community consensus. It also extends to sporting prowess – a good goal, a good tackle, etc. So we apply these judgements all the time.

The fact that experiences have accompanying brain activity doesn't, in a general sense, dictate the truth or value of the judgements we make – even if they are necessary for given types of judgement to be made. The same is generally true of religious experience. But there is a particular relevance of a scientific anthropology to particular questions. So, for example, a thousand years ago it was easier for people, including intellectuals, to operate with what you might call a naïve realism about the content of religious experience, such as sensations of ascent into heaven, a return to earth, prophetic or inspired speech. The demonstration that some forms of experience – which are subjectively very convincing – can be produced through entirely natural mechanisms does have bearing upon any naïve interpretations of what those experiences are. I think it makes it less plausible that they can be taken at face value, and makes it more likely that they have to be considered as a product of brain behaviour dependent on ideas and context in very particular ways. With respect to religious experience, this is partly to do with understanding the relationship between the brain and experience, but I think it's also, perhaps even more importantly, to do with broader changes in philosophy. Philosophies, for example, following on from Immanuel Kant, which underscore the idea that we don't have an unmediated access to a world of experience and understanding independently of cognition. I think that point is absolutely fundamental, because it argues very strongly against a naive realism. It means that the types of religious experience that may be consistent with, for example, belief in God, don't carry the weight of self-evident truth that has historically been ascribed to them. It becomes more a question of inference in a much weaker epistemological sense than was in the main accepted in premodern religious traditions.

When I say that it's a question of inference, I do *mean* it's a question of inference. For example, some versions of theology incorporate religious experience as part of the abductive inference of God – using cumulative arguments for the existence of God. This involves looking at numerous lines of evidence which cumulatively point towards the idea that believing in God makes sense: God as an omniscient, omnipotent creator of the world, and so on. I think certain kinds of religious experience more readily support those kinds of inference. For example, I was at a conference called 'Cognitive Approaches to Ancient Religious Experience', and Rowan Williams was talking about Christian monasticism and certain types of religious experience which arose for some of the early desert practitioners. He was discussing the case of Evagrius and I pressed him quite closely as to what he thought was going on in between the attenuation of symbolic thought and its resumption; modes of experience which were essentially non-verbal, and which are consistent with apophatic theology, in which there is a profound reluctance to make positive statements about what religious experience points to. Rowan said that his sense was that these modalities of experience, to the extent that one can discuss them, were about what he termed 'connectivity', by which I think he meant an altered sense of self, or an attenuation of the normal sense of self, a kind of intimate, profound relationship with the universe, which is experienced as inherently valuable, and which has ethical implications. Within one way of thinking, this is the nearest a mere mortal can come to the direct intuition of God. I think this makes sense within its own terms, and it is certainly a mode of experience which has evoked and reinforced the inference of God – even if this is not the only ontological inference that can be made on the basis of this form of experience.

THE BRAIN AND REVELATION

QD: Revelation is much more problematic. Revelation, in the sense of direct control of mental and vocal apparatus by God or other supernatural agents to introduce messages about the nature of the world into the world, is a different case. It seems to me that the fragility of human cognition, of the human mind, is evident in how, with astonishing ease, it is possible to evoke comparable experiences in many people by simply administering suggestions to them. I think that raises a challenge as to how we interpret those experiences. There are accounts in the Christian tradition of revelation as 'divine dictation' which are perhaps theologically most problematic. But a tradition that the Holy Spirit works concursively with the human mind in the production of revelation allows for the idea that there is an evocation or inspiration rather than direct control of human communication by God. It therefore also makes greater space for epistemic limitations – the influence of the human mind on what is communicated. In this latter tradition, one could argue that it is an evangelist's own understanding, in some deep sense, which is being communicated, but which is nevertheless being influenced by an apprehension about the nature of the world. Even then that's problematic, because that's not what they thought they were doing, and it has never consistently been interpreted as such within the respective traditions.

An alternative view is not to be troubled by this, because it's in the nature of the divine agent that they can intervene in the world, and enlist the cognitive resources of mere mortals to speak through them. If that argument is made, then that requires a different kind of world picture, and a different sort of theological view, which is not mine. So I do think questions are raised, and the naturalistic approach to the world, in broad terms, continues to pose a profound challenge to theological realism.

When you break theological realism down into particular issues, it requires radical revision, compared to premodern understandings of the world. There's no doubt about that. Now whether what you're left with after that is the same religion as the one of former ages is a matter of individual judgement, I think. But you end up in a very different place and the people you may find yourself closest to, in terms of their sensibility about the world, may not even be religious. If you think about religion as a kind of umbrella term, which encompasses all sorts of subsystems, experiences, practices, ethical orientations and different resources that people draw upon to navigate and make sense of the world, then there'll be subsystems in Christianity, as it now is, that are much closer to subsystems within Islam, some forms of Sufism and some forms of Buddhism, Hinduism, than they are to most of their co-religionists, and indeed, also to romantic poets.

JA: And to secularism as well?

QD: We're in an odd stage of history, where many traditions are being pulled in different directions, and arguably quite radically fragmented. People are asking: what do you have to believe and how do you interpret the world in order to be a genuine inheritor of a tradition, without self-contradiction or dissimulation? In that context, it doesn't make a lot of sense for a Christian to be a kind of social worker who practises out of a church. There has to be meaningful institutional continuity, otherwise the Christian project is lost.

Modes of experiencing oneself as part of the totality of being, as Ricoeur put it, are a source of value, and they do point towards forms of understanding, relationship with oneself, with the world, with fellow human beings, which have been tracked within different traditions and identified as a source of value. There are local characteristics and interpretations within different traditions, so different schools of thought within Buddhism are not the same, different forms of Hindu tantras are not the same, different forms of Sufism are not the same, etc. Those variations do make a difference, but I can see family resemblances between different sensibilities that point towards a kind of common resource, which one can recognise across different forms of life, including the secular.

Like many people, I find myself in this position that I can see a great deal of value and good in religions, along with a great deal of harm, while not belonging to that religion. The question: 'are you religious or not religious, or are you an atheist or not atheist' is a very nineteenth-century question. We're in a kind of multi-polar Hegelian dialectic, the outcome of which is not known, and may not be known, because we may all have destroyed ourselves before we get there, which at the moment is starting to look a bit more likely than not. The people who will shout loudest on our way to the whole thing spinning really out of control will of course be the people who see themselves as the inheritors of the traditional systems. We're in a world in which people are shouting at each other through megaphones all the time. That seems to have happened very quickly, because I don't remember such a pervasive sense of this growing up: it's just changed. We're dealing with all sorts of fundamentalisms, including secular and nativist fundamentalisms, and we find our societies fragmenting and some being attracted to extremism. That's creating very new dynamics and predicaments for people.

I think there is more work of imagination, partly poetic work and partly philosophical work, needed to understand how to recognise and articulate a vision of the world other than a sort of simple subjectivism. People who've given up premodern ontologies often don't feel that there's a shareable discourse about the world, and about the structure of our place in the world, which can form a common basis for value orientation. I'm not sure that that's the case, but the really powerful thing about religions is that they're very, *very* good at concretising beliefs and ontologies and making them externally very compelling. Ideologies like fascism and communism have, at times, also been very good at that.

The other place I think problems with naturalism come up is in cosmology. We're in this odd position where the scientific account of the universe is, at one level, extraordinarily impressive as an intellectual and scientific achievement, even though there are bits of it that clearly are still matters of profound uncertainty, and changing very rapidly. But scientific discourse doesn't function simply as descriptive or explanatory; it tends to be read as an effort after a broader or even ultimate meaning. At the same time, science struggles to convey a total vision of the world, because it's not designed to do that. This illustrates the power as well as the limitation of the scientific and naturalistic ambition, not least because we encounter the question: why is there something rather than nothing? I'm not proposing that there would be an answer to that either. I'm saying that there's an epistemological limitation around the project, and also a question about the sufficiency of scientific language for human beings – for articulating radical awe, or ontological shock – because the language is not really designed to do that. When you see science documentaries and read science journalism, they're often framed as an encounter with some awe-inspiring feature of the universe, but this points to a problem of epistemic limitation to do with the sufficiency of the causal explanation about why this world exists. This is not just to do with the restricted focus of explanatory discourse or explanation in science, it's also the symbolic, linear, temporally and spatially bound nature of understanding that is problematic. What is epistemologically disruptive is the troubling intuition of the vastness and complexity of a world that we cannot fully grasp or understand; to intuit that is to be awestruck, and perhaps, at times, to be fearful as well. Not fearful of damnation, but just fearful of mystery.

AFTERTHOUGHT

Quinton's sense of intuitive awe, and even fear, in the face of a vast and complex world brings me back to the importance of music within the mental and physical processes involved in our human experience of encounter and relationship, with the world around us and with each other, as well as experiences that shape our perception and reception of reality. Music, especially when used in the intense arena of trance-inducing ritual, as Quinton has explained, can be a powerful psychological and neurological stimulant. When examined within the realm of religion, we find that music, in this context, is part of a more powerful experience than mere cognitive belief in a creator god. As John Gray has written, 'A godless world is as mysterious as one suffused with divinity, and the difference between the two may be less than you think.'[31] Moreover, as Anthony Storr concludes, 'Although music is not a belief system, I think that its importance and its appeal also depends upon its being a way of ordering human experience.'[32] It is this experience, for Storr, both physical and neurological, that helps him make sense of the 'fearful mystery' that takes the listener beyond both of these embodied processes:

> Music exalts life, enhances life, and gives it meaning. Great music outlives the individual who created it. It is both personal and beyond the personal. For those who love it, it remains as a fixed point of reference in an unpredictable world. Music is a source of reconciliation, exhilaration, and hope which never fails ... It is irreplaceable, undeserved, transcendental blessing.[33]

Storr here refers not to a transcendence that is imagined, but to a real hope that allows for the 'vastness and complexity of a world that we cannot represent to ourselves'. In this context it leads not to a vague 'transcendence' of a meaningless 'other', but substantial influence on the genuine process of reconciliation and exhilaration, leading to a greater optimism for the future. Through this experience we approach, with meaning, the awesome mystery of our existence.

CHAPTER SIX

MUSIC AND FAITH UNDER PERSECUTION

> Music ... will help dissolve your perplexities and purify your character and sensibilities, and in time of care and sorrow, will keep a fountain of joy alive in you.[1]

The former Chief Rabbi, Jonathan Sacks, has stated that 'religion isn't born in someone's bright idea. Religion is born in collective pain.'[2] If the pain becomes too severe, someone will emerge to lead a new religion forward:

> People find themselves wandering through a desperately cruel, random universe, where a few people flourish and many people don't. A cry goes out and someone comes along and finds a way of reaffirming human dignity and reigniting human hope.[3]

Sacks considers that the Western world has not yet reached such a place of despair, but that it will: 'We in the West have not yet reached that cry of pain but we may in the predictable future.'[4] One society that did reach that cry of pain was pre-revolutionary Russia. The uprising of 1917 and the communist era that followed did not give birth to a religion but a political ideology that sought to crush all faith practices. What then happened to people's Christian faith and the culture that went with it? Was it extinguished? Quite the reverse.

We have considered how music has played a fundamental role in human evolution and neurological development. We have seen how music is a universal characteristic of human existence, experience, encounter and relationships. In the third chapter in this part of the book, I explore how the relationship between music and faith has endured, even in the most hostile circumstances in recent European history, including the rise of communism in Russia and Eastern Europe. As Michael Bourdeaux has written, religion, and sacred music with it, were intended to be extinguished by Marxist and Leninist ideology:

> The catastrophic experiment forcibly to impose 'state atheism' (gosateizm) in the Soviet Union lasted just 70 years. Until Lenin's first decree on the Separation of Church and State of January 1918, no government in history had sought to impose a system which rejected all forms of religion.[5]

However, this was never the case, despite the best efforts of the communist regime:

> The revival of religion, especially among the intelligentsia of Moscow and Leningrad, even as early as the 1960s is amply documented. Those writers who have attributed it in some way to the perestroika of Gorbachev are seriously in error. What Gorbachev did was to take the lid off a seething cauldron, facilitating the rebirth of religious institutions nationwide and giving voice to the pent-up spiritual aspirations of the Russian people (one meaning of 'glasnost'). This is the context in which we must view the events of 1988, when all this suddenly broke the surface.[6]

Faith survived. In fact, the attempt to eliminate faith from society was always doomed. To see Marxism as a replacement for religion, Terry Eagleton argues, was, and is, a 'kind of category mistake' because 'Christians hope still to believe on their deathbed, whereas political radicals trust that they will be free to abandon their efforts long before that point'.[7] Far from replacing religion, Eagleton sees close affinities between religious thought and Marx's vision of history:

> Justice, emancipation, the day of reckoning, the struggle against oppression, the coming to power of the dispossessed, the future reign of peace and plenty: Marx shares these and other motifs with the Judeo-Christian heritage ... Marxism should feel enriched by this legacy, not embarrassed by it. He himself was an enthusiastic reader of the Old Testament prophets.[8]

In order to explore how faith and sacred music survived, and indeed thrived, in communist Russia and Eastern Europe, I interviewed two people with first-hand experience of the most oppressive decades of the communist era. One is an English man who became the 'voice' of the religious oppressed in Russia, Canon Michael Bourdeaux. The other is someone who was at the heart of the sacred music revival in Hungary from the 1970s onwards and who is now a senior academic in the University of Budapest, Balázs Déri. The men's personal stories reveal not only their own strength of character in the face of fierce opposition, but also the phenomenal tenacity of people in the most adverse circumstances to cling on to faith, hope and love. In the midst of stifling limitations, music so often gave expression to the enduring desire for hearts and minds to reach out towards the numinous and unknown, and to explore regions of reality not ratified and validated by a restrictive regime and ideology.

The Revd Canon Michael Bourdeaux spent a year in Moscow in the 1950s, as one of the first wave of British exchange students to visit the Soviet Union. It was during that time that he took up the cause of believers who were persecuted for their faith under the Soviet regime. He was a co-founder of the Keston Institute, which focused on studying religious belief and practices under communism in the former Soviet Union and Eastern Europe, and he has written authoritatively and extensively in this field. He is also a great lover of Russian music and a long-standing member of the Great Britain-Russia Society.[9]

In 1969 he co-founded the Centre for the Study of Religion and Communism. In the early 1970s he bought the old parish school on Keston Common and the centre was renamed Keston College. Later it broadened its purview to include former communist countries, with its main concerns being the former Soviet Union and the Eastern Bloc. Over the years it played a key role in the revival of the Russian Orthodox Church, and has become a leading voice on religious freedom in former communist countries, with an emphasis on the former Soviet Union. Eventually the enterprise was relocated to Oxford. In 1984 Michael Bourdeaux won the Templeton Prize.

I began by asking Michael how music might have been involved in his life as a priest, and in all the various activities he has undertaken, and what kind of sacred music has had a particular importance to him. He began by telling me something about his connections with Russia and how his associations with religion in communist countries came about.

MB: In 1959, when I was eighteen and doing National Service, I was seconded to the joint services school of linguists, and I learned Russian for eighteen months, starting at Cambridge University. Then I read Russian at Oxford and then Theology. I was lucky enough that a door opened in the most amazing way. I found myself on the boat to Leningrad. I was a member of the very first Russian/British exchange in history. Seventeen students from this country went to Moscow and Leningrad universities. I was at Moscow, and the equivalent number came here. I was one of the first British students to live in Russia and that was an exciting and challenging experience.

It was the heyday of great Russian music, and we could get tickets for everything at Moscow University. There was a department called the Foreign Department, and we had the privilege of being able to go there and ask for tickets for the Bolshoi to see great performers. Shostakovich was at the height of his career. [The cellist Mstislav] Rostropovich was playing regularly, as well as [the pianist] Emil Gilels and [the violinist] David Oistrakh. I was thrown right into the middle of them.

In fact, I got to know Rostropovich and his wife, Galina Vishnevskaya. Benjamin Britten wrote the soprano part in the *War Requiem* for Vishnevskaya. When it was first performed in London, I was privileged to be in the chorus. That was a wonderful experience. She had been in London to sing *Aida* and she planned to stay on and go straight to Aldeburgh to rehearse with Britten, and the Soviet embassy bundled her on a plane and said she was ill. When the famous performance of the *War Requiem* took place in Coventry Cathedral in 1962, the soprano was Heather Harper, and none of the press mentioned the fact that Vishnevskaya had been struck off, or if they did they said she'd been ill, which was absolute rubbish. When the Coventry Cathedral performance took place, she and Rostropovich listened to it on the BBC, and she wept bitter tears. Can you imagine taking that away from somebody, however wonderfully Heather Harper sang it? That was in the 1960s, when our arts world was blind. Britten was really a good friend of the Soviet Union in the best sense. He wasn't a communist or anything like, but he had excellent relations with Shostakovich and with a lot of other Russian musicians, especially Rostropovich and Vishnevskaya. He wrote a song cycle for Vishnevskaya when he was in Armenia.

The only music I had performed up to 1959 was quite a lot of singing when I was at school, and at Oxford I sang in the Bach Choir for five years. But in Moscow I found myself being able to listen to live music of the highest possible international standards. I didn't get to know the Russian Church music very well at that stage, because the Russian Church was so repressed. There was very little going on. There were churches in Moscow where music was sung, but I didn't take a great deal of interest in Russian Church music at that point. However, my first piece of original research was to find out exactly how many churches were open in Moscow, because that simple statistic was not known, because the Russian Orthodox Church would not come clean and say how many churches they had open. It turned out to be forty-one. A rumour went round, sometime early in 1960, that Sergei Rachmaninov's choral *Vespers* were going to be performed. Normally Rachmaninov would not be in the repertoire because he'd been in exile and was under a cloud. So I turned up at the church where it was going to be performed. It was absolutely packed – we were shoulder to shoulder, as there are no seats in an Orthodox church.

We all stood in a huge crush. It was a fully liturgical performance and it went on for some three hours, but I was young and fit in those days, I could stand it. It was the most wonderful experience, by candlelight. I've never forgotten it. And in subsequent years I've had the great privilege and pleasure of training choirs to sing the Old Church Slavonic of the Rachmaninov *Vespers*.

JA: Do you still help choirs to get the language just right with their conductor and the performers?

MB: I have been the coach for the BBC National Chorus of Wales, so we've done *The Bells* by Rachmaninov, and I trained them to do the first night of the Proms recently, where they performed Prokofiev's *Alexander Nevsky*, which I know well as a singer – I know it virtually off by heart.

JA: Do you enjoy singing yourself?

MB: I've had a fair amount of experience now. I sang in the Philharmonia Chorus for thirty years with my first wife, who was a pianist and had a lovely light contralto voice. So we sang in the Philharmonia together for over twenty years.

JA: What were the restrictions on music and musicians in communist Russia in 1959?

MB: Personnel and repertoire. Let's start with personnel. You had to conform to be accepted. If you were absolutely outstanding, you could get away with things, but you were constantly under observation. The Borodin Quartet were very famous in those days. They got together first of all when Stalin died, when he was lying in state, because the authorities needed music ongoing all day, so they played a long stint. They wanted to call themselves the Beethoven Quartet, but were not allowed to.

Once established, the Borodin Quartet did extremely well but their personnel was controlled. They were considered sufficiently reliable to be allowed to go abroad, but with a minder. Every group or individual that went abroad had to have a minder. There were famous cases of defections – [the ballet dancer Rudolph] Nureyev most famously of all – and the Soviet regime were absolutely horrified when a top musician [like Sergei Rachmaninov] announced that he wasn't coming back. So a top group like the Borodin Quartet would be accompanied by a minder.

On the question of repertoire they were severely restricted at home, but they got away with things on tour that they couldn't play when they were in Moscow. Some of the restrictions are explicable, some are not. Why, for instance, were they not allowed to play [Leoš] Janáček? The group put Janáček's two quartets on the map eventually, but they weren't allowed to play them in Russia. I suppose they could play them on tour because the Soviet regime thought it would give a better impression if they were going to play some 'modern' music. Janáček died in 1926 so he wasn't that modern but it sounded modern.

JA: But Shostakovich would be fine, of course.

MB: Yes, they played all of Shostakovich's quartets. Anyway, the day came when they did a trip to America, and they were allowed to go without the minder. What did that tell the first violinist? That one of the other three was the minder. Indeed it was true; they were going to be betrayed by one of their own. It turned out to be the cellist, who was exposed as a Soviet informer, which eventually led to the breakup of the group.

The repertoire, in Russia, was so restricted that all one would hear would be Russian music *ad nauseam* almost. Not only great composers like Shostakovich but lesser composers like Khachaturian, Shebalin and Weinberg.

Weinberg was a Polish Jew who emigrated to Russia and became a Soviet citizen. He was friends with Shostakovich, who admired his music, and told me so, because I met Shostakovich. Weinberg was a wonderful composer but, because he was a Polish Jew, his music simply was not played. He was edited out. He wrote a few film scores, which provided money for his family, but not one of his many operas was ever performed. English National Opera staged one, called *The Prisoner*, about five years ago, and it was the most wonderful music.

JA: Do you think he's almost been lost to history because of that restriction?

MB: Yes. He had to teach music in school as his career. He was sent to prison once, for a very short time: Stalin, in his last paranoid days, had a purge of Jews – it was called The Jewish Plot – and all sorts of Jews were being rounded up and imprisoned, but luckily Stalin died before these people had long sentences. Weinberg was released, along with many others, just after Stalin died, and that saved his life probably.

In 1959–60 there was a great emphasis on improved international relations. Khrushchev was the general secretary of the Communist Party and he was keen on improving relations with America. My most significant scholarship has recorded Khrushchev's anti-religious campaigns, although his public persona promoted 'Peace and Friendship', which made allowances for American music, as long as it was controlled by an organisation called '*Gos* Concert', meaning 'State Concert', which controlled personnel and the repertoire. A week of Soviet-American music was announced and the American Ambassador, Llewellyn Thompson, hosted American composers, such as Aaron Copland, who had Russian origins in his grandparents. Copland's music was very acceptable to the Russians. They loved it. He came with another American composer called Lukas Foss.

My then fiancée, Gillian, was virtually in charge of domestic arrangements in the ambassador's household and Mr Thompson, whom I knew socially, said to me, 'You're interested in music, aren't you? Shostakovich will be coming to the reception after the concert, I want you to take personal charge of him. Because he will not stay longer than ten minutes, your job is to buttonhole him at the reception, and keep him there for longer than ten minutes if you can.' We had a wonderful concert, including a Shostakovich symphony and music by Copland and Foss. Afterwards, I was put into one of the American embassy cars with Shostakovich and, when we reached the room, he made a beeline for the corner, so I made a beeline after him. He was an introverted man. You've seen pictures of him, and he always looks frightened, no expression on his face. I thought, 'I'm not going to be able to talk really, but I'll try'. My Russian was pretty good by that time and he began to open up and ask me what British composers I knew. I mentioned Benjamin Britten's *Serenade for Tenor, Horn and Strings*. He said that he knew the piece because he sometimes managed to listen to the BBC World Service and that friends would sometimes send him musical scores of Britten's works. That opened my eyes. Shostakovich didn't know the wonderful recording with the tenor Peter Pears and horn player Dennis Brain, so we talked about that. He started to open up, and then he mentioned that he would like to meet [Aaron] Copland, who was over the other side of the room, so I went and brought Copland over to him and I interpreted between Copland and Shostakovich. It was wonderful! Ambassador Thompson was very pleased.

JA: Shostakovich's music was both patriotic and secretly subversive. Did you get the impression that audiences knew that? Do you think they could read the scores in that sense?

MB: No, I don't think so. They simply thought that it was patriotic music. Even when Shostakovich was at his most brutal, there was always something really arresting going on, and I think people were just carried along with it. I don't really think that they asked themselves questions about what Shostakovich was really saying. They might have done with the String Quartets, which are much more internal and questioning music in my view. Shostakovich was enormously popular, and I feel it was just a tremendous privilege to get to know a lot of his music. I attended the Moscow premiere of his first Cello Concerto, played by Rostropovich.

JA: These concerts drew large audiences presumably?

MB: Oh you couldn't get a ticket for Shostakovich. It was difficult enough for Gilels and Borin and other great pianists, who were all at the height of their careers. But they didn't have a programme that was published long ahead of time. You would only know that these great musicians were playing by a poster that would be stuck up outside the Moscow Philharmonic or outside the Bolshoi. At the Bolshoi, you wouldn't know a week ahead which operas they were going to do on which night. So people would buy tickets on the day more or less.

JA: And what sort of people went to operas and concerts? What strata of society could you identify?

MB: I think it would be fair to say that ordinary people went. Love of music was very much common.

JA: Was the '*Gos* Concert' for ordinary people, as a state-sponsored event?

MB: Shostakovich was successful in that, in carrying his public along as well as writing great music. It was accessible enough for everybody to be carried along with the experience.

JA: In terms of your own reception of the music at the time, did you feel that there was a meaning to it? Or did it have any particular resonance to you in terms of the political situation, the historical situation?

MB: Although I didn't know a huge amount about the anti-religious persecution in 1959–60, I could feel the atmosphere, which was forbidding. I felt that the concert hall in those days was my home rather than the church. I didn't go to the Orthodox churches all that often. At the same time I was acting as an unofficial chaplain to the British Embassy, which was a great privilege. I was not ordained until I returned to England, but I did have my theology degree, therefore I was reasonably competent to take services. The Anglican Church in Moscow was used by 'Melodiya' as a recording studio, and was completely secularised. It did not return to being used as a church until the Gorbachev era – 1988 or '89, I think. But services in those days were in the ambassador's study in the lovely old British Embassy on the banks of the Moskva River. The only other Protestant services were held at a single Baptist church, which was oppressed at the time, but not completely suppressed, although their services were in Russian and Russian-ised.

JA: So with the suppression of religion in Moscow, it's quite surprising that there were forty-one Orthodox churches managing to hold services.

MB: Jonathan, it's about to get a lot worse. I didn't realise at the time just how bad it was getting, because the main oppression was in the provinces rather than in Moscow and we didn't get much in the way of information. A few newspapers would report trials and imprisonment of clergy, on what turned out to be trumped-up charges, usually financial embezzlement, which they didn't do. I think occasionally sexual crimes. Who knows?

JA: They'd be incarcerated?

MB: Yes. I was trying to monitor the press systematically, and when I returned from Moscow I was able to order Soviet newspapers through an agency, so I could read the Soviet press through the 1960s and find out about the anti-religious campaign simply through that means. But there was one publication called *Silencing Religion*, which turned out to be the flagship of the anti-religious campaign, and began publication in September 1959, which was the exact month that I arrived in Moscow, and I was able to buy the first copy.

JA: Was it propaganda?

MB: Yes, the propaganda campaign was what I experienced more than the physical attack on religion. The propaganda campaign was huge. Every student in every Soviet university had to pass exams in dialectical materialism, Marxism and Leninism. They called it 'Diamat'. Diamat was the most hated subject, but if they didn't pass their exams in Diamat, they'd be thrown off the course. Moscow University comprised the body of the most handpicked students in the whole of the Soviet Union, so they were ideologically very difficult to talk to, because they were so convinced, or if not convinced, they would pretend to be convinced of their anti-religion position. My conversations on religious topics did not get very far with my fellow students, but I did hear of one or two fellow students being thrown out of the university for having been seen in church. Those forty-one open churches were about to be reduced in number by an assault in the 1960s.

JA: So that performance of the Rachmaninov *Vespers* in 1959 was highly unusual?

MB: It was about the only time it was performed. I think I would have heard about it if there had been another performance.

Regarding repertoire, a huge swathe of Western music was excluded because it was Christian, so we didn't hear any settings of the Mass, or Beethoven, or Bach. We didn't hear Bach Cantatas or any Renaissance music at all. I heard about a group that secretly formed to sing some Renaissance music. They performed unofficially in some of the closed churches, which you couldn't have done in an active Orthodox church. It had to be closed for them to perform Christian music in it.

JA: Did any other choirs manage to last?

MB: The choirs managed to keep going, and some of them were very impressive. The main church choir in Moscow was the Yelokhovsky Cathedral Choir. Yelokhov is a district of Moscow. All the central Moscow churches had been closed down, so you had to go into the suburbs to hear an Orthodox choir. They were still allowed to employ professional singers. So singers from the Bolshoi, for example, would earn themselves a bit of extra money by singing in the cathedral. So you heard some very fine music. It was all traditional chant and I got to know it and love it. When I did manage to attend this church, I was absolutely bowled over by the music and by the religious atmosphere.

RELIGION, PAIN AND REBIRTH

Michael's first-hand knowledge of music and musicians in 1960s Russia is profound, but he also witnessed the active life of faith under persecution, especially at Easter in 1960. It was a life-changing experience for him, when the resurrection of Christ became a known reality, as he witnessed the

worship of those who had suffered imprisonment, torture and hardships under the communist regime, gathered to proclaim the Easter Good News, even under fear of attack.

MB: The only time I've been in Russia for Easter was in 1960. I was told that there would be a particularly lovely service at a certain church, so I went there with a Russian friend. We couldn't get in, but my friend managed to obtain access at the side entrance. We stood in a completely dark church by the iconostasis. It was about eleven o'clock on the Saturday evening of Holy Saturday, preparatory to proclaiming the resurrection at midnight. The experience I went through that evening I'll never forget. I had studied theology at Oxford and learned all about the proofs for the resurrection, but it was on that night that the resurrection became a reality for me. I've often thought about it, and indeed written and preached occasionally about it.

The tradition in the Orthodox Church was that around eleven o'clock, perhaps eleven thirty, a group, led by a priest, would walk around the outside of the church singing a chant, the words of which were something like, 'They have taken away my Lord and I know not where they have laid him.' There were many occasions on which the procession would be attacked by groups of atheists and often people were physically injured while trying to proclaim their faith through the Easter procession.

That night there were no attacks. The procession stopped at the west door of the church, and a single voice came from inside the church right at the back. A deacon or a priest saying, 'Why seek ye the dead among the living? He is not here. Christ has risen.' And the congregation whispered, 'He has risen indeed! He has risen indeed!' The whispering went around, and one candle had been lit. Then that candle gave light to another candle, from two to four, and four to eight. Gradually, as the proclamation of the resurrection increased in volume, as people sounded more and more triumphant, so the light in the church increased. Gradually, the church was blazing with candles, everyone had a candle in front of their face, and there was I standing in the front, so I could look back on the faces. They were all old people. Young people didn't dare go to church in those days, but those old people had suffered. They had been through the Stalin period, who had only been dead for seven years. Almost all of them, if they hadn't been in prison themselves, had relatives that had been in prison, or they'd lost loved ones in the war. The number of Soviet dead in the Second World War was an indescribably large number. What I'm trying to say is that you could see the suffering on the faces of these people, illuminated by their single candle, and you could see the suffering turning into joy – the certainty of the resurrection. That's what taught me that the resurrection was a physical fact, a reality for those people, and it became a reality for me on that night as it never had done before. I've never forgotten that.

I went on from that to experience a much worse persecution of the Church than I'd ever imagined. We thought that things were going to get better under Khrushchev, but when I learned more about him, I realised that that man could never have been anything other than a religion hater. For instance, the Ukrainian Greek Catholics (a Catholic Church that uses all the forms of the Orthodox Church) were completely suppressed in the Ukraine in 1946, and it was Khrushchev that did it. Nobody knew that about Khrushchev's biography at the time, but I discovered it later on and have written about it.

JA: What's life like in Ukraine now following the recent Russian occupation in 2015?

MB: It depends what part of Ukraine you're in. My wife, Lorna, went close to the war zone in February this year [2016]. She was taking in relief medicines. There are so many people that are exiled from their homes, and living in what used to be the Communist Party summer camps for kids. That part of Ukraine is terribly depressing. I went with Lorna to western Ukraine, to a city called Lviv, or Lvov as it is in Russian, in October [2016], to lecture at the Ukrainian Catholic University, and it's the most wonderful city with absolutely lovely people. Ukraine is a divided society, and what the Russians have done in eastern Ukraine is just beyond imagining. It's gone out of the news. Nobody thinks about the fact that 10,000 Ukrainians were killed there. In fact, sporadic killing still goes on, and many thousands are exiled from their homes and living in temporary accommodation. It's a very sad story.

RUSSIA AND FAITH TODAY

We tend to think of Russia as moving out of communism into something more liberated, but of course things are volatile these days. I asked Michael how he saw the place of the Church and Church music in Russia now.

MB: I've been now to Russia over forty times, but I had two periods of ten years when, because of my human rights work, I couldn't get visas at all. The second period of ten years was a kind of exile, because I do love Russia, and had some wonderful experiences there. I love Russian literature, love Russian music, and I love the people, when they're not being misled by present authorities. Lorna and I were there for what is called the millennium of the baptism of Russia or Rus in 1988. Russia became Christian officially in Kiev in 988. It was seen as God's organisation of the whole of the Russian race. We were in Russia at the very right time to celebrate a thousand years since the Christianisation of Russia. By that time, the bans on Russian churches were lifted and so a full celebration took place and my visa was restored. It was the most amazing experience. The culmination of a week of services, with new churches and new monasteries, was in the Bolshoi Theatre no less. Wonderful artists performed Glinka's *A Life for the Tsar*, which was not suppressed, but they gave it a different title and ended with a great church service. Right up in the top of the Bolshoi, miles above the stage, there is a set of bells that I'd never heard, because bells were suppressed in communist times. The door in front of these bells opened up at the end of *Life for the Tsar*, and all the bells rang. It was the most amazing moment. But even more amazing, just after that, the Choir of the Holy Trinity Monastery at what used to be called Zagorsk – it's now Sergiyev Posad – came on to the stage. I thought it was the first time since the Revolution that a religious choir had sung on the stage of the Bolshoi. It was the most moving moment. They sang about fifteen or twenty minutes of music. Gorbachev wasn't there but his wife was, along with clergy and politicians. What I saw was, in fact, the second performance of sacred choral music at the Bolshoi since 1917, but it was wonderful to see Russian religion opening out in front of our eyes, with people parading icons on the streets in the way they used to take icons to war.

JA: So there was sacred music pouring out of the churches and sacred music on the stage of the Bolshoi?

MB: Absolutely everywhere. Lorna and I went on to Kiev and we were taken to the most ancient cave monastery on Soviet soil, which was the original cradle of Russian Christianity. I had also been there in 1960, when the priests were visibly under constraint and didn't say anything, but I could tell the atmosphere was terrible. Shortly afterwards it was shut down. In 1988 we were back, twenty-eight years later, and we were the very first foreigners to visit after it reopened. It was a great occasion.

In 1998 I was approached by BBC producer Stephen Shipley and asked if I would broadcast a service from Russia for the millennium, to which I agreed. We were invited by Archbishop Kirill of Smolensk [now Patriarch Kirill of Moscow] to broadcast from his diocese. He was absolutely marvellous and, whatever my criticisms of him in subsequent years (because he is a great friend of Putin and consequently the Church and the State are in cahoots), I still have great respect for what he did for us in that year. He opened up every opportunity and the BBC was so pleased with what we did. You cannot just record a service of Orthodox music. If it's going to be a service, it has to be artificially constructed, because a Russian Orthodox service goes on for three hours, and in any case there's so much singing you have to interpolate what's going on. So the broadcast became a semi-documentary, explaining what was happening in the liturgy, but with absolutely genuine recordings from the Sunday service in the cathedral with a wonderful choir. And when the BBC heard it, they decided to broadcast it as the first in a series of services from around the world.

Stephen and I went to Russia seven times altogether. We recorded four Sunday morning worship services and Orthodox vespers. I always decided where we were going to go, so we went to St Petersburg in 2003, celebrating the three hundredth anniversary of the founding of St Petersburg. We went to the Solovki Islands, which had been a prison camp and a great monastery; we did one in Moscow eventually in the Danilov Monastery, which is now the headquarters of the Moscow patriarchy; and the one in Smolensk. So in some cases we recorded two services, including a vespers for broadcast in the 'Choral Evensong' slot on BBC Radio 3.

JA: And you always used local musicians? You never took people with you?

MB: Not a soul. I would decide on which church we were going to, set up a friend or two to help us with the contacts, make contact with the local priest or bishop, and Stephen would organise the recording.

JA: The standard of music-making is very high, isn't it?

MB: Yes. Especially in the case of the monastic choir at the Danilov Monastery. It was an all-male choir, but quite often a lot of the choirs are mixed.

JA: Did you receive good feedback from audiences?

MB: Very good, yes.

JA: Is that from a non-Russian audience, would you say? Or did you have feedback from Russian people listening to it?

MB: No feedback from Russia. I don't think it was even broadcast in Russia because it wasn't on the World Service. But I received a lot of feedback from Russians based in the UK, and they were all pleased.

JA: But those broadcasts are now available online. You have enabled people around the world to hear the quality of this Russian music that's survived all the way through the Revolution.

MB: That's right. For instance, we recorded a monastic choir from Solovki Island Monastery in the Arctic who paraded an icon around the outside of the monastery, so some of the singing was a bit rough and ready because they were walking while they were doing it, and some of the congregation joined in, but it was a very genuine liturgy.

FAITH IN THE MUSEUM OF ATHEISM

MB: But the broadcast that really sticks out in my mind was a Sunday worship from the Kazan Cathedral in St Petersburg. I emphasise Kazan Cathedral, because that was the museum of atheism in Soviet days, and I had known it well as such. To be able to go back and, as it were, almost to preach from the steps of the cathedral saying this was the museum of atheism and now we're going to hear worship with the Russians, was a marvellous occasion. And the choir – it was a mixed choir – were absolutely world class.

JA: And is sacred music still able to thrive under the Putin regime?

MB: More than survive. Under Patriarch Kirill's regime, backed by Putin, churches have been reopened and newly built in hundreds of regions. So if you visit even a fairly modest Russian village, where people are living in poverty, there will be a fantastic new church.

JA: That's a state-funded church?

MB: Not completely. The believers are very generous. But also some are imposed upon. In Moscow the huge new Cathedral of Christ the Saviour was paid for by the plutocrats. The Mayor of Moscow, in conjunction with Putin, made a deal with certain oligarchs that, if they funded the cathedral, they would avoid investigation into their taxes. So a lot of very dubious money went into that cathedral. That wouldn't be the case in the provinces because there are no oligarchs there, but people have given generously, as well as the local authorities.

JA: Do they still sing ancient chant in these churches?

MB: Oh yes.

JA: Would they perform pieces by well-known named composers as well?

MB: Both. They've restored ancient chants, Kievan chants as they call them. There are several strands of ancient chant. But most of the Russian Church music is harmonised in a very obviously nineteenth-century fashion, in the style of Tchaikovsky. In fact, Tchaikovsky wrote a series of *Choral Vespers*.

In the Cathedral Church of Christ the Saviour in Moscow, there is tradition built on tradition. There is nothing innovative about it at all. That is also true about modern Church music – you either write in a nineteenth-century style or your music will not be heard. That is very disappointing about the Russian Church, I think.

JA: So there's no modern innovation in terms of the development of Church music in the West, as we would know it?

MB: This is symptomatic of where I'm disappointed with Patriarch Kirill. I met him and considered him a good friend. When he helped us with that broadcast in 1999, I thought, 'Here is a man who would really open up the Church. He had his own run-in with the KGB. People rather carelessly call him a KGB agent, which to my way of thinking helps nobody, and it's only partly true. I mean he had a live-and-let-live relationship with the KGB. He's now in his sixties, so he was in his forties at the time when communism collapsed, but he had built up a relationship with the authorities in Leningrad as it then was. He was head of the theological seminary in Leningrad, and he built it up to be a great educational institution, which the communists allowed him to do. Then they thought he was getting too powerful and having too strong an influence on the younger generation, so they moved him to Smolensk. When people call him a KGB agent I say, 'Remember he was also a victim of the KGB.' He might have collaborated, but everybody had to collaborate, or you wouldn't become a bishop. But then he became so strong, so they moved him to Smolensk where they thought he couldn't do any harm, and he built up a wonderful diocese in Smolensk.

JA: But you think his reforms have kept music and religion back in the nineteenth century?

MB: He's rebuilt the nineteenth-century Church, as well as recreating the same relationship between Church and State as there was in Tsarist Russia, and that was profoundly disappointing. He's just been in London [2016] and *The Times* went to town on excoriating the Foreign Office and the Archbishop of Canterbury for securing a visit by the Patriarch to the Queen. *The Times* thought that was absolutely terrible. I think I would have advised against it as well, but I wouldn't have gone to town on criticising the Palace for receiving the Patriarch.

Michael's knowledge of Russia, its politics, religion and music, is breathtaking. He has published widely on the survival not only of the Christian faith in Russia but also the revival of many other faiths. He has not only documented, in this interview, the endurance of great music in the era of the Soviet Union, but also demonstrated how he was at the heart of bringing our attention, in the West, to the thriving choirs, churches and monasteries keeping sacred music alive within the liturgy of Orthodox Christianity. Perhaps it is the intuitive, implicit nature of music and faith that keeps them from being extinguished by any opposing ideology. Whatever the national politics, people's love of music and their sense of faith in something beyond themselves is impossible to eliminate. One can declare that religion and God are dead, that certain music is not to be played in public, that some composers' works are to be banned. Literature can be censored, radio airwaves can be controlled. But what we hear in our inmost beings and what we reach out for, searching for the transcendent, numinous and unknowable experience with intuitive faith, is every person's privilege. At the end of the Middle Ages, Desiderius Erasmus espoused the inner life of faith, a *philosophia Christi* or philosophy of Christ, by which we orientate our lives according to the life and teachings of Christ. It is this inner life that was kept alive in the hearts and minds of so many Russians during the twentieth century.

BALÁZS DÉRI AND SOVIET HUNGARY

The surprising perseverance of sacred music and the musicians who performed it is also an amazing story in the history of another former communist country: Hungary. When I met Balázs Déri from Budapest, I was fascinated by his tale of maintaining church music, and especially sacred plainchant, as a living reality in Hungary from the 1970s onwards. Balázs is now Head of the Latin Department and Director of the Centre for Religious Studies at the University of Budapest, also known as the Eötvös Loránd

University. It was founded by the Jesuit Cardinal Péter Pázmány in 1635 in order to research and teach theology and philosophy. Balázs grew up and was educated in politically turbulent times in Eastern Europe, so I began by asking him about his experience of university in the 1970s and the political difficulties.

BD: The politics were more than difficult. That time was a very hardened period. You remember that the 1968 revolution was all over Europe, including Hungary, which was part of the alliance against Czechoslovakia. At that time I was a Baptist and a fundamentalist. It was at first a stupid idea and everybody thought that I could not be accepted for the university. But God's ways are special. The Ministry of Culture and Education let me join the university, but they were suspicious of me, and that's why I was given a place in a research group of the Hungarian Academy of Sciences, working on the dictionary of the Medieval Latin of Hungary. The room next to mine was the workplace of Benjamin Rajeczky, László Dobszay and Janka Szendrei, the leaders of the Schola Hungarica, founded in the 1970s. I always wanted to be a member of the Schola Hungarica.

JA: And what is the Schola Hungarica?

BD: The Schola Hungarica is one of the best musical groups of Gregorian chant. It was a very special choir in a communist country. It was revolutionary that Gregorian chant became known to the wider public. There was opposition. Everything was opposed: the theatre, books and music: everything was.

JA: Opposition to what?

BD: To the existing system.

JA: The communist regime?

BD: Yes. I thought that all my life would be in the communist regime. I never thought that it could be ended.

JA: So art and literature and theatre were all rebelling against this system?

BD: But I must tell the truth. The state control was not good, it could not be good. But the aesthetic level of the books that appeared, and theatre, was quite good. And there were some possibilities to widen the barriers.

JA: Widen the barriers? Or break down the barriers?

BD: No, no, no. Widen, only widen. And the recordings of the Gregorian chant were extraordinarily successful. They sold in tens of thousands. There was an LP with a hundred thousand copies pressed.

JA: And could people go to church at this time? Was it difficult?

BD: It was difficult, but difficulty is good for the Church.

JA: But to hear this music in church would have been very difficult, would it?

BD: The Gregorian music was not the favourite music of the Hungarian Catholic Church. Some pieces, such as *Tantum Ergo*, or *Ave Maria*, were popular, but the consequences of the Second Vatican Council in the 1960s were brutal for Hungary. The changes from Latin to Hungarian happened overnight. But Hungarian Catholic music, and the other Churches too, had some specialities. We had a big repertoire of very good-quality hymns from late medieval times. It's not the same as in France or Spain or Italy, where there was money, good organists and choirs, etc. It was similar to England, because there was a big repertoire of hymns, hymns in the sense of the congregational hymns, so Hungary became largely Protestant.

JA: You mean after the Reformation?

BD: After the Reformation. There were some enclaves of Catholicism, but Hungary was in three parts: Transylvania, Turkish Hungary and Royal Hungary, dominated by the Habsburgs, the Protestants of Hungary, the Lutherans, the Calvinists, even the Unitarians. The anti-Trinitarians of Transylvania translated many medieval or ancient Church texts, the whole repertoire of the Mass. A good part of the breviary was translated, sometimes in a very rough way, but it was sung in Protestant schools. There are those that think the strophic hymn poetry created a lot of very interesting and very good repertoire, both theologically and musically. And it was a huge repertoire, like it was in the German states.

After the *Genevan Psalter* was translated into Hungarian, at first this had a bad influence on the Calvinist Church, because old [medieval] and good hymn repertoire was suppressed and replaced by *Genevan Psalms*. But the *Genevan Psalter* was sung by the Lutherans, by Unitarians, and the best ones were sung by the Catholics too. It was like the development today, where all the hymn books of the Catholics, the Anglicans and the Methodists are the same in England. But medieval hymns survived, along with a small number of priests, during the Turkish invasion.

JA: When was that?

BD: It was from the sixteenth century till the end of the seventeenth century – 150 years of Turkish occupation. But the lay singing of hymns, and even of the Gregorian repertoire, survived until the middle of the seventeenth century. Even today, in some parts of Transylvania, the Good Friday Passion is sung in Unitarian churches.

JA: Is that in Latin?

BD: No, Hungarian.

JA: So it would originally have been medieval Hungarian and then late medieval Hungarian, and now today it would be modern Hungarian?

BD: Exactly. What happened in the nineteenth century was that the Regensburg Caecilian movement introduced some Latin Gregorian chant. There was some level of Latin Gregorian chant in monasteries, such as the Benedictines, and the Mass was naturally sung in Latin, but in parish churches the people sang the congregational hymns: a hymn for the Introit, a hymn for the Gradual, a hymn for Gloria, and so on and so on. Everything was this very interesting repertoire of the Catholic hymns, which are, even today, in use everywhere in the Catholic churches.

HUNGARY AND CHURCH MUSIC FROM THE 1970S

BD: I grew up as a Baptist, but at my father's side I was Catholic. It's a very difficult thing to be born in a divided family. My normal spiritual life was in the Baptist Church and I was baptised as a fourteen-year-old boy. I had a Catholic father and a Baptist mother, who brought us to Catholic Masses, and to burials, because funerals were events in the village. The funeral was beautiful, so I loved it and was very proud that we had a fundamentalist and very simple liturgy, where there was nothing more than preaching and chanting. Congregational singing is, for me, very important. But when we went to visit my Catholic grandparents, we attended the Catholic Mass, which all the village went to, and everything was marvellous for me.

JA: You liked it?

BD: More than liked. I was divided. I thought I was Catholic when I was in the house of my grandfather and grandmother, and there was conflict naturally. My Baptist mother didn't want me to be baptised as a child, but my grandmother insisted that I must be baptised as a Roman Catholic.

JA: Were you baptised as a Roman Catholic as a child?

BD: Yes, as a child, when I was five months old.

JA: And then you were re-baptised as a Baptist when you were fourteen?

BD: Yes.

JA: That must have been difficult, because from the Catholic point of view that would have been seen as heresy.

BD: It's a heresy, yes, it is heresy. When I returned to the Catholic Church, we discussed it a lot, what to do. Through my music academy years, my medieval studies, and through Gregorian chant I became closer and closer to the Roman Catholic Church. In the secondary school I attended the Masses and, even as a Baptist child, I was a Roman Catholic cantor from the age of nine.

JA: So you were always a musician from childhood?

BD: Yes. There was no music education in the village but my father wanted to lift me out of this very poor intellectual situation. He had some ideas that his little boy became something. My mother's family was one of the very first Baptist families in Hungary. In the middle of rural Hungary, in a cultural desert, they founded a Baptist colony.

JA: So being a Baptist was extremely rare?

BD: Yes, but from the beginning of the twentieth century it was a recognised religion, influenced by the American parliament, surely. There were only a small number of adult Baptists in the first years of the twentieth century. Even today there are the same number.

JA: So it's a very small minority.

BD: A very small minority but a known minority. But when we visited my Catholic grandparents in the western part of Hungary, I played organ in the Roman Catholic Masses, and my grandmother was extremely proud that their little child could do it. From the age of ten my mother sent me to a music school in Budapest. So I began my musical formation. Every week I travelled the forty kilometres to Budapest by train, but during the winter time it was not possible, and that's why she found a local piano teacher for me, who was a very bad teacher, but it did not matter. From my secondary school years I studied music in Budapest, and at that time it was the country of Zoltan Kodály, so I learned music by the Kodály method. From the age of sixteen I thought that I must learn the organ in a special school. The authorities were very suspicious of me, because the organ was an ecclesiastical instrument. But I did it anyway.

JA: What was unusual about learning an ecclesiastical instrument? Was that difficult with the state?

BD: That was difficult with the state. There were only three or four musical state schools that taught the organ, because the state knew that all the organists would be playing church music.

JA: So it became politically subversive to learn to play the organ?

BD: Absolutely, absolutely.

JA: Was there an organ or a piano in your Baptist church?

BD: The Baptists were very poor, and even the influence of Calvinist ideology and fundamentalism was so hard that, in the very beginning of the Baptist Church in Hungary, every instrument was forbidden.

JA: So there was no music at all?

BD: Only unaccompanied singing of hymn tunes, without harmony, just the tune. Harmonised singing was an interesting feature of the Nazarene Church and an Anabaptist Swiss Church, called the Fröhlich Church, which had been planted in Hungary too. They even exist there now.

JA: So the Free Churches allowed harmony? Did they sing metrical psalms like the *Genevan Psalms*?

BD: Yes. But then the Baptists began the revolution by starting to use instruments. At first, the congregational singing was nothing more than the German Baptist tradition, so early Lutheran chorales, and late Pietist chorales, which was special because the Lutherans didn't sing these types of chorales, only the Baptist church. Then the inner mission of the Calvinist and Lutheran Churches introduced music by Sankey.

JA: You mean Moody and Sankey?[10]

BD: Yes, Moody and Sankey. From the 1930s, this repertoire became part of the Baptist singing and it was like a revolution for the young generation. This was music accompanied by guitars and mandolins.

JA: So this was Americanised, popular, folky kind of spiritual choruses and songs, translated into Hungarian?

BD: Yes, but it also became responsible for the decline of Baptism and the loss of Continental Baptist fundamentalist practices and ideas. This type of singing was practised by all Baptist congregations, but there was a new class of very clever and well-educated musicians in the Baptist Church who tried to reform Baptist singing by a more ecumenical approach.

JA: What was it like for you growing up in a small village with a Baptist mother and Catholic father?

BD: When I was small I was ill because I was very little and a shy boy, the littlest in the class, and everybody beat me.

JA: You were bullied?

BD: Yes. I was the *prügelknabe*, as they call it in German – everybody beat me. In a Roman Catholic village I belonged to the Baptist minority. When I was six I received the very first Reformed hymn book of the Baptist church in our congregation with music in four parts. The editors of the hymn book tried to make the hymns more ecumenical, including many old Lutheran chorales and Genevan chorales and even some Roman Catholic music, as well as many Methodist English hymns.

JA: Like John and Charles Wesley?

BD: All the Wesleyan hymns, including Samuel Sebastian Wesley, and Isaac Watts.

JA: Did you introduce this new ecumenical style, which brought together traditions from lots of different denominations, to your village congregation?

BD: Yes I did, even when I was nine, but I remember there was a big resistance from part of the congregation against the new hymns. There was a very simple, very clever man, who tried to teach the music to the congregation before the services, and there were a lot of services in the Baptist church.

JA: So everybody had to learn these new hymns before every service?

BD: Yes, and I had to learn them by ear because, at the age of nine, I had not been taught to read music, so I tried to play the harmony on the church organ, and I discovered everything for myself.

JA: You taught yourself?

BD: Absolutely. There were three of four years of transition from the introduction of the Moody and Sankey hymns to the publication of a new hymnal, which used more traditional four-part harmonies by Prudentius, or Luther, and so on. The book included a short bibliography and short notes about each hymn, which introduced me to the science of hymnology. I was a musicologist from that time.

JA: How did this music fit in with the liturgy?

BD: As it was a fundamentalist church, there was no ornament, gesture or elaborate liturgy. The liturgy was hated, because it was perceived as a Catholic practice.

JA: Did the Baptists celebrate the Eucharist?

BD: Yes, but in the simplest Calvinist way. I remember the pastor would say, 'This is the *sign* of the body, is the *sign* of the blood', rather than 'This *is* my body.'

JA: So no sense of the real presence of Christ in the Eucharist?

BD: That's right. I had some troubles around the age of fourteen and lost my faith for some years.

JA: At the end of the 1960s? Was your loss of faith connected to a state persecution of the Baptist and Catholic churches?

BD: The Catholic priests were persecuted and many of them became spies. I cannot judge them.

JA: You think that was inevitable that they became spies?

BD: Yes.

JA: In order to keep their parishes? I mean, otherwise they would have been removed?

BD: Yes. I could avoid it during my student years, but I did not want not to judge those who were spies. It was by a special grace of God that I could avoid it. Because I was not connected with the Church, I could not be under suspicion. For a very poor boy from a poor family, it was the only possibility for me to rise from these conditions, and to gain a university education.

JA: It was your only way to escape poverty?

BD: For instance, when I was a boy I attended a Baptist church summer camp, but we were afraid, because it was absolutely forbidden, so it was useful, in some ways, that I lost my faith as a teenager. After some years I found my faith again, and it was in the Roman Catholic Church.

JA: When did you become a Roman Catholic cantor?

BD: At the age of seventeen. I became a cantor because the old cantor was against the liturgical changes of the Second Vatican Council and left his position. The assistant priest, a young priest, was my very first Latin teacher. Even my mother didn't mind because, as a child, she had attended a Roman Catholic Mass sometimes, even as a Baptist, because she enjoyed the music of the organ. She loved the beauty of it.

Beauty is an obsession in our family. My religiosity is a very aesthetical one. The beauty of the liturgy, the beauty of music, and the beauty of truth. Discovered truth is a kind of beauty. My mother had to leave school at the age of twelve and was not musically trained, but she prayed: 'Oh God, if I have a boy, a son, please let him play the organ,' and her prayer was fulfilled.

JA: In you?

BD: Yes. God heard her prayer, because I'm an organist and I'm a church musician. It's a fantastic thing that a Baptist young lady, without any hope of rising from this awful, very hard communist situation in the 1950s, prayed in a Roman Catholic church, that her son might be an organist. Moreover, at university I discovered the Latin and Greek world and it was my fate, I think, to join the Schola Hungarica, and to know its director, László Dobszay, who is one of the most important Gregorian chant experts in the world. He invited me to join the Schola Hungarica and the International Musicological Society, even before my university studies had ended.

THE SCHOLA HUNGARICA AND LÁSZLÓ DOBSZAY

BD: As a musicologist and a liturgist, Dobszay highlighted the negative influences of what followed from the Second Vatican Council: the loss of beauty. He held the same views on plainchant within the liturgy as Josef Ratzinger [Pope Benedict XVI], and his last book was dedicated to Ratzinger.

As one of the cleverest disciples of Zoltan Kodály, a good composer, a fantastic director, and the leading light of Hungarian musical life after Kodály, Dobszay created a performance repertoire of Hungarian plainchant, transcribed from manuscripts. This 'new' ancient Gregorian was so beautiful, so heart-touching, even as a Baptist church organist in Budapest, after most services I went quickly to the city's main church of the new Gregorian liturgical movement. That was the church where Janka Szendrei, a colleague of Dobszay, had a liturgical *schola*.

The Schola Hungarica was always a concert choir and a lay organisation. Students at the Academy of Music would join the choir, such as the composers Zoltán Jeney and György Kurtág. Many Catholic churches had changed their music to modern rock, but these concerts of Hungarian plainchant were full, especially with young people. It was a big revelation.

JA: When did the communist regime fall?

BD: In 1990.

JA: And what happened with the political changes?

BD: We were free from the Russian army and it was a marvellous experience to have a passport so that we could travel. For me it was an obsession. I travelled to Switzerland, Italy, the south of France, Cordoba and Seville and many other places, sleeping in the train or in parks.

JA: Towards the end of the 1980s, before the fall of the communist regime, what was the music like in the Catholic churches? Did the congregation join in with the plainchant? Was there any participation from the congregation?

BD: In most of the congregations the cantor and the organist accompanied the congregational singing. But after the changes, after some years, the majority of church singing became evangelical Christian rock.

JA: Is this an influence from the West?

BD: Surely. They knew the American type of evangelical megachurches and they wanted to introduce that to Hungary.

JA: Is there a cathedral choir tradition in Hungary?

BD: There's no cathedral tradition.

JA: So where does a believer find aesthetic beauty for their faith now in Hungary, in music? Do they go to the concert hall?

BD: Sporadically. There are some new players. For example, our Church Music Society gathers Lutheran, Calvinist and even Jewish music together. Catholics and some Baptists and Methodists, who are liturgically minded, try to maintain the science of liturgical music to convince the people.

JA: And you put on sacred music within the liturgy, do you?

BD: Yes. There are some cathedrals, Roman Catholic cathedrals, which continue the tradition of symphonic Masses. For example, in the castle of Budapest, the King Matthias Church maintains a tradition of performing Mozart, König, Marcel and Haydn, and so on. In the Basilica of Budapest the music is mainly from the 1930s, in the Hungarian Kodály style. There are some fifty or sixty Gregorian *scholas*, liturgical choirs, all over the country, and in good contact with each other.

JA: Do they sing concerts or do they sing within the liturgy?

BD: Within the liturgy. Many people don't like the services, but like concerts. I think that real Church musicians like the services. The Mass, the Vespers and so on, and additionally, if they have time to perform concerts then that's OK. But what is more important is serving the services, the Church.

THE FUTURE OF CHURCH MUSIC IN HUNGARY

Balázs is concerned for the future of sacred music in Hungary and considers the ancient chant of the Church's heritage to be a key part of the potential revival of traditional church music in the future. Therefore I ask him if he is trying to change the future of church music alongside Calvinists, Lutherans and Catholics.

BD: Yes. There are a handful of Calvinist churches where the ancient Gregorian repertoire is sung and has been revived. The Lutheran Church is a little bit more liturgical in Hungary. Not so liturgical as in Germany or Scandinavia, because there was a big influence of the Calvinist Church, but there are some places where there is Gregorian Vespers, or combined with Lutheran chorales. Although the Lutheran Church is in decline, in the main Lutheran church of Budapest, they sing the *St John* and *St Matthew Passions* of Bach, and several Bach Cantatas are sung in one Sunday service.

JA: With orchestra?

BD: With orchestra and with the best soloists they can find.

JA: And they're paid professionally as well?

BD: A little bit. There aren't professionals in Hungary as there are here. The Church believes that the priest, the bishops, the sacristans and the church warden and so on are paid.

JA: And no one else?

BD: No one else. The church musicians live by the grace of God.

JA: So they either do it for free, or a little bit of money?

BD: They give a little bit. It's pocket money. For example, in our traditional little community, which uses the ancient rite, all the members of the liturgical choir are unpaid. I'm financing the church's music from my salary, such as the addition of new liturgical books. Because it's the only traditional community who sing the Gregorian plainchant masses and the vespers regularly, and it's a big development, so we must think about the future and you must dream.

It's a small church in inner-city Budapest and the leader of the *schola* is a young associate professor from my department, who has created a large database of Latin medieval liturgical books from missals, breviaries, ordinaries and pontificals. So one of the most important research projects in my department is liturgical medieval history. We are creating

> the liturgical books, all of them bilingual in Latin and Hungarian. Only the Ordinary [of the Mass] is in Latin.[11] All the Propers are in Hungarian and Latin. I hope that, when all the liturgical books are finished in some twenty years, maybe the Roman Catholic Church will revive the ancient rite. I don't think that there is any other solution to save music in the Catholic Church. My Pope is Francis, but spiritually my Pope is Benedict [who advocated plainchant].

Balázs ends on a note of hope for the future and that there is more work to be done. As with Michael Bourdeaux, tracing the developments of communism through the twentieth century leads to a consideration of ongoing reforms in the twenty-first century. For Balázs, more is required in the field of liturgical reform as he hopes for another revival, that of ancient Catholic liturgy and chant within all churches. Benedict XVI, Joseph Ratzinger, is an advocate for precisely the kind of revival that Balázs hopes for. In his work *The Spirit of the Liturgy*, Ratzinger sets out his reasons for claiming Gregorian chant as the best sacred music, but also the benchmark for all subsequent polyphonic and instrumental music:

> In the West, in the form of Gregorian chant, the inherited tradition of psalm-singing was developed to a new sublimity and purity, which set a permanent standard for sacred music, music for the liturgy of the Church. Polyphony developed in the late Middle Ages, and then instruments came back into divine worship – quite rightly, too, because, as we have seen, the Church not only continues the synagogue, but also takes up, in the light of Christ's Pasch, the reality represented by the Temple.[12]

Moreover, in the same volume, Pope Benedict explains his Trinitarian understanding of the role of singing within the liturgy and its source of love:

> The singing of the Church comes ultimately out of love. It is the utter depth of love that produces the singing. '*Cantare amantis est*', says St Augustine, singing is a lover's thing. In so saying, we come again to the Trinitarian interpretation of Church music. The Holy Spirit is love, and it is he who produces the singing. He is the Spirit of Christ, the Spirit who draws us into love for Christ and so leads to the Father.[13]

Love becomes the final theme of this chapter. Love that is about the relationships, encounters and experience of the Russian people that Michael went through; the love Balázs has for his country, its music, its religion, its people and his ongoing relationship with music and faith with his ambitions to bring more and more people into contact with the transformative effects of sacred plainchant. Perhaps it is this source of love that makes music and faith endure in such places, because that source, whatever we call it, is a never-ending spring.

INTERLUDE II

AN ECHO OF THE SPHERES IN THE SHIRES: THE ENDURING APPEAL OF SACRED MUSIC AT THE THREE CHOIRS FESTIVAL

You cannot be schooled in Hereford, as I was, and not be aware of the Three Choirs Festival, the 300 year-old tradition that brings together the cathedral choirs of Hereford, Gloucester and Worcester, the Festival Chorus and world-class orchestras, as well as recitalists and fringe events for a week of musical and liturgical festivity.[1] But my first proper introduction to the Festival came when I joined Hereford Cathedral Choir as a 'supernumerary lay clerk' (choral scholar) in my gap year. It was a testing year for the lay clerks as they were forced, patiently or otherwise, to endure my ignorance and mistakes as I learned the Anglican cathedral repertoire. For the Gloucester Festival of 1989 my accommodation was basic – a tent in a field – but the music-making, liturgical or otherwise, was grand and inspiring. The Hereford contingent of the chorus had spent many an evening rehearsing under the direction of the exacting Dr Roy Massey, whose memorable quips to errant singers I have never forgotten: 'He who never made a mistake, never made anything' or simply: 'Sort yourself out!' Thus, like many a singer before me, the Three Choirs Festival became an inspirational part of my musical education and I was delighted to return, years later, as a soloist. In my youth I was entranced by music and the atmosphere, but largely unaware of the rich and long history of the Festival, nor indeed how influential it has been upon the British and worldwide musical landscape, and how it has not only championed English choral music, from Purcell and Handel to Elgar, Parry, Vaughan Williams, Howells and Finzi, but has also been an enormously significant promoter of new music throughout its history. Through commissions and brave programming, the festival has been increasingly at the heart of advances in contemporary choral and orchestral music. Many established composers today cut their teeth composing for the Festival.

Daniel Lysons's early nineteenth-century history, republished by Gloucester Cathedral Organist John Amott in 1865, along with more recent accounts by Watkins Shaw (1954), Anthony Boden (1992) and Barbara Young (2000), attests that the medieval choral foundations had long been connected. For instance, Thomas Tomkins (1572–1656), 'master composer', was Organist at Worcester (c. 1596), having been a boy chorister at Gloucester, where his father had been precentor. The origins of the annual Music Meetings were outlined in a 1729 sermon preached by Thomas Bisse, Chancellor of Hereford Cathedral. It sprang, he said, from 'a fortuitous and friendly proposal, between a few lovers of harmony and brethren of the correspondent choirs ... tending to the furtherance of God's glory, in the exaltation of His holy worship, to the improvement of our choirs, the credit of our foundations ...'. Bisse had also suggested that the meetings should benefit 'the widows and orphans' of poor clergy within the three counties.

From the earliest days, new compositions were written for the morning and evening services, the music being 'in wonderful harmony with the associations and architectural characteristics of our ancient hallowed Cathedrals', as Amott wrote. For instance, Purcell's *Te Deum* and *Jubilate* canticles were sung liturgically almost annually for the first forty years. But later, as Amott opined, 'it is not, perhaps, too much to say, had it not been for the Music Festivals, the people generally would never have become acquainted with the highest form of musical composition, the Oratorio'. With the rise of this new musical form, objections were made concerning the performance of oratorios in 'sacred edifices' and to the hiring of professional singers, 'some of them fresh from the applause of the theatre; as though the Cathedral were profaned both by the performance and the performers.'

In fact, the first oratorios at the Festival were performed in secular buildings, as they 'were associated with secular music'. But, Amott argued, the sacred texts and the musical settings of these large choral works were best suited to the sacred space of a cathedral. A work such as Handel's *Messiah*, performed in a town hall, he argued, 'is but grand music; in a cathedral, it is a noble exponent of the religious feelings suggested by the daily uses of the edifice. From a mere composition it is elevated into a fitting expression of that worship which has been offered up daily within the same walls for a thousand years, and is pouring forth of the deepest aspirations of the devout soul.' *Messiah* was sung at every Festival, bar two, from 1757 to 1963.

Following the introduction of female singers in 1772, the classical repertoire expanded, including such works as Haydn's *The Creation* in 1800, with a typical morning concert programme of 1812 including recitatives and choruses from *The Creation, Israel in Egypt* and other oratorios. No single oratorio was performed complete in these renditions, but rather extracts. Similarly, a programme of 1821 contained overtures, recitatives, arias and choruses from various pieces by Handel, Jomelli, Haydn, Mozart, Pergolesi and Attwood.

When Samuel Sebastian Wesley became organist at Hereford Cathedral in 1832 he wrote scathingly of provincial music: 'Painful and dangerous is the position of a young musician who, after acquiring great knowledge of his art in the metropolis, joins a country cathedral. He can scarcely believe that the mass of error and inferiority in which he has to participate is habitual and irremediable.' Nevertheless, Wesley achieved great things over the next three years. The first meeting to be given the name 'Three Choirs Festival' was in 1838. In the following years, chamber recitals were introduced and performances of Mendelssohn's *Elijah* and Bach's *St Matthew Passion* were given under Wesley's direction.

The advent of the railways increased attendance dramatically and the late Victorian period gave the festival its distinctive reputation for many years to come. Also, the influence of Sir Edward Elgar can hardly be overestimated. He first played in the Festival orchestra in 1878 and went on to conduct the first performance of his Overture *Froissart*, the première of *The Light of Life (Lux Christi)* and, of course, his *Enigma Variations*. In the early twentieth century he conducted *Caractacus* (Scene III), the *Cockaigne* overture, and the first Three Choirs complete performance of *The Dream of Gerontius*. Elgar regularly directed his own works at the Festival for the next thirty years, including *The Apostles*, the overture *In the South, The Kingdom*, and his Violin Concerto with soloist Fritz Kreisler. Likewise, Sir Hubert Parry's influence was profound. He conducted the premiere of his *Scenes from Shelley's 'Prometheus Unbound'* in 1880, a work hailed by Sir Henry Hadow as the birth of modern English music. In the following years he conducted his oratorio *Judith*, his *Ode on St Cecilia's Day*, the premiere of his *De Profundis* and his *A Song of Darkness and Light*. Other British composers, such as Sir John Stainer, Frederick Delius and, of course, Ralph Vaughan Williams made a huge impact upon the direction of English choral and orchestral music. Vaughan Williams conducted the premieres of his *Fantasia on a Theme by Thomas Tallis, Fantasia on Christmas Carols, Magnificat, Hodie, Five Mystical Songs* and many other works.

The World Wars interrupted the Festival twice. After the first resumption (following the First World War) the musical landscape was dominated by such composers as Elgar, Vaughan Williams, Holst, Bliss, Howells and Bax, with contributions from Dame Ethel Smythe, Dyson, Kodály, Bantock and Walton. After the Second World War there was a shortage of lay clerks, prompting *The Times*, in 1955, to report that the cathedrals' choral tradition had been 'sadly mutilated'. However, numbers revived and significant compositions followed by Finzi, E.J. Moeran, Dyson and Rubbra, and continued output by Vaughan Williams. Despite repertoire including Ravel, Stravinsky, Britten, Shostakovich, Paul Huber, Hindemith, Walton's *Belshazzar's Feast*, Frank Martin and Howard Ferguson in the 1950s and '60s, there was a call for more radical musical compositions by William Mann in *The Times* in 1967: 'do we have to admit that an existence of 240 years inevitably induces some sort of senile decay and that, in its present form, the Three Choirs Festival needs to be retired or replaced for the musical health of the country?' Whether or not in direct response to this criticism, the repertoire in 1969 was noticeably more adventurous, including the premiere of Jonathan Harvey's *Ludus Amoris*, the first Three Choirs performance of Janáček's *Glagolitic Mass*, Elizabeth Maconchy's *And Death Shall Have No Dominion*, Luigi Dallapiccola's *Due Liriche di Anacreonte*, *Quattro Liriche di Antonio Machado* and *Canti di Prigionia*, as well as Peter Maxwell Davies's *Five Carols for Boys' Voices*. In addition, William Mathias's setting of Psalm 150 was heard for the first time at the Opening Service. Clapping after a performance (for the National Youth Orchestra) was first recorded in 1969; this had been 'discouraged and deplored in previous years' (Alan Charters). In the 1970s, compositions abounded from John McCabe, Alun Hoddinott, John Joubert, Lennox Berkeley and Geoffrey Burgon. In a letter of 1977, Gloucester Organist and Festival Director, John Sanders, set out his vision for commissioning works:

> one obviously wants to choose a composer who is going to be sympathetic to the Festival audience and also to the ability of the chorus ... Had it not been for the Three Choirs Festival very few modern English choral works would have seen the light of day! ... In the past the Festival tended to concentrate on a few composers, e.g. Handel 17th century, Elgar at the end of the 19th century, and Vaughan Williams very recently. Nowadays it is our policy to make the programme more representative of the international music scene.[2]

Thus, for the 250th anniversary of the Festival in 1977, works were commissioned by Harrison Birtwistle, Peter Maxwell Davies, Rory Boyle, Ronald Tremain and Tony Hewitt-Jones, along with the *Mass of Christ the King* by Malcolm Williamson – then Master of the Queen's Musick. However, all did not go smoothly as Williamson failed to finish the piece on time and attempted to complete the score in Gloucester on the day of the performance. The conductor, Sanders, met with Williamson before the concert and, despite Williamson's fury, went ahead without the *Gloria, Credo* or tenor solo psalm, and with the *Agnus Dei* accompanied by the organ only. The rest of the programme was hastily revised to include some Howells and Handel. However, the *Church Times* reported, 'Sanders had to achieve a viable performance of an incomplete work from an incomplete score, while the composer offered to copy out parts for the unfinished sections on the day, and seriously expected the orchestra and choir to perform from these, sight unseen. Sanders gently vetoed this, and performed what was ready to score.' He saved the day. The work was eventually completed and performed in Westminster Cathedral in 1978. Williamson later praised Sanders for his actions: 'You behaved with the patience of a saint and with a professionalism that I appreciate deeply. I see by hindsight the quandary in which I placed you ...'

Through the 1980s and '90s new works by ground-breaking composers, such as Jonathan Harvey's *Resurrection*, Paul Trepte's *God's Grandeur* and Pierre Villette's *Messe en Français*, were performed side-by-side with British and Continental classics such as Elgar's *Dream of Gerontius* and Mahler's Eighth Symphony. Of the British composers, Paul Patterson, Francis Pott, William Mathias, John Joubert, Michael Berkeley, Peter Maxwell Davies and Paul Spicer were often evident in the programme. Highlights of new music in the twenty-first century have been world premieres of *Sun-Dogs* by James MacMillan, *Three Preludes & Fugues: Hommage à Marcel Dupré* by David Briggs; and world premieres of John McCabe's *Songs of the Garden*, John Joubert's *An English Requiem* and Cheryl Frances-Hoad's *Songs and Dances*. Other notable commissions have been Jackson Hill's *Still in Remembrance*, Ian King's *A Worcestershire Song Cycle*, Nicholas Brown's *On the Operations of the Sun*, Dobrinka Tabakova's *Centuries of Meditation*, James d'Angelo's *Venite*, John O'Hara's *The Bargee's Wife* and Torsten Rasch's *A Foreign Field*, which commemorated events in the First and Second World Wars.

Thus, the Festival has been responsible for an enormous output of creativity throughout three hundred years and has played a vastly significant role in British music history. It may seem a far cry from the simple gatherings of the eighteenth-century cathedral choirs that in today's post-secular society one might expect to hear Mahler's 'Symphony of a Thousand' among a panoply of world-class music and artists, but at its heart the Festival's ethos remains the same: it is a week for 'lovers of harmony'.

PART III

BELIEF AND UNBELIEF

CHAPTER SEVEN

MUSIC, FAITH AND ATHEISM

Lord, I believe; help my unbelief[1]

In our Rectory garden we are fortunate to have a lawn shaded by three large flowering cherry trees. Last year my wife Emma, who is the parish priest, suggested that the garden would make a marvellous place for a labyrinth. There are many examples of labyrinths around the world which are used for spiritual purposes. Perhaps the most famous is in Chartres Cathedral, but others are created in natural environments, such as mowed into lawns. I thought the idea of having a labyrinth in our garden that anyone could come and walk would be an excellent idea and I relished the challenge of researching how to make one. Having found a suitable pattern and method, I set about creating it one sunny spring afternoon: measuring and marking the centre, the boundaries, twists and turns, and making sure that each path was even and clear. It took all afternoon for me to make sure that the labyrinth was properly mapped out before I started to mow. The process was totally absorbing. I had to concentrate entirely on the project in hand and I had no other concerns or interests while engaged in it. I believe that my mind had gone into what the psychologists call a 'flow' state of complete focus – a state I have known partially in other physically demanding and absorbing situations, such as long-distance walking or cycling. Once the mowing and the labyrinth were complete, I felt that I had spent a thoroughly fulfilling and purposeful afternoon [Figure 8].

The joy of the experience was not so much in the completion of the project. Indeed, I could have asked someone else more professional to complete the task and then I would simply have had to admire it. The joy was in the process. Likewise now, when anyone walks the circular route of the labyrinth, finding their way slowly to the centre, where they find the meagre rewards of a water-filled bird bath, the benefit of the experience is not in the final destination, which after all is only another piece of lawn, it is in the journey. It is the thought processes, prayers, meditations and the focus of the mind through the walking that makes a labyrinth a worthwhile spiritual exercise. In this chapter I wish to explore the idea of faith as a process or journey, rather than a destination, and the ways in which music, even for those who do not believe the Christian creeds, works powerfully in a process of discovery, which is immensely valuable, even when firm conclusions seem illusive.[2]

I began this book by distinguishing between a religious world of belief and the word and one of faith and experience. In drawing a line between the word-centred world of post-Reformation modernity and pre-Reformation Christianity, I found some parallels with the twenty-first-century phenomenon of a rise in 'spiritual but not religious' people and the decline in biblical literacy in Western Europe, which aligned to some extent with late medieval experiential Christianity (through an orated tradition of stories, drama, colour, art, music and other aesthetic and spiritual encounters) at a time of widespread illiteracy among most of the population. In the light of this I distinguished between belief, which required a language-based cognitive ascent to a set of tenets, and faith, which is less prescriptive in its need for doctrinal or dogmatic assertions and concerns what we *do* rather than what we happen to think or believe. Belief, therefore, in a postmodern and post-secular society is an increasingly interesting notion, as Abby Day has acknowledged:

> Christians who belong to mainstream churches rise together each Sunday to recite jointly their creeds as collective statements of their church's and – one assumes – their own beliefs. As they begin 'I believe' in their God who made heaven and earth, and in Jesus Christ, one could wonder if they mean that as a truth claim or a statement of faith and trust. It could be one, or both. So ingrained is *belief* to their tradition they may never consider what, exactly, they mean by that word.[3]

Indeed, many people attending those churches may *not* believe the words of the creed that they recite, but they are doing so because it is part of a communal ritual from which they benefit in various ways. The need to examine the veracity of every doctrinal detail may be secondary to the primary importance of belonging to a community which performs, and puts into action, important values of inclusion and belonging. Day refers to 'cultural performativity,' in which communal actions are seen as binding and unifying social groups.[4] An implication of the idea of 'believing in belonging' is, according to Day, 'the necessity to dispense with binary, subsidiary categories of belief, such as "religious" or "secular", and focus instead on multidimensional, interdependent orientations.'[5] The idea of believing without belonging has been considered by several sociologists and theologians, as we shall see below.

Grace Davie's *Religion in Britain Since 1945: Believing Without Belonging* presented theories concerning 'unchurched believers' and has been followed by Day's suggestion that the best way to describe people who consider themselves to be Christian but who do not attend church regularly is 'anthropocentric,' because they believe 'that human life is social, with meaning, power, and authority located in the social without a divine origin or authority.'[6] However, this recent focus on belief without belonging still uses the word belief as indistinct from faith and therefore, in the sociological focus, misses the fruitful theological distinction between these two ideas. Thus, belonging without believing means something slightly different to these sociologists. Either way, their examination of the changes in Church allegiances involves a concept of belief. Brian Mountford takes the theme into more theological territory with his concept of the Christian Atheist, and I shall now explore the relationship between faith, music and atheism.

CHRISTIAN ATHEIST

John Gray's recent *Seven Types of Atheism* argues that contemporary atheists are struggling to escape from a world in which any notion of a God, higher power or ultimate justice has been replaced by a surrogate faith: faith in humanity. However, such faith ends up replicating old ways of thinking inherited from Monotheism.[7] If an atheist is someone who has no need for a creator-god, Gray argues, then it is not a rejection of religion. Moreover, religion has always been more defined by its practices than its beliefs:[8] 'The idea that religion is a matter of belief is parochial.'[9] Even Christianity, which is the religion most allied to belief, defies this definition:

> Eastern Orthodoxy holds that God is beyond any human conception – a view fleshed out in what is known as negative or apophatic theology. Even in western Christianity, 'believing in God' has not always meant asserting the existence of a supernatural being ... Thomas Aquinas was explicit that God does not exist in the same way that any particular thing exists.[10]

Gray's seven types of atheism include 'new atheism', which he dismisses outright:

> The new atheists have directed their campaign against a narrow segment of religion while failing to understand even that small part. Seeing religion as a system of beliefs, they have attacked it as if it was no more than an obsolete scientific theory. Hence the 'God debate' – a tedious re-run of a Victorian squabble between science and religion. But the idea that religion consists of a bunch of discredited theories is itself a discredited theory – a relic of the nineteenth-century philosophy of Positivism.[11]

New atheism lacks validity because what it is rejecting does not exist. New atheists are not even knocking down a straw man – there is no man there at all. Religion is not a belief system and cannot be rejected as such. So Gray searches for other types of atheism: secular humanism, scientific atheism (such as evolutionary humanism), political atheism (such as communism) and God-haters. Grey finds two types of atheism more helpful: firstly, the atheism of George Santayana and Joseph Conrad, who rejected the notion of a creator-god but without replacing that notion with an elevated view of humanity; and secondly, the mystical atheism of Arthur Schopenhauer and the negative theologies of Benedict Spinoza, which 'point to a God that transcends any human conception'.[12] If we agree with Gray that the last two types described are more attractive and coherent than contemporary militant new atheism, then we may also agree that they are not so far from the views of many Christians: humanity is not equipped to replace the notion of a divine creator, and any concept of God must be implicitly unknowable, transcendent and mystical.[13]

For Schopenhauer in particular, music was a kind of surrogate religion that pointed beyond the material world and expressed the ineffable nature of the world that language is unfit to do: 'What music hinted at ... was the God of the negative theologians – a state of pure being.'[14] The seventeenth-century philosopher Spinoza, for example, was the kind of atheist who could deny that God created the world while also affirming 'a God that permeates the world but about which little or nothing positive can be said'. In this sense, for Gray, 'theologies that affirm the ineffability of God and some types of atheism are not so far apart'.

One theologian who is not afraid to connect this type of atheism and Christianity, and who bravely proclaims the term 'Christian Atheist', is Brian Mountford. In his book of the same name, Mountford finds many people who fall into this seemingly oxymoronic category. In 2009 the novelist Philip Pullman, in discussion with Mountford, made this remarkable statement:

> I am a Christian Atheist; a Church of England Atheist; a Book of Common Prayer Atheist. You could add a King James Bible Atheist, if you want. All those things go deep for me; they formed me; that heritage is impossible to disentangle, like a piece of barbed wire fence embedded in the bark of a tree. I've absorbed the Church's rituals and enjoy its language, which I knew as a boy, and now that it's gone I miss it.[15]

Pullman is an example of someone who values the cultural heritage of Christianity without accepting its beliefs or creeds. The term Christian Atheist is very difficult to define, as Brian Mountford has explained,[16] but the relevance of it for the purposes of this book is that it can be a useful term to describe those who find great worth and meaning in the music of the Christian faith, both within and outside its liturgical context, but who do not believe in God. The Christian Atheist, as Mountford discovered, is someone who is committed to Christianity's 'moral compass', but who also values the aesthetics of the Christian faith: 'the sense of transcendence that can be felt in response to art, music and the resonant language of the Bible and Christian liturgy'.[17] Indeed, there may be many within the Church who find themselves in this category, or one close to it. As Jane Shaw has suggested, they are those 'who don't believe what they "ought" to believe, but need and want to be there for a whole host of reasons. They "belong without believing" and they are significant parts of our worshipping communities.'[18] Philip Pullman characterised himself as having a religious temperament, rather than a secular one, even though he holds no religious beliefs: 'What characterizes a religious temperament in my mind is having a sense of awe and wonder, and I have a sense of awe and wonder. It's also about asking those questions: who we are, and what are we here for, and whether there's a purpose.'[19]

One atheist that Brian Mountford interviewed for his book was the venture capitalist Nigel Hamway, who was a cathedral chorister and a choral scholar at university, and who values the 'culture of the Christian West ... shaped by the Christian story, the incarnation, and the death and resurrection of Christ and by the ethical values encapsulated in that narrative'.[20] Hamway explained that he enjoys the outstanding music of his own church that he attends, which 'provides a focal point for the community with concerts, plays, and events'.[21] They have even performed an Easter anthem composed by Hamway, 'Christ is risen'. But he is clear about the importance of the natural world in the Christian story and the experience of aesthetics:

> What I get from services is no different from what you might get from a beautiful mountain scene. I take spiritual comfort from aesthetic experience – 'belonging to everything' – but I don't think transcendent experiences require religion to explain them.

Mountford gives several examples of music played within the context of community, 'which brings about a common experience in which people find some sort of transcendent depth in art, some sense of being taken beyond themselves, of being the better or the greater for having been there and heard a performance', for as George Steiner has written, 'Music means. It is brimful of meanings which will not translate into logical structures or verbal expression.'[22] The reason, therefore, that so many atheists hang on to the 'coat tails' of religion, according to Mountford, is that 'art, music and literature provide their closest access to religious experience and the reason many of them are still involved with institutional Christianity is because of its commitment to the search for truth through beauty.'[23]

I find this phrase extremely helpful in describing the joint enterprise involved by all who engage with music seriously. The search for truth through beauty is one that can be undertaken by the believer, the agnostic and the atheist alike. However, for theologians Hans Küng and Karl Barth, the experience of transcendence still needs the language of God to explain it. Similarly, for the philosopher John Cottingham, 'one can discern in the world unmistakable traces of that unexperienceable reality that transcends it.'[24] But for Mountford, the experience of transcendence through music need not point towards a supernatural reality but is 'of this world.'[25] Although no one has discovered completely how music affects the brain or how it moves the listener, he argues, 'sound can enhance a sense of height, depth, sadness, joy, fear, loss or triumph. Important too is the expression in sounds alone of emotion, intensity, imagination, dream, dissonance and resolution.'[26] For Mountford, God is in the natural order: 'I wouldn't claim transcendence leads to the supernatural; but that the deep things we see through it are where God is to be found.'[27] Moreover, everything that the word 'God' stands for 'has the capacity to give shape and purpose to a life that otherwise seems empty.'[28]

MUSIC AND THE ATHEIST 'SOUL'

Most of the people Mountford interviewed he termed 'soft' atheists, but his friend and colleague Richard Dawkins, whom he calls the godfather of 'hard' atheism, observes that sublimity of art does not require a divine origin:

> Obviously Beethoven's late quartets are sublime. So are Shakespeare's sonnets. They are sublime if God is there and they are sublime if he isn't. They do not prove the existence of God, they prove the existence of Beethoven and Shakespeare ... If there is an argument linking the existence of great art to the existence of God, it is not spelled out by its proponents.[29]

For Dawkins, the presence of sublimity in art does not mean we have a God-given soul. His rejection of the notion that sublime experience of the natural world necessarily leads to the divine ironically concurs with the reformed theology of Jeremy Begbie, who also rejects sublimity as a route towards divine transcendence.[30] In Dawkins's provocatively entitled collection *Science in the Soul*, he muses on the 'breathtaking' scenery of the Grand Canyon – a sacred place to many Native American tribes – and wonders from where the concept of 'soul' derives:

> Was there some point in the mile-long evolutionary progression up the canyon's strata when something you could call a 'soul' sprang into existence, like a light suddenly switched on? Or did 'the soul' creep stealthily into the world ... eventually a soul on the scale of a Beethoven or a Mandela?[31]

Rather, Dawkins prefers to define soul as 'something like an overwhelming sense of subjective, personal identity.'[32] Nevertheless, he is 'unashamed to embrace' the poetic usages of the 'soul' in the artistic.[33] Albert Einstein's assertion, 'I am a deeply religious nonbeliever – this is a somewhat new kind of religion,' is employed by Dawkins:

> Though I wouldn't use the exact phrase, it is in this sense of a 'deeply religious nonbeliever' that I consider myself a 'spiritual' person, and it is in this sense that I unapologetically use 'soul' in the title of this book.[34]

This definition of soul has no relation to the idea of a spiritual part of a human surviving after death or a disembodied spirit of the dead (which Dawkins calls Soul-1). It is more akin to the second *Oxford English Dictionary* definition of soul: 'Intellectual or spiritual power. High development of the mental faculties. Also, somewhat weakened sense, deep feeling, sensitivity.'[35] Dawkins calls this Soul-2. If there is a notion of transcendence in Dawkins's experience of the world it is the one expressed by the Indian astrophysicist Subrahmanyan Chandrasekhar of 'shuddering before the beautiful ... beauty is that to which the human mind responds at its deepest and most profound.'[36]

Only Soul-2 will survive in fifty years' time, Dawkins predicts: 'Science has already battered and wasted Soul-1. Within fifty years it will extinguish it altogether.'[37]

However, this does not mean, for Dawkins, that the teachings of great religious thinkers should be thrown away. In an amusing and insightful essay entitled 'Atheists for Jesus,' Dawkins observes: 'What was interesting and remarkable about Jesus was not the obvious fact that he believed in the god of his Jewish religion but that he rebelled against Yahweh's vengeful nastiness.'[38] For, as Darwin himself noted, natural selection is a 'deeply nasty process': 'What a book a devil's chaplain might write on the clumsy, wasteful, blundering low and horridly cruel works of nature.'[39] And yet, human kindness and selflessness can often go against the principles of Darwinism. 'Superniceness,' as Dawkins calls it, is a singular event in evolution, achieved by the large human brain being capable of 'calculating long-term consequences beyond short-term selfish gain.'[40] How can we spread the notion of 'superniceness' in our world? Dawkins asks. Perhaps a T-shirt with the slogan 'Atheists for Jesus' (or, indeed, 'some other role model from the ranks of the supernice, such as Mahatma Gandhi'). Perhaps if Jesus were reborn today he would even wear the T-shirt, and be appalled by what had been done in the name of Christianity, Dawkins muses. 'But, of course, modesty would compel him to turn his T-shirt around to read "Jesus for Atheists".'[41]

ATHEISM AND CONSUMER CULTURE

Dawkins's writing is captivating, challenging and thought-provoking. But, for Roger Scruton, atheist arguments against the existence of God are not the reason for a decline in belief. The fault lies in consumer culture:

> The consumer culture is one without sacrifices; easy entertainment distracts us from our metaphysical loneliness. The rearranging of the world as an object of appetite obscures its meaning as a gift ... It is inevitable, therefore, that moments of sacred awe should be rare among us. And it is surely this, rather than the arguments of the atheists, that has led to the decline of religion. Our world contained many openings to the transcendental; but they have been blocked by waste ... By remaking human beings and their habitat as objects to consume rather than subjects we revere we invite the degradation of both.[42]

Scruton's rather pessimistic, or perhaps sadly realistic, view of modern society is tempered by his assertion that, even if one wishes to reject the concept of God, the idea of God will remain in the created void: 'God is in intimate relationship even with those who reject him. Like the spouse in a sacramental marriage, God is *unavoidable*, or avoidable only by creating a void.'[43] Scruton would take issue with Dawkins's evolutionary biology, as 'Biology sees us as objects rather than subjects, and its descriptions of our responses are not descriptions of what we feel.'[44] Rather, the study of humanity is an exercise in interpersonal understanding: 'I have in mind the kind of understanding exhibited when we explain why ... "smiling through tears" is an apt description of the Cavatina in Beethoven's B-flat quartet.'[45] Scruton considers another work of musical genius to explore the nature of unbelief and faith. Although *The Ring of the Nibelung* opera cycle was written by an unbelieving Wagner and was influenced by Feuerbach's projectionist account of religion, Wagner nevertheless asked what god would have to be in order for them to be objects of our love.[46] For Scruton, this agnostic series of operas 'contains an important moral for believers too. It attempts to show at the deepest emotional level that all that we truly esteem, love included, depends in the end on suffering, and on our freedom to accept suffering for another's sake.'[47] This human characteristic might equate with Dawkins's respect for 'superniceness' in people, but Scruton sees, in Brünnhilde's sacrifice and the water of the Rhine covering the wreckage of the drama, restoring nature, that 'suffering is made available to God himself by the act of incarnation, and it is the way – perhaps the sole way – in which he can show that he loves us with a human intelligible love, by suffering for our sakes.'[48] Thus, even this 'secular' work points towards a religious reality.

THE THIN LINE BETWEEN SACRED AND SECULAR

Between the theist viewpoint of transcendence as an experience that leads one to the divine and the rationalist approach which explains it as 'a heightened level of feeling' there is a kind of pre-Christian Platonism, where 'justice, goodness and beauty (for example) exist as perfect paradigms and universals in some other world, and when we speak of these things, or try to apply them to our daily lives, we experience an imperfect version or shadow of that ultimate reality.'[49] This non-theistic standpoint elevates art and nature as access points to a better moral life, as Iris Murdoch has written:

> The appreciation of beauty in art or nature is not only ... the easiest available spiritual exercise; it is also a completely adequate entry into ... the good life, since it *is* the checking of selfishness in the interest of seeing the real.[50]

For Murdoch, the introduction of selfishness into art also introduces fantasy and makes the art form mediocre. But if we let go of our Romantic Ego, selflessness can help us to see the complexity of meaning found in the aesthetic. Music is 'multi-layered': 'In music meaning is created by the tension between dissonance and harmony, between unresolved sounds and resolution.'[51] Poetry, in its widest meaning, embraces 'all the layers of meaning communicated and evoked by words, music, art and symbolism, to express transcendence and the consequent recognition that for religious language poetry is of the essence.'[52] This essence of the poetic and musical in the world around us is beautifully expressed, as Mountford has observed, in Carol Ann Duffy's poem *Prayer*:

> Some days, although we cannot pray, a prayer
> utters itself. So, a woman will lift
> her head from the sieve of her hands and stare
> at the minims sung by a tree, a sudden gift.
>
> Some nights, although we are faithless, the truth
> enters our hearts, that small familiar pain;
> then a man will stand stock-still, hearing his youth
> in the distant Latin chanting of a train.
>
> Pray for us now. Grade 1 piano scales
> console the lodger looking out across
> a Midlands town. Then dusk, and someone calls
> a child's name as though they named their loss.
>
> Darkness outside. Inside, the radio's prayer –
> Rockall. Malin. Dogger. Finisterre.[53]

This poem helps us to understand that the 'traditional language of religion' is often ambiguous and inadequate, and that the music of the created order shows us that 'the atheist/theist divide is often nowhere near as clear cut as is often supposed.'[54]

> Institutional religion is helpful because it's strengthening to support each other, uplifting to have critical mass, inspiring to meet in large buildings of great beauty, good to organise aid and support from one community for another, liberating to think seriously about what ultimately matters, whether God, or faith, hope and love, or whatever is true, honourable, just and pure.[55]

Certain themes emerge from Mountford's work, pertinent to the notion of music and faith as 'process,' as I have called it, which are worth exploring.

PROCESS

The first observation to emerge from reading Mountford's work is not only that the benefits of belonging to a Christian community are social and cultural but that belief in the propositions of creeds are not essential for belonging: 'I would think that, as a matter of sociological fact, belief in God and assent to creeds is not the principal motivating force for Christian allegiance.'[56] While Boyce-Tillman has argued that the secular community choir has replaced many of the social and musical needs that used to be fulfilled by the local parish church or choir,[57] there are still important benefits of belonging to a community of faith, even for the unbeliever, because it is a place that considers matters of ultimate importance. However, while the traditional doctrine of 'God, Christ and Salvation' may be difficult for some to believe, Snowden's revision of 'God, Jesus and Revelation' is a more accessible concept for some, because it is resonant of ideas of encounter and relationship. This may seem to some as typically woolly liberal thinking that simply waters down the 'truth' of the Gospel, but as the ecclesiastical historian Diarmaid MacCulloch reminds us, doctrine is always changing: 'Many Christians do not like being reminded of Christianity's capacity to develop, particularly those in charge of the various religious institutions which call themselves churches, but that is the reality and it has been from the beginning.'[58] Therefore the search for truth and holiness, the process, is often more fruitful than the objectification of religious truth in creeds. 'In the process of trying to live a Christian life, holiness is discovered,' Mountford observes.[59]

Another theme in Mountford's argument is that the border between faith and scepticism is permeable and that the paradox that exists between doubt and faith is a strength, not a weakness.[60] Drawing upon Paul Tillich's theology of God as the 'ground of our being,' by which he means that 'God is the ultimate depth and meaning of being, from which ... humans draw their own being,'[61] Mountford advocates the notion of faith as processes of action, inspired by the actions of Christ. As D.H. Lawrence put it, faith 'tells us how to act, not what we ought to believe.'[62] If this is so, then faith is essentially experimental and existential. Does this mean we do away with a sense of transcendence? Mountford redefines transcendence as not supernatural but embodied human 'heightened feeling.' However, Terry Eagleton is critical of the Durkheimian theory that sees religion as primarily social.[63] Durkheim's statement that 'because he participates in society, the individual naturally transcends himself when he thinks and acts'[64] may lead to a conclusion that religion is a source of social cohesion. But, as Eagleton perceptively points out, the teaching of Jesus in the Gospels is often disruptive and divisive, rather than socially unifying.[65]

ENCOUNTER AND DEEP HARMONY

My own argument concerning faith, music and process does not attempt to reduce faith to the limited sphere of social bonding and human thought. Rather the process is one of opening up to the limitless wonders of existence around us, which brings me to the area of science, the natural world and rationality. We saw in the chapter on music and the brain how Quinton Deeley ended his interview by musing upon the awesome complexity and mystery of the world.[66] Many atheists, such as Richard Dawkins, as we saw above, claim science as a replacement for religion. One response to such 'militant' atheism is to adopt an 'anti-militant-atheism,' as Mountford does, by replacing their 'unattractive' and 'extreme' brand of atheism with a more imaginative outlook. As Howard Jacobson puts it:

> Nothing returns one quicker to God than the sight of a scientist with no imagination, no vocabulary, no sympathy, no comprehension of metaphor, and no wit, looking soulless and forlorn amid the wonders of nature.[67]

Another approach is to explore, as Robert Gilbert has, the relationship between science and 'the truthfulness of beauty' to be found in the world. Based upon his experience as a research scientist and a priest and his explorations into 'sacramental spirituality,' he argues that a personal experience and encounter with the natural world is essential if we are to have a loving knowledge of it. That personal perspective is not to be dismissed as subjective but is 'authentic' and 'irreducible.'[68] Within our experience, music is an 'especially communicable form of beauty.'[69] Gilbert cites the Nobel Prize-winning physicist Frank Wilczek as someone who uses music to explore the 'mathematical beauty of fundamental physics,' a mathematical beauty that was highlighted by Pythagoras in ancient Greece and can also be found in other natural phenomena:

> Our appreciation of mathematical beauty is also exemplified in the 'golden ratio' of rectangle edges of 1.618:1, beloved of the Greeks, which is also the ratio between adjacent numbers in a Fibonacci progression – the Fibonacci progression that also determines the shape of a spiral shell of a nautilus (an equiangular spiral) and the patterns of growth in some plants. Whether this is surprising or not, it is the case. It just highlights that it's not just mathematicians who find mathematical relationships beautiful; subconsciously, so do we all.[70]

Thus Wilczek, when asked about God or a possible design in the universe, replies that he lets the world 'speak for itself' because, as he has written in his book *Finding Nature's Deep Design*, 'when the world speaks for itself you find an extraordinarily tight, conceptual, beautiful structure underneath.'[71] Does this lead, then, to a God-of-the-gaps who is lurking invisibly in the voids that science cannot yet explain? No. It's not so much about an 'answer' to our gaps in knowledge. The interest lies in the exploration: 'This has been a real voyage of discovery to get in touch with those questions again.'[72] So belief, for Wilczek, is belief in the process of experiencing the world:

> Just believing what you find, engaging with the natural world, is an engagement with deep beauty and surprises and strangeness that has some of the elements of religious experience. I engage with the world as it is and I find what I find and it's beautiful and it's wonderful but does not match any existing dogma but to me gives some of the experience which was very meaningful to me as a child in religion.[73]

For Gilbert, Wilczek's enthusiasm for experiencing the world inspires his own search for 'the *deep* harmony and coherence that physics reveals in the world and the ways in which it echoes more everyday experiences of beauty'.[74] It validates the idea that truth can be found through beauty: 'He wants us to note, again and again, how the Ideal turns out to be Real, and how reality embodies idealised relationships.'[75]

Thus we end our exploration of music, faith and atheism with a vision of science and rationality that positively promotes an exploration of the world where truth and beauty can be found in the process of encounter, experience and relationship. In the mathematics of music, relationships between melody, rhythm and harmony are communicated through the relationships between composer, performer and listener and resonate with a deep sense of physical coherence in the universe which, paradoxically, is seemingly able to lift us out of the material plain to a more numinous level of experience. No doubt debates and disputes between religious and scientific fundamentalists will continue for generations to come, but Wilczek and Gilbert help us to see that the process of faith, if we are to understand that word as a verb which involves encounter with the world around us and each other, has nothing to fear from scientific exploration, especially the fundamentally physical and mathematical discipline of music, whose essence is to be found deep within the origins of the universe.

CHAPTER EIGHT

'CHANGING THE RUMOUR ABOUT GOD': MUSIC AND ANGLICAN CLERGY

How beautiful are the feet of him that preaches the Gospel of peace.[1]

Clergy are given the task of communicating the Gospel of peace. The Ordinal of the Church of England states that they are 'to proclaim the word of the Lord and to watch for the signs of God's new creation. They are to be messengers, watchmen and stewards of the Lord ... With all God's people, they are to tell the story of God's love.' This proclamation is, of course, often achieved by using words, in sermons, in the scriptures and in the liturgy. So we now explore how music relates to the Word: the story of God's love. Our way into this exploration begins with the work of Maeve Louise Heaney, who has addressed this relationship in her book *Music as Theology: What Music Says about the Word*. If theology is 'faith seeking understanding,' as Anselm wrote, then, Heaney argues, 'could music not also be theological? Does it not offer us, at the very least, a form of understanding of our faith ...?'[2] Of course, her answer to this question is 'yes.' Her conviction is that music offers a way to understand our faith which is complementary to 'linguistic and conceptual' comprehension.[3] When she uses the term 'Word' she refers to the *logos*, the incarnate God, the Word made flesh, Jesus Christ. If theology aims to mediate an understanding of this *logos*, then music is a powerful mediator. So far as this goes, it is a music theory with which reformed theologian Jeremy Begbie would be able to concur.[4] However, Heaney also alludes to music's ability to reveal the divine in a more intuitive sense that would appeal to those who do not assent to the salvation narrative of scripture surrounding the figure of

Christ: 'I therefore intuit that the acts of listening to and making music have something to teach us about who God is and who we are …'[5] Or, as George Steiner put it, 'Music has long been, and continues to be, the unwritten theology of those who lack or reject any formal creed.'[6] Thus, Heaney explores 'what music is "saying" to us in this moment in history, and why it is emerging as a form of faith transmission.'[7] In attempting to understand how music works in this linguistic way or is 'saying' something, Heaney suggests that music's power lies in three of its essential characteristics: it is free, it is embodied and it is truthful.[8] As such it is capable of transmitting theological meaning and, for Heaney, specifically the Christian Gospel: 'understanding music and its role in Christian spirituality and theology implies a greater appreciation of how we inhabit and relate to the world around us, as well as *how* we come to faith in Christ.'[9] Seen in this light, music becomes a missionary activity:

> A theological understanding of the musical vocation within the same paradigm that grounds the calling to consecrated missionary life opens potentially fruitful avenues of future work in the area of spirituality and the arts.[10]

Music and mission can go hand in hand, and in this chapter I relate interviews with three contrasting Anglican clergy: a parish priest, a former cathedral dean and a bishop. So how, from a clerical perspective, does music communicate the Gospel or, on the other hand, does it point towards or reveal something of the nature of God that might lead to a deeper encounter? I begin by asking parish priest Nick Brown.

NICK BROWN

For parish priest and musician Nicholas Brown, this idea that music can 'speak' the Gospel is true, but it is not easy:

NB: When I'm performing music I am participating in something of the divine or the transcendent, while also trying to speak to people whose worship is offered to God because of revealed doctrine of God. My difficulty then is how to translate the non-verbal language of music into something that can be a dialogue with the very verbal formation of doctrine.

JA: So, perhaps for other people, worship might involve thinking about God in terms of how they could express that in language? So, for instance,

'God is almighty', or 'God is powerful', 'God is loving', 'God is merciful', all these kind of descriptive adjectives?

NB: Yes. But then for me God is an experience, transmitted largely through music and aesthetics. Not just music, but art and architecture, hence the specialness of holy, sacred places as well.

JA: So your experience of God involves the context of place. Is that because the building or space impacts upon the experience of the music that's performed?

NB: Yes. For instance, if one has a spiritual experience that's influenced by a particular piece of music in a particular place, then repeating that music later, in a less sacred or special space, can evoke that same spiritual experience. I don't think that's uncommon.

JA: Are clergy taught to communicate ideas about God purely by means of verbal language and vocabulary?

NB: Many people who maybe are in a tradition like that eventually reach the limits of verbal theological language and then move to more contemplative experiences, involving silence without words. But there's the gap in between, where aesthetic experience through the arts might be another way of experiencing the divine.

JA: For someone who thinks in linguistic, verbal ways, why would they need any aesthetics in their experience of God?

NB: Because a great deal of popular theological writing about the Bible or God uses music as an analogy for doctrinal, creedal ideas.

JA: But is there a conflict between being a priest, who leads the people to the Word of God by using words, and one who experiences God through non-verbal aesthetic experiences?

NB: That's a conflict I've had within myself. When I left university I tested myself as to whether I was doing music for the right reasons. I tried to give up the Church because I couldn't reconcile the doctrines of the Church with my experience through music. That experience taught me that I wasn't doing it just for the music.

JA: Was the music a means to something else?

NB: For me, it was a means to the transcendent. The experience of trying to give up the religious element of being a musician taught me that there *was* something spiritual going on, which ended up taking me on the track to ordination. My experience of 'Initial Ministerial Education', working with other junior clergy and curates, is that there's a hunger and thirst for more understanding as to what the role of music and musicians is in the Church. There's a deep spiritual experience that people find through sacred music. It relates somewhat to Schleiermacher's work on experience of natural religion.[11] It's a very broad simplification but, on the one side, there's the revealed religion of the Church which has truth to it and, on the other side, there's natural religion of everyday experience. Schleiermacher suggests that you should have a dialectic between the two, which then ends up with the deeper truth beyond it.

JA: The question here is whether music *is* theology or natural religion, whether there's something innate in the music that, whether people realise it or not, they are in fact participating in something theological?

NB: Yes, and there's an interesting parallel in poetry as well. I was speaking with a lay reader a while ago, and they were saying that they're really interested in the relationship between poetry and God, because the words start off just being words about God, and then, through the very act of the poetry, the words begin to speak beyond themselves. Eventually the words become a mere starting point, and the reader or listener finishes with an experience that cannot be put into words. Music does the same for me. You start off with verbally formulated doctrines, put them into music, and end up somewhere that you cannot ever describe.

JA: It's taken you beyond words completely?

NB: Now there's a risk, and some people criticise music for this, that music takes one away from God and anything to do with the original doctrine, so that God exists merely in emotional 'soupland'.

JA: And critics would say that that's not God? It sounds rather like Augustine's criticisms in the fourth and fifth centuries.

NB: But my own personal experience would say that whatever the transcendence of God is, I've touched it.

JA: And it remains numinous and nameless?

NB: Yes, and I could equate it to other experiences I've had of God that people, working from another theological understanding, would agree with. So, for instance, the experience I had at ordination was identical to the experience I've had in those spiritual experiences of music, in terms of what it's done to me and my spiritual feeling. I can directly equate the two.

JA: Is that experience the feeling of the presence of God?

NB: Yes, it feels like a very personalised experience of God.

Thus, for Nick Brown, the spiritual experience encountered through music is not a mere extra to the Christian life but *is* the Christian life. It does not replace revelation through the Word, but contact with the divine is made just as effectively through music as through doctrinal revelation. Like Heaney's ideas on transmission, Nick sees music, particularly within the liturgy, as a means to something greater than itself. A form of communication that leads to an experience of God. Another clergyman who has spent a great deal of his ministry working with music and faith is the Very Revd Christopher Campling, former Dean of Ripon Cathedral in Yorkshire, to whom I now turn.

CHRISTOPHER CAMPLING

Author of *The Food of Love: Reflections on Music and Faith*, in which he writes 'Music creates and expresses feelings that are too deep for words',[12] Christopher Campling finds that there are close connections between music and faith because they 'say the same thing and demand the same sort of commitment', but he acknowledges that there are differences between music and religion: 'Religion must be universal in its claims if it is anything at all. Music need not be so. Religion makes moral demands upon men and women. Music does not. Music entertains ... Religion demands ... music invades our senses' but religion 'is also concerned with the truth and it makes demands upon the will.'[13] Plato and Aristotle, as well as Augustine and Luther, among others, would have argued that music has both an affective sensual influence but also a moral demand upon the will. To these distinctions we might add the further distinction between religious belief and faith. If we do, then we find the bond between music and faith is revealed as much closer than the bond between music and religion. When I met Christopher in his home in Worthing, Sussex, therefore, I asked him whether music's role within institutional religion was a missional one.

CC: I remember we once had a tremendous debate about music in General Synod. There were people who were saying, 'If you have light popular music you'll draw people in.' Other people said, and I think I said, 'By all means broaden the cultural scope of the music, that's a good thing to do, but you must see it from the point of view of worship, not from the point of view of attracting them in. If they want to listen to pop music they can go to pop concerts, much better than going to church.'

JA: What are the weaknesses of light music?

CC: Well, I feel that it doesn't nurture the worshippers. Music expresses mood. Now there are many moods in the business of worshipping God, there's joy, there's penitence, there's excitement, there's deep sadness, and the best music can hold these complexities together. But what contemporary worship music seems to me to be saying is, 'The more we are together, the happier we shall be.' Now that's not very deep theology. No doubt they enjoy it and it does some good to them. But really, there is more than that. Christianity is not all about excitement.

JA: So if you go to a pop concert, you're expecting to be taken to a particular place of excitement and exhilaration, but if you're approaching God with all of your problems and difficulties in life, then you may be feeling sorrowful or guilty or joyless or many other emotions?

CC: Happiness isn't joy. I can see the happiness of some music, I can feel that, but not joy. Joy is a deeper thing altogether. For instance, there's nothing more joyful than the last chorus of the *St Matthew Passion* [by J.S. Bach], which has a tremendous sense of release and triumph, and yet there's an underlying sadness to it.

Christopher's view here regarding the aesthetic choice of musical style suitable for worship is echoed in our next chapter by lay Christian Shanika Ranasinghe. Conversely, in the same chapter we find a contrasting view regarding the role of light or popular music within worship by Firoozeh Willans. For a defence of the theological significance of rock, pop and general non-classical forms of music, wherever they are heard, Gavin Hopps puts a strong case, arguing against the 'theological imperialism' of recent music theology that only allows for certain classical aesthetic styles. Rather, Hopps suggests, along with Frank Burch Brown, that 'there is room for all sorts of different art in the life of faith – including, I suggest, the "softer" and "sentimental" forms'.[14] I ask Christopher whether the setting or the personal beliefs of the performers matter.

JA: How do you feel about sacred Christian music being performed in concerts by non-believing performers?

CC: Many musicians and organists seem to be fairly untouched by the Christian truth, the Christian story. But in their music, they find tremendous spirituality and joy. Ron Perrin at Ripon [Cathedral] composed the loveliest *Magnificat*, which has a dancing, beautiful joy to it, and he did feel it very deeply. But I have known organists who read lessons (for example, at a carol service) as if they meant nothing at all. But there certainly are musicians who find spirituality through music. Music's a very spiritual thing.

You can analyse music physically, you can say what it is in terms of sound waves. I suppose you can analyse it in terms of what it does to your brain. You can write it down on paper. But none of these methods define music. Music is beyond that. It is something that the composer feels, and we feel. Music itself is something beyond, and I find that's the same of God – you can write about God and do your theology, but that isn't God.

At Ripon Cathedral we had a superb choir. I used to prepare the choirboy choristers for Confirmation myself. My argument was that if they and I worshipped God every day together, then I was going to share with them the truth of Christianity besides letting them share with me the music. I always remember one child who was asked, for a broadcast, 'Who did he sing to?' He said 'Well, in the practice I sing to the organist, but in the service I sing to God.' I thought that was lovely.

When they left we had a leaving ceremony and I used to make speeches about them all. I said to one of them afterwards, 'Tell me honestly, Ralph, at Christmas and Easter we really worked you hard. Was it too much for you?' He said, shrugging his shoulders expressively, 'Magical, magical.' That was, to my mind, lovely proof that it got through to them.

JA: I wonder if people who were rather less than religious might have found the music helpful to bring them to a place of prayer.

CC: Well one hopes it does. Besides the parish congregation, we had ever so many visitors naturally, every quarter we put on a full orchestral musical Mass, by Haydn or Mozart. That was packed with people.

JA: Do you think this kind of music can be effective in every church context?

CC: As a curate I had an awful experience. I was given the charge of a mission church in Basingstoke. So at Christmas I decided to hold a carol service, with lessons and music. There was a little girl in the main street who had a beautiful voice, so I asked her to sing the beginning of *Once in Royal David's City*. So I trained her up, got it all ready, and there was the choir and congregation. When it came to the service, she completely broke down in tears and couldn't do it. So it was all a great failure. I went and told my vicar about all of this, and he said, 'Well you see, it's the culture. You can't push your culture onto them.' Which was a very good point and taught me a lesson. You can't push your culture onto everyone.

Again, this anecdote highlights the dangers of a theological imperialism of imposing certain 'acceptable' or 'aesthetically refined' art forms onto a situation and a community that is not suited to it or experienced in the culture of it, and is therefore unreceptive.[15] However:

JA: In terms of your own spirituality, do you find that music is a help?

CC: Tremendous help to me. You have to listen to music, and you have to listen to God. Faith is a kind of listening. It's paying attention, opening yourself up to receive. If you want to receive something from music, then you have to listen. There's no good in having musical wallpaper, you've got to listen to it attentively. I find music and faith back each other up. My present love is Shostakovich quartets.

Before I preach, which I still do occasionally, I always go and play the piano first. I play from memory. It gives me a sort of release, calmness, and settles me down. Because I preach without notes, but I'm always nervous doing it. Music takes away the tension. Playing from memory especially does as it helps me communicate when preaching from memory. If a pianist can play a Beethoven concerto from memory, why for heaven's sake shouldn't I remember my sermon and preach it?

JA: That's a very interesting connection there about communication. Just as a pianist or a singer communicates the thought or the inspiration of the composer to the listener, as directly as possible, so the preacher needs to communicate the Gospel in the same way.

CC: As directly as possible, yes.

JA: In your book [*The Food of Love*] you've written about specific pieces of music and what they've meant to you down the years. Do you find that your taste in music has changed, or that you're drawn to different pieces of music at different times?

CC: Of course when I wrote the book, I'd hardly heard of Shostakovich. But I think my taste has broadened. Benjamin Britten I love. It's a question of being open.

JA: What do you think about the use of plainchant?

CC: Oh I love plainchant, yes. The very bareness and repetitiveness of it is prayerful. There is much repetitiveness in prayer, because you have to be content to attend to God and yet wait. Therefore there is something that moves in a pattern, slowly and gently, that is helpful. So I find plainsong helpful in that respect. The words of the Psalms, for instance, can be very mood-changing. There are barbaric, joyful and sorrowful themes. Plainsong lets the words speak beautifully.

JA: Some of the music you mention in your book is oratorio, written for the concert hall but with sacred texts, such as Handel's *Messiah*. Is there a difference between sacred music that's sung liturgically and music which is sung for concert purposes?

CC: I immediately think of the *B Minor Mass* [by J.S. Bach], which is after all not liturgical, and yet it sums up Christianity, with its joy, pain and complexity of human emotions. All the moods of Christianity are in the *B Minor Mass*, but it can't be used liturgically.

JA: But it was unusual for Bach to write non-liturgical sacred music. Whereas Handel was quite used to writing pieces that were specifically for the concert hall.

CC: Haydn's *Creation*, for instance, he said, was written for the glory of God. It's an astonishing piece of music.

JA: I wonder whether the boundaries have somehow now been blurred between what is sacred music in terms of its function within a church and a cathedral, and where we might find sacred music today. If you wanted to listen to some sacred music, for instance, how would you do that? Would you use a recording, go to a cathedral service or a concert?

CC: Occasionally we spoil ourselves by going to Chichester Cathedral on a Sunday morning, where the singing is very beautiful. In my local church the music is typical of an Anglican congregation; and when I go to a church with pop music I pray that the music that the congregation enjoys be offered to God, even if I don't like it myself.

JA: Are there are different types of participation then?

CC: Yes, exactly. You join in by listening. The service of worship depends on the skill of the performers performing as well as they can, but it depends also on the devotion of the congregation, the priests and other people offering it to God and making it into a prayer. If they don't, then indeed the service just becomes a concert, and it's no good to anybody. But if there are people who are worshipping, then the efforts of the musicians get lifted up to God.

JA: So, in a cathedral service you have a professionalised high standard of music-making and of liturgy in general, and a congregation who may not be vocally participating much, apart from the hymns and the creed, but the intention and devotion of their hearts and minds make a difference to what's going on?

CC: Yes. I used to say it often and loudly at Ripon to the congregation, 'It depends on you, this service. You have to pray through it and make sure that we make this a musical and prayerful offering to God.'

JA: So they are not just passive observers or listeners?

CC: They're not just passive, no. Concerts are different. People don't go to concerts consciously to pray, and yet I think they're sometimes deeply moved spiritually, and yet they don't see that that's something to do with God. Well, never mind. God is still there. I think that is a spiritual experience.

JA: What about non-texted and non-religious abstract music? Is there something equally spiritual about that? A Mozart Quintet, for instance, which is not specifically for any kind of sacred purpose. Do you find something sacred within it?

CC: Oh I do, yes. There you have sadness and joy. For instance, there is one trio section in the G Minor Quintet where, in a minor tonality, Mozart touches upon a major chord, and it moves me to bits every time he does it. Suddenly out of the darkness there comes this moment of sunlight. I find profound spirituality in that. But that doesn't mean to say that somebody else has to. But, if they're moved by it, they're moved towards what's spiritual. And after all, if you can begin to believe in the spiritual, it's difficult then to see why you shouldn't let in God. If you think everything's material, then there's no room for God at all.

JA: What is spirit?

CC: I remember a young medical student in the war on my ship, saying to me that he didn't believe in God. He'd started anatomy, and he'd never found the soul, as if he could find a little thing called the soul in human anatomy. I said, 'The soul isn't that. The soul is a quality of the whole person in relation to the spiritual reality of God.' Spirituality is beyond the material and physical.

Music is the perfect sacrament. It's physical, it's in time, and yet it's about something else beyond itself. But if you say to me, 'It's not spiritual, it's emotional', I say, 'Well, of course it's emotional because it works through our emotions.' Emotion is part of our human nature. You can say it's a physical response in the brain. And of course it works through there, and you can analyse it. But ultimately it isn't emotional. The ultimate is the spiritual.

Christopher has spent a great deal of his clerical life working with musicians and immersing himself into the music of both the church and the concert hall. While his emotional sympathies are strongly with the classical tradition of Western music, he has a broad view of what qualifies as a spiritual experience, even allowing for God's presence to work within a concert setting where no explicit theological allusions may exist. Christopher spoke eloquently about the connection between music and prayer, describing music as the perfect sacrament, while also demanding that the congregation actively participate in the music through prayer, even if that prayer is not vocalised. Prayer, sacrament, faith and music all combine, in Christopher's view, to produce a spiritual experience wherever those elements are present. One priest who also has a broad outlook with regard to music, but whose musical preferences include rock, pop, folk and jazz, as well as more traditional classical works, is Nick Baines, to whom I now turn.

NICK BAINES

The Right Reverend Nick Baines is the Anglican Bishop of Leeds and has written extensively about how popular music has been connected with his life of faith. He also has a wide experience of ecumenical dialogue and collaboration. Within his diocese he oversees churches and cathedrals with a variety of musical, liturgical and ecclesiological traditions. In his book *Finding Faith* he explores many twentieth-century pop and rock songs, finding in them theological significance. For instance, musing on John Lennon's *Imagine*, he writes about its sense of wonder but also of the failings of secular humanism:

> *Imagine* ... is more about fantasy than imagination ... Imagination is rooted in the capacity to wonder and exercised in the pursuit of curiosity ... The early Jewish writers and Psalmists gave expression to their experience of wonder at the enormity of the universe and the need to respond to the One who pours himself into it – leaving fingerprints of his activity and touch everywhere, if only we can see them. They make a connection between their experience of the 'numinous' and the need to respond to what is greater than themselves and their own particular experience. They recognise within the human person the image of the loving Creator who exists in relationship and beckons the imagination to reach out beyond what is merely or apparently evident.
>
> It is surely the capacity to wonder, to see and imagine beyond ourselves and the reality we experience, that is one of the features that makes us human and unique. So, why does that capacity appear to be so

> starved and the implications of wonder seem to be so feared in contemporary Western culture? Maybe it is because the dominant cultures of the late twentieth and early twenty-first centuries have taught us that the only things that matter are those that can be measured.[16]

Nick is dismissive of Lennon's simplistic sentiment that the eradication of religion would solve the world's problems:

> He [Lennon] seems to assume that if only we could excise religion from human society everything would be all right, conflict would end and people would live in harmony with each other.
>
> Now this might fit within the remit of a pop song with a good tune, but it is pathetic when subject to a few seconds' rational critique by a 5-year-old child. The secular humanist (if that is a reasonable way to describe John Lennon) assumes that his own worldview is neutral and that religious people hold a 'loaded' worldview that is, therefore, dangerous. The commitment religious people apply to the object of their worship or worldview is to be suspected because it refuses to deny implications and consequences for all other worldviews. Lennon lets the cat out of the bag in this song when he merely assumes that his own worldview is neutral, not loaded, is somehow 'natural' and self-evidently true. Yet it is precisely this arrogance that he condemns in religious people.
>
> It is a fantasy of epic proportions to think that human beings are governed by their rational faculties alone and can somehow 'mature' morally into something benign without a single shred of evidence from history that this is even remotely realistic. The Soviet model (of atheistic humanism – or inhumanism – that cost millions of innocent lives) was not notably successful in this respect.
>
> Yet this nonsense is reflected every day in our so-called 'mature' society. A whole generation of teachers has been trained in the United Kingdom with the assumptions that (a) religion is not neutral (and therefore dangerous), (b) that all religions are basically the same, but allow for peculiarities of diet and fashion, and (c) that their critically unexamined secular humanism *is* neutral and self-evidently true.[17]

Baines' attack on the atheist project is followed up by the assertion that faith and belief are intrinsic to human life and that there is no such thing as a purely rationalist existence. This applies to propositional belief as well as to experiential faith:

> Everyone believes something about the world for which they do not argue and which they merely assume: that life can be meaningful, for example; or that relationships matter; or that it is 'wrong' (as opposed to 'merely inconvenient') to kill someone ... No human being has no faith and no human being believes in nothing ... John Lennon never got as far as exploring the problems of the world he was calling for; he simply tried to call for the abolition of the bits of this world that he found personally inconvenient.[18]

Far from agreeing with John Lennon's vision, therefore, Nick Baines sees the act of faith, especially in worship, as being about relationship and encounter:

> Worship, for the Christian, is the expression of freedom to be loved and, in response, to love the Creator. This liberates us to live responsively in the world now with trust in the Creator for whatever will follow.[19]

But what Nick demands in worship is honesty. Like the Psalms, which contain almost every human experience, from utter despair to joy, so our hymns and songs in church should not always be about being happy. In this respect he concurs with Christopher Campling's view:

> Few, if any ... hymns and songs could be said to complain to God, ask God questions, lament our circumstances, voice our more unpleasant desires or leave our desires unmet ... Where would the woman whose child had died find space and language for 'worship'? Where would the man whose wife had left him for someone else find himself acknowledged and his experience recognized? Where would the teenager abused by a leader find her own experience given even subtle expression and know herself to be heard by God and his people? These are not theoretical cases.[20]

Examples of honest sacred music are gospel music, which has its origins in black slavery in America, and its offspring, the blues, which often expresses the complex and difficult nature of human existence. The poets of blues music are honest about dread, despair, wounded-ness and brokenness.[21] Thus Baines finds implicit religious meaning in much of modern music, one example of which is Eric Clapton's song *Pilgrim* from the album of the same name:

> His own pilgrimage, though not explicitly Christian, is worked out in his music and speaks at every turn of the reality of human loving and

> disappointment, the pain of rejection and the need to keep travelling and looking and wanting. In one sense this is the unavoidable outworking of what Augustine recognized when he said that 'our heart is restless till it finds its rest in [God]'. The honesty of Clapton's poetry is hauntingly impressive.[22]

But this sense of pilgrimage is not an individual exercise, and Baines condemns the growing phenomenon of 'spiritual but not religious', because it fundamentally ignores the fact that a spiritual experience involves relationship and encounter:

> What is crucial in all this is the fact that pilgrimage cannot be a solitary exercise. Pilgrims meet other people and are changed, encouraged and challenged by their encounters ... In Britain there is now a widespread rejection of what they call 'religion' ... Instead, such people claim to be 'spiritual' – and spirituality has become an unthreatening word to describe that non-rational part of people's internal life (or soul). But it is also understood to be something private and to do with the individual, not something for a community. This is really questionable – owing as it does more to a sort of narcissism than it does to altruism.[23]

Thus, for Baines, faith is communal and so is music, not a solitary spirituality.

In a post-secular society it is becoming increasingly clear that individualistic concepts of personal spirituality are inherently disappointing, because they miss the central truth that personal fulfilment, especially within one's life of faith, is found in communal experience.

When I met Nick Baines, I began by asking him how he became so interested in the relationship between music and God.

NB: I started playing music when I was eleven or twelve. I learned the trumpet in Liverpool. I played orchestral music and joined a couple of jazz groups, but I had to give up the trumpet because it was damaging my teeth, so I took up the guitar. I'm the only bishop I know who's been arrested for busking on the Paris Métro, in the tunnels under the Élysée Palace.

JA: So did you move from playing classical music because you had to give up your trumpet, to an enjoyment of pop music more than classical, or did you keep an interest in both?

NB: It depends how you define 'pop', but I've always been interested in music. Sometimes we even have to overcome our own prejudices. I'm always a bit behind the curve so, at the moment, I'm listening to people like the Arctic Monkeys and Killer and Creed. I do 'Pause for Thought' on The Chris Evans [Radio 2] Breakfast Show. I'm in the studio quite a lot on a Friday when they have guests and live music. So I get to hear people I've never heard of. I often go out and think I've got to get that album. You can't beat live music of any kind.

When I became a vicar in Rothley in Leicestershire, the choir were terrified because they thought I was inevitably going to scrap them. It took me a year to convince them that I wanted to build them up, not cut them down, but I also wanted to add to the menu. We developed a family orchestra for first Sunday of each month. Then we put a band together, and a vocal quartet and a string quartet. I taught them a lot of music that none of them knew, so no one group could say, 'Oh he's with them' or 'He's with them'. I remember one year where we had the band playing in the morning and it was really quite lively, and in the evening we had Fauré's *Requiem* with the choir. There's a band called Lies, Damned Lies from Scotland, who came and played tracks from their album on the Lamentations of Jeremiah on Ash Wednesday. We had said Holy Communion first in the chancel, then did the Lamentations, and it was really powerful. So I do believe in the idea of a musical menu, with a variety of options on offer, and I'm very eclectic in my own music tastes.

JA: Do you think there's a fear about learning new music in some churches? Even just a new hymn?

NB: I think there's a fear about teaching them. Even now, as a bishop, if I think a service needs it I might get up to preach, but before I do, I say, 'I want to teach you a song that goes with it. So if you're on this side of the church and you're male, sing this', and I sing it. Then everybody sings. It's all about leadership. It's all about confidence.

There is a connection here between Nick Baines's use of music homiletically and Christopher Campling's use of music to prepare for preaching. Baines employs music as part of his sermon, in order to prepare the congregation to receive the Word. Campling uses music to calm himself and to prepare his own mind for the task of preaching from memory. In both cases, music is utilised as an aid to the process of transmitting the Word of God. I continue my conversation with Nick Baines by asking him how his vocation to the priesthood was discerned and developed.

NB: I think that was when I went to university. I was training to be an interpreter, a translator. I studied modern languages and I was interested in international politics. But when I left university, Linda and I got married and moved to Cheltenham, and I retrained as a Russian linguist at GCHQ before finding a vocation to ministry in the Church. But music was a common thread through the whole of that time. Then, at theological college, I was introduced to a wider range of music.

At one point I went to Iona. Partly through exposure to John Bell's music, it radically changed my ministry. It became more humane. One night John asked me if I would sing a song in the abbey. The service was in complete darkness and in sub-zero temperatures. My song was one of emptiness really, by a Glaswegian called Brian McGlynn. During the singing of that song, the questions in my head of 'why me?' or 'why not me?' became 'thank you'.

At a later date John said to me about my work in the parish, 'I've been trying to work out what it is you're doing here, and I think you're changing the rumour about God.' I thought it was an interesting phrase. That we constantly have to change the rumour about God and the Church. You don't do it by reason, by having an argument. It's a slow process and music is part of that experience of change.

JA: Do we have to break down old stereotypes about the Church and provide a new form of access for people?

NB: Yes. But I don't think we should do it in order just to break down stereotypes. We should do it because it's part of the great menu. People who come to church come from lots of musical backgrounds and are exposed to lots of different types of music. Why do we shove them down one musical alley and say that that's what the Church does?

I've got three cathedrals in the diocese – Wakefield, Ripon and Bradford. But with Choral Evensong, I'm conscious that many people who attend are not familiar with the service. So I've now asked the Dean of each cathedral, in welcoming people at the beginning of the service, to explain that there isn't a great deal of participation and self-expression. The choir does it for you, so it creates a space where you can be quiet and reflect, you can dream, you can pray. So don't judge it by another particular type of worship. When it is explained, then people enjoy it.

JA: It seems to me that music is obviously not only important to you in terms of your own faith but also in terms of your ministry as well. You are able to incorporate it imaginatively because you really know a wide variety of repertoire. Is that something that is particular to your ministry? I can imagine that other ministers might struggle to know, let alone communicate, any music.

NB: You have to go where your interests are, don't you? That's how you inspire and enthuse people. They can tell when it's fake.

JA: I wonder then about the relationship between words and music, and how that is important in transmitting a message. How much is language important?

NB: The language we use should open up the imagination – it shouldn't close it down. We're living in a culture where you have to grab people's attention. You have to waken people's curiosity – it's not just intellect, you have to tease the imagination. It's the way Jesus used story, image and language that scratches away ten hours later at the back of your mind and haunts you.

It's the same with the dissonance between words and music. It's not neutral. I go along with Wesley that, if you sing, you learn your theology from what you sing, not from what you hear or what you say. And if you sing rubbish, you believe rubbish. Language matters. For instance, there's a limit to how many times you can gaze into the eyes of Jesus and tell him he's beautiful! Confessional worship songs are not about God: 'I worship you, I lay down my life for you, I give my all to you.' It's not true! It may be a great aspiration but it's not true. There are very few church songs that question God, or lament, or that don't have a happy resolution. Where are the songs about lament or questioning?

JA: Often, however we feel, we go into a church and we are forced to be happy, to be praising, to be filled with uplifting fantastic emotions about God. Is that because the music persuades us that that's how we should be feeling? Is that sometimes a problem, do you think?

NB: I think it is. Music should create the space in which people can find God and God can find them. I was in the Radio 2 studio once, and was asked, 'What's the point of the Church?' I had to think on the spot, and I said that the job of the Church is to create the space in which people can find that they have been found by God. We think we find God but we don't – we discover that he's already found us. The music in worship is a vital part of that. You can't compel people to confess, or to be absolved, or to be blessed, or to remember the story, but you can create a space in which the imagination as well as the intellect are teased. And people can live with it. And that's why I think you need

> different media. I couldn't have Choral Evensong as my sole musical diet. But I couldn't have only 'happy clappy' music either. You need a varied diet, as you do in the rest of life. Why do we think that in worship you must get the same thing all the time? I find it odd. And it's incumbent on those who lead churches to enable and encourage, and perhaps cajole people sometimes, to expand their experience into cultures with which they are not familiar in order to see and feel afresh.

Nick Baines' honesty with regard to the music of faith is extremely refreshing. His definition of the role of the Church as a place in which we have the space to find that we have been found by God encapsulates a profound idea of what the community of the faithful is about at its heart. Good music, in all its rich variety, enables those who are there to discover the divine in that place and time, and find that the divine was there all the time. Nick is not sentimental, and has little time for songs which simply extol God's virtues. For him, both the music and the language must be real, honest and heartfelt, whether expressing despair, dread, pain or disappointment as well as joy.

These three conversations demonstrate how, within one Christian denomination, the clerical responses to the relationship between music and faith can be very varied. Nick Brown sees music as having the potential for an encounter with the divine in itself, Christopher Campling sees music as the perfect sacrament and Nick Baines sees music in terms of relationship and encounter. Each has his own story of faith in which music has played a critical and life-changing part, whether in Brown's decision to dedicate his life to ordained service, having tested his motivations as a classical musician; or Baines's extraordinary moment of revelation in Iona Abbey, playing his guitar in the freezing cold; or Campling's insistence that cathedral music is worth more to a congregation if they participate in prayer. In each case, to use Nick Baines's words, people are finding that they have been found by God and, through music and a life of faith, these three clerics have changed the rumour about God.

CHAPTER NINE

MUSIC, FAITH AND THE LAITY

> Music is an agreeable harmony for the honour of God and the permissible delights of the soul.[1]

> Music is one of the most glorious gifts of God ... for it removes from the heart the weight of sorrow, and the fascination of evil thoughts.[2]

We have considered how the theological connection between faith and music might be meaningful to those, either within or outside the Church, who do not hold traditional or orthodox Christian beliefs, or indeed any Christian beliefs at all. We have also heard the voices of three Anglican clerics with their divergent musical tastes and theological stances. I now turn to explore two interviews with lay women who have contrasting experiences of cultural, national and denominational aspects of Church.

Firoozeh Willans is of Iranian descent, was educated in France and travelled widely with her family before settling in England. She now worships at the charismatic evangelical Hillsong church. Her Sunday morning experience of worship involves being part of a large congregation who meet in a hall with a worship band performing and accompanying the songs. There is also a commitment to social outreach work and study groups during the week. In addition, however, Firoozeh and her husband Olly have a son, Sacha, who is a chorister, and so they also regularly attend services in Magdalen College Chapel, where they hear the classical repertoire of Western sacred music. This forms an interesting mix of musical and liturgical encounters in the Willans family.

Shanika Ranasinghe, on the other hand, is a Roman Catholic of Sri

Lankan descent who has lived in London for most of her life. She is a PhD student in music at Royal Holloway, University of London. Her field of research is pop music, and in particular an ethnomusicological approach to the phenomenon of the Swedish pop band ABBA. She is also a classically trained pianist and, like Firoozeh, to some extent, came to know classical sacred music well at an Oxford college chapel when studying as an undergraduate at Worcester College. I began by asking Shanika how she came to enjoy music as a child and discovered that singing was an important part of her musical development.

SR: Well, the first thing to mention is that my mother is a pianist and she had a sense that I had an ear for music; that was her inclination. So when she started to teach me how to read and write she also started to teach me piano, when I was about three. Another early influence would have been the church that I was attending, because they had a choir, in Barnes, called St Osmund's. The choir wasn't very good but I really liked hymns and I realised quite early on when I was a child in primary school that my voice wasn't high enough to sing descants or even sometimes the melody. I felt a bit down about that because 'Hark the Herald Angels Sing' or 'Oh Come All Ye Faithful' have got such great descants and I couldn't sing them.

When I was about nine I was introduced to ABBA. Obviously there's a lot of harmonising between the females in ABBA, so I realised that you don't always have to sing the tune all the time. I used to try to copy Frida, who is the redhead, and try to emulate her vocal line instead of Agnetha, the blonde one. And that's how I got into singing.

My primary school, attached to the local Catholic church, had a big singing ethos because our headmistress was half Welsh and she'd grown up singing a lot and she had a really good voice herself. So we would sing and learn new hymns. When you were in year six you got to sing the harmony part or the descant part. I aspired to be in year six, because then I could sing the really cool bits in the hymns. Those were my early influences: school, church and ABBA.

JA: So Western classical music, and pop music?

SR: Yes, but it was old-fashioned pop music, it wasn't so much current music. My parents used to listen to a lot of Boney M and The Bee Gees, not so much The Beatles because I don't think they had the same impact in Sri Lanka, which is where my parents are from.

JA: When did they leave Sri Lanka?

SR: They left in 1978 ...

JA: So The Beatles had split.

SR: Yes, but I think there was a communist government in Sri Lanka at one point who really didn't like The Beatles, so there was a ban on The Beatles or something ridiculous like that. But not on The Bee Gees, not on ABBA.

JA: And what about traditional Sri Lankan music, is that something that you've inherited?

SR: My mum does play that kind of music but only at family parties. She'll play the piano and they'll have a sing-song. Someone will get a guitar and someone will play bongos on a bin. Traditional Sri Lankan music is called *Baila*, which is a Portuguese-derived word from when the Portuguese occupied Sri Lanka. It's very complicated music because, although it's simple harmonically, the time signature is two beats overlapping three beats. So it has a syncopated feel.

JA: As you got older, did you think you might become a musician?

SR: When I was around fifteen or sixteen I decided I wanted to do music as a degree because that was the only subject that I was really interested in. Very much at that stage it was about performance. I really enjoyed piano-playing so I wanted just to continue it. I did find my Music GCSE quite interesting, especially learning about other cultures, so we did a bit about gamelan and Indian music. I also enjoyed musical theatre a lot.

JA: Then you studied music at Oxford and in a college which had a very good chapel choir?

SR: I didn't know that when I applied though. I had no concept of these things. It was all quite new to me, but one of my tutorial partners was in the choir and one was the organ scholar, so I wanted to support what they were doing because they spent so much of their time doing it. I wanted to see what it was all about and support what they were doing so I started attending Monday services because they told me that was when the really good music was sung. I'd come from a very Catholic background where Mass is always the same. Suddenly I didn't know any of this music whatsoever because I didn't have a background in choral music. It was a real awakening for me that there was other music out there. It was a shock to the system, because I had no idea whether to sit or stand, or when do to any of that stuff, because I'd never been to an Anglican service before. The first year was mainly spent trying to figure out when to sit, when to stand, when to bow and kneel, all those kinds of things.

JA: So it was a complete culture change then, in terms of attending church, as it were?

SR: Yes it was, but Worcester Chapel soon felt more like home and more comfortable for me.

JA: Can you say why?

SR: I think it was a welcoming space and I also really liked the music. It took me a long time to get used to the music, just because it was so new to me with all the different parts and especially – and this was the most shocking thing – when they started to sing music by William Byrd, which is so intricate and complex and I thought 'Woah! This is what polyphony sounds like.' I'd never heard anything like that before.

JA: So up to that point had you heard a live performance of a choir singing contrapuntal, complicated polyphony?

SR: I don't think I had, certainly nothing like Byrd or Tallis. I had heard my church choir and piano recitals. I had gone to the BBC Proms. Once in a blue moon I might go to the Festival Hall. So I think it was probably the first time I'd heard anything like polyphony. It was absolutely mind-blowing.

JA: Did you go to the Proms and the Festival Hall for orchestral concerts?

SR: Yes, and for piano recitals. Now they do semi-staged musicals, with the John Wilson Orchestra, so I've started going to those because that's good fun. And one-off things, like one year Nigel Kennedy did the [Vivaldi] *Four Seasons* with a Palestinian youth orchestra, and his improvising was amazing. But even now I don't really go to concerts for choral music. I do love choral music, but for me it has to be in the setting of Evensong. When I go to a concert, even if it is the Worcester Chapel Choir, I feel less connected to it because it's not part of that structure of worship.

JA: Would you go to listen to a professional choir sing Renaissance polyphony?

SR: I've often thought I should go and listen to Monteverdi *Vespers* at a late-night Prom, but I never end up going because of a lack of motivation and curiosity. I think, for me, I'd prefer it not in a concert setting.

JA: So what do you get from sacred music in a liturgical setting?

SR: I think it helps me to feel more connected to God, because there was a point in my life where I used to experience God quite a lot and he was very much present in my life. Those days have almost gone, so I feel this disconnection from my faith and disjunction from God. But when I'm listening to that music and when the first sopranos hit the really high notes, it's like a vault opens in the ceiling and, if it was a play, there'd suddenly be streams of light coming from the ceiling as if the heavens have opened. It makes me feel like God is there because it's so beautiful and at times very profound, and I don't pay that much attention to the words even if they are in English. I don't tend to pay attention to the words. It's more the music.

JA: You're not worried about, particularly, how the choir is conveying the text so much as the actual sonority of the experience?

SR: Yes, it's more about the sonority for me. It's partly because I have a hearing problem, so it's difficult for me, even with a very good choir who have very good diction, it's hard for me to make out the text if it's not in front of me.

JA: So it's a different kind of experience from any kind of detailed engagement with words?

SR: Unless it's something like the *Magnificat*, where I know the words, or if it's the setting of *Ave Maria*, then the words come into it but otherwise it's more about the sound and the feelings, rather than the text.

JA: Would you call that an emotional effect or a spiritual, or mental, intellectual effect?

SR: I wouldn't call it an intellectual effect. I think it is something very emotional. Sometimes it's a mix between emotional and spiritual. On very rare occasions it is *just* spiritual and that's a kind of feeling, I guess Buddhists would call it 'enlightenment', where there's a sudden clarity about God and my relationship with him, or God in the world and God's presence.

JA: So years ago when you were having a more direct, regular feeling of the presence of God, was that with or without music?

SR: It was with music actually, because I think I was having those experiences when I started going to chapel a lot more. By the time I finished at Worcester I was coming to every service. And that was partly me seeking answers, partly me just enjoying and valuing the community and wanting to be a part of it. But it was also partly to do with the music. I think the music helped a lot. And especially for me, something that

> was really helpful, was the service of Compline or Night Prayer. I don't think I'd ever properly experienced plainchant. Coming to Worcester and learning that there was this thing called 'The Office' [the daily round of services] that some [religious] orders follow and I thought 'Oh this is a thing, okay!' It was just completely mind-boggling to me because I had no idea how to read neumes [medieval plainchant notation]. I had no idea how anyone knew how to change from one note to the other or how long to sing a note, so that took a while to get into. But actually that was one of my favourite parts of the week during my whole time at Worcester. And actually for one academic year I was in the Oxford University Philharmonia Orchestra and the rehearsals clashed with Compline, and one of my reasons to give up my place in the orchestra was based on the fact that I wanted to go back to Compline, because I really missed it.

For Shanika, there seems to be a three-fold motivation for her participation in the musical and liturgical life of a chapel: it is partly an attempt to recapture that intimate knowledge and experience of God that she once felt – a kind of faith seeking understanding; it is partly the sense of belonging to a community and, as Boyce-Tillman, Dunbar and others would tell us, there is an intimate connection between music and community; and it is partly the music itself which, interestingly, has words but which are not particularly important to Shanika compared to the musical sonority and composition. Thus, I ask Shanika if she was able to participate in the services more vocally.

JA: Did you sing along?

SR: By the end of my first year I could sing along. I think it took me about two terms to an academic year. I'm a bit slow at singing.

JA: But it's interesting how long it does take to pick up all the Gregorian melodies of Compline, and the Anglican liturgy of standing and sitting at Evensong.

SR: But then it just became a natural rhythm.

JA: Is there any particular style of Church music that you prefer? We've mentioned polyphony and William Byrd and so on but the music of the Baroque, Bach, Handel or Classical music, Mozart or perhaps the Romantic music of Brahms and Mendelssohn, or perhaps more contemporary music?

SR: I think my favourite choral music, in terms of sacred music, is probably from the Renaissance period, so Byrd, Victoria. There's something really, exquisitely beautiful about polyphony and the subtle changes in the harmonies, so I think that's my favourite period. But I do like bits of other periods as well. My favourite *Magnificat* and *Nunc Dimittis* is Wood in E-flat.

JA: That's very Romantic.

SR: I don't know why but it's always just kind of stuck in my head. Because I don't tend to remember music that I've never played because of my memory problems and communication problems, but that I do remember. And I remember thinking, 'Wow, that's beautiful' and wanting to cry because it was just that beautiful, so I have quite varied taste I guess.

JA: When you listen to the [J.S.] Bach *Preludes and Fugues* or a violin piece by Handel, do you get the same sensations of that connection with God or is it different?

SR: I hear God in Bach's music, I really do. And I think there's something transcendental about it and I've never quite pinpointed why. It feels like something is just opening up and some kind of understanding or shared experience with the divine is going on. And I feel like that with some Handel as well. I don't think there are many other composers that do that for me. I know lots of people love Beethoven, and I do love Beethoven, don't get me wrong, but I don't have this deep sense of 'Beethoven-ness' that other people seem to have. I don't really know why, but for me I think my favourite period for violin is Baroque, definitely. Piano ... I do really love Debussy, but I wouldn't say I have spiritual experiences when playing or listening to it. I think it's rare for its time and it's incredible music but I wouldn't go as far as to say there's a spiritual or divine connection there. So for me that's really with the Baroque music.

JA: So Bach, for instance, you would be able to hear his connection with the divine, but with Debussy it's a completely different experience?

SR: Yes. With Debussy it's more about the colours and images that it conjures up and it's another sound world completely. For me there's not a connection with anything spiritual and I don't know if that has anything to do with his own life and beliefs. Obviously Bach had a much stronger Church connection.

JA: Well we know that Bach was a Church musician and a man of faith. Maybe that does make a difference – the intention of the composer?

SR: Maybe, I don't know. We spent a great deal of time in our undergrad degree debating whether the intention of the composer is important or if it actually comes across at all. But I think with Bach, if he intended for it to have a spiritual effect, I think it definitely does come across.

Shanika is also an expert on, and a fan of, the music of ABBA. It is interesting that although she gains a spiritual encounter through certain sacred music in a liturgical context, where for her the words are not important, when it comes to pop music, her experience is entirely emotional and the words become crucial to her experience.

JA: Now you're doing a doctorate on pop music – on ABBA and a particular period in pop music history. Do you find that's a completely different world or is there any connection at all with the sound world and the experience that you have in the chapel?

SR: No, with ABBA's music it's a purely emotional response. Because I use ABBA's music to regulate my own mood, in terms of if I'm feeling low and I want to feel lighter or upbeat then I'll listen to *Dancing Queen*, because that's a sure-fire way of lifting your mood. Or if you want to feel really depressed and push loads of self-destruct buttons then you listen to *The Winner Takes It All*. I think *The Winner Takes It All* is a really clever song because there's so little to the music and yet they make a whole song out of it. I just find that incredible. With pop music for me, the words are more important than they are in a sacred setting. So for me in *The Winner Takes It All*, the music is really beautiful by itself but the words have a huge impact as well.

JA: So you don't understand the emotional centre of the song unless you know that it's about a divorce?

SR: I think you can appreciate it even if you don't know that but there's just something knowing that it's about a divorce and as much as Bjorn says 'it's not about our divorce', it clearly *was* about your divorce and you made your poor ex-wife sing a song about your own divorce. No wonder she had psychological problems after that!

JA: So it was a rather cruel thing to do?

SR: I think it's hugely cruel and if everyone talks about Agnetha being a recluse, well no wonder. If you had to go round *Top of the Pops* and the other international shows singing about your own divorce then of course that's going to destroy you.

JA: There are other ABBA songs I was thinking of, such as *The Day Before You Came*, which when you listen to the words, is rather positive isn't it?

SR: Well, that's what the ABBA fans think and say, but the truth is I find it really sad. I find the combination of the tune with the words 'I'm sure it must have rained the day before you came' very moving. With this ABBA song, one wonders, 'Did he come into your life and destroy you or come into your life and make everything better?' I don't like not knowing.

JA: It's ambiguous.

SR: It is very ambiguous and ABBA claim that they don't know what it means either. But I'm pretty sure they must know what it means or what it meant to them at that time.

JA: That's where the intention of the composer makes a big difference, isn't it – in the dynamic, in the story of their relationships and the story of the music?

SR: It's an incredible story, because you do see, as ABBA's marriages start to fall apart, there is a slight correlation with their music becoming more mature, if you want to call it that, and moving from the glam rock and the dazzling costumes to more serious subjects, such as your child going off to school and not needing you anymore, or what happened the day before this person came, or divorces. So yes, I think biography can play a huge part in pop music, definitely. And I think that comes across more easily than it does in Western art music.

JA: So you may not be relating to the music in a spiritual way, but I guess what can't be ignored is the human connection that's being made between the listener and the performers or the composers. Because it's almost impossible to listen to that music purely as music, there's no such thing. It's certainly not abstract and it is, would you say, highly emotionally connected with the lives of the composers and performers?

SR: I think it is, and it has to do with this biographical story and the fact that you can really sense the pain.

JA: And people relate to the human experience.

SR: I think a lot of people do. Every pop band has love songs or love ballads or songs about love or a break-up, but for some reason ABBA did that more effectively than most other bands.

JA: Is some pop music able to convey spirituality or some kind of spiritual, prayerful or divine message?

SR: Probably, there must be, but I'm struggling to think of any pop song that I would consider spiritual. There are pop songs that make you think and there are pop songs that stay with you or that become part of your life because you were listening to them at a particular time or when something happened, and they become entwined in the fabric of your life, but for me it's not spiritual. There must be people out there for whom it is.

JA: What about music that's performed in some churches that is basically a rock or pop band on a stage?

SR: I'm not going to lie. For me that has nothing to do with God at all. I don't pretend to understand how that works or why. For me it's irreverent. I feel quite strongly that that's not spiritual, not dignified. I once read this really funny meme on Facebook which I think sums it up for me, which was this guy who was looking completely plastered and he's at an evangelical church with this rock band and he says, 'Not sure if they're singing about Jesus or my girlfriend.' I don't have that much experience of evangelical rock bands but that for me sums it up, because they're talking about love in a very specific, touchy-feely kind of way and for me that's just not what it's about.

JA: Because you mention reading C.S. Lewis's *Four Loves*, and so in a sense you're saying that this kind of music is tapping into a more erotic, kind of sensual feeling of love, rather than the selfless *agape* kind of love.

SR: It's not just about the selfless *agape*. It feels disrespectful the way they sing about Jesus. It's a very different type of Christianity from what I'm used to. I'm not saying that I think the Catholic Church is right about everything, because I really don't, but I think there has to be reverence because it is a deity you're talking about or addressing. Do I think Jesus is my best buddy? No. Am I going to go down the pub for a beer with Jesus? No. So he's not my best mate and he's not my lover ... it bemuses me, it really does.

JA: I'm putting together from this that, for you, this kind of experience of God within the context of sacred music has to include a number of coinciding characteristics, such as contemplation within the liturgy, it has to be within a sacramental context, has to be reverent as you say, and also there are certain styles of music that lend themselves more easily to spirituality. I was just wondering, then, if the standard of that music has to be at a certain high standard or whether anybody's efforts are helpful? When is music a useful aid to that worship, and when is it a distraction?

SR: It's a distraction when it's bad. And I'm all for inclusivity to a degree, but I think for it to be a spiritual experience, if that's what people are aiming to produce through music, that spiritual experience, there has to be a degree of competency. Stand-out moments for me would be when Saint Pope John Paul II died. In the Sunday Mass immediately after that, we were going up to receive the Eucharist when the choir master and his daughter, who is a very good singer, performed *Panis Angelicus*, which was excellent. Likewise, on Good Friday, if I'm about to venerate my Saviour who's died for me, there has to be a degree of competency to the music. Not that every choir has to be The Sixteen or The Monteverdi Choir.

JA: But both of those two liturgical experiences that you've just outlined seem quite intense ones. The day after the Pope died and Good Friday are quite big occasions for a Christian, especially for a Catholic.

SR: It's hard to tell. I'd like to be nice and say it's just trying that counts but I think for it to be a proper spiritual experience it has to be done well. I think a good singer or a good conductor or a good choir does make a real difference. There has to be a degree of craftsmanship. In any art form the intention of the composer, or the painter, or the dramaturge, or playwright has to come across as well, because you can intend things that don't always come across. So it's somehow getting that magic formula.

JA: You say also that your contact with God is rare but that you find it again through music. How is that going now?

SR: I think music is the best way to get through. Either music or reading, because a number of years ago now around 2010–11 I did a lot of reading of the Carmelites, so I read St Teresa of Avila, for example, and that was quite powerful at the time because it felt as though someone had written about my life five hundred years in advance. These days it's probably, though it rarely happens, through music still. There are those moments where a soprano will hit a very high note, or where the polyphony is really sublime and beautiful. There are kind of glimmers.

Shanika speaks very openly about her difficulty in connecting with God in the way that she was once able to do. She is also clear about the distinctive nature of sacred music in a liturgical context, which opens up the possibility of a spiritual experience that is not found in the primarily emotional experience of listening to the pop music of ABBA. She clearly loves the music of ABBA but is certain about the nature of the effect the music has on her. Shanika is an interesting case, because it has been possible, through her relatively recent discovery of classical choral music, plainsong and Anglican liturgy, to track the impact of the music, such as Renaissance polyphony and plainchant, upon her psyche and spiritual life. Her story is one in which, through the musical and intellectual development at university, she also encountered the revelation of sacred music within a new (for her) liturgical framework which, for her, needs to be contemplative, reverent and sacramental, with music that is 'dignified'. Such musical and liturgical settings led to a spiritual search for faith and an experience of relationship with the divine, as well as with her fellow worshippers and musicians in community. Shanika continues her spiritual journey, seeking to find the elusive and rare spiritual encounter again.

For Firoozeh Willans the encounter is not so rare or elusive. Firoozeh is a woman of faith *and* belief. Her background and history is rich and complex. She has a firm commitment to following Christ, but would not necessarily associate that faith with religion or a particular Christian denomination. As we shall see, this emphasis upon a strong conviction of faith, while adopting a liberal and non-denominational or religious allegiance, is fascinating. For Firoozeh, the international nature of her upbringing and her inclusivity of spirit with regard to worship and liturgy means that she can appreciate a wide variety of musical styles in worship and gain from them all, including silence. I began by asking her about her childhood.

FW: My background is very international. My mother is from Iran and she's related to the Shah, so due to that political situation she was brought up in this country. My father is English and he is a direct descendant of Sir Titus Salt, the Victorian philanthropist. So my maiden name is Salt, and his side of the family is very well documented because of this philanthropy. Saltaire became a UNESCO World Heritage Site, made famous by Sir David Hockney. My father worked for British Airways and so we lived in lots of different countries. I went to thirteen different schools in nine different countries. At my school in Paris, which was a convent, every single child was from a different country. We moved pretty much every year and then I went to boarding school. I loved it. Even though I was incredibly worldly in some ways I was naïve in realising that people actually lived in the *same* house all their lives. On my father's side, his mother (my grandmother) started *Woman's Hour*, *Children's Hour* and *Letter from America* on BBC radio. She was Oxford educated and her best pal was Barbara Castle. They got into lots of trouble together and were imprisoned in Paris for organising communist riots. She worked for the BBC, like my grandfather, who sadly died when my father was only four, leaving my grandmother with a four-year-old, a three-year old and a baby, so my father was pretty much raised in the BBC canteens, he said. Thanks to the Salt money, they had a big house in Didsbury in Manchester, and my grandmother always wanted interesting people living there, so when we were visiting from abroad, she had twenty-seven Vietnamese refugees living there in the late 1970s.

In the 1970s we lived in Iran. By the time I was nine we'd been evacuated four times, twice from Beirut and twice from Iran. Many of my mother's family left and now live in the California area. Sadly my grandmother and uncle stayed, because they didn't want to leave their country. They were under house arrest for about fifteen years, maybe longer. It was very difficult for them. My mum went back to Iran as well, and she didn't come out again. Of course there was no internet, we were not allowed to telephone. She did receive our letters, but we didn't know that, so as far as we were concerned there was no communication at all. At the age of seventeen I met my future husband, Olly. The same year the Foreign Office let my father know that my mum had died, under house arrest. So I didn't do as well at university [studying French at Oxford Polytechnic, later Oxford Brookes] as I maybe could have done. But my aunt Marian has always been a great role model for me, and her home was always my home.

JA: When did your Christian faith begin?

FW: I think all my life. My mother really loved God. I tell people that I was raised in a Christian family. I wouldn't say worship or prayer were a part of daily life, but certainly Jesus, God, the Bible and obviously Christmas were very much part of the way we were as a family. I'm the eldest of two sisters and my sister tells me that I'm very greedy, and that that's how I found Jesus, because I wanted the best. In all the countries we lived in, the missionary mums were very good cooks! There were these American missionaries in Tanzania, Kenya and Uganda. I kept on going round to their house because they baked really well and I enjoyed it.

JA: So you must have experienced many different types of worship, then?

FW: Many, from barefoot under a baobab tree, to Roman Catholic, High Church Anglican, and my Aunt Marian is Quaker. I think every single school I went to was a worshipping school in some way or another. The convent in Paris had a very strong Catholic ethos and we went to Rome several times from Paris. I think it was C.S. Lewis who wrote that you are invited into the hallway of God's house and you choose the way of worship that's personal to you. I feel comfortable in pretty much all ways of worship.

My upbringing was very liberal as well. My grandmother would always have people in her home that needed a place to stay, so you never knew who was going to be there. You walked into the kitchen and you never knew who might be there, an archbishop or a Somali refugee, and that's the way we've always been. Olly and I, and we as a family, have gravitated towards trying to be what we believe Jesus would want us to be.

JA: Would you say that you're part of a denomination at all?

FW: No, I wouldn't. So when people say to me, 'Oh I know you're quite religious, Firoozeh', I don't know what that means. I just know that I have a relationship with Christ and I really enjoy that. I know people get quite pickled up about that. My Aunt Marian does and gets quite confused about it, but I'm not. I'm embracing of it all and I don't understand a lot of it, but that's fine by me, I'm plodding on.

JA: I know you've done some work with Justin Welby.

FW: I am a counsellor and psychotherapist, and also with the Association of Christian Counsellors, and that work leads me to do lots of different things and speaking for lots of different Christian organisations. I've done quite a bit of work with Chris Russell, who is the Adviser for Evangelism and Witness, and works closely with Justin Welby. He's also the Vicar of Reading and he's in Lambeth Palace three days a week. This is how I also got involved with 'Hillsong'.

The term Hillsong perhaps needs some explanation. Praise and worship music, as it is known by some, developed in the 1960s and '70s. The initial folksong influence gave way to praise choruses and then to rock music styles. The biggest early growth was in the United States, but soon spread through the UK, Europe and Australia. The latter is home to 'Hillsong UNITED', which sprang from a youth ministry in Hillsong Church, near Sydney, in the 1990s. From there it has spread into a global phenomenon, run by Joel Houston. Hillsong now publish many albums of music a year, having developed enormous worshipping communities throughout the world. Worship rarely takes place in a church because there are very few churches big enough to host the large congregations. Cinemas, stadiums and other large community buildings are often hired for the purpose. Hillsong are now making their way into television broadcasting. Through recorded media, television and local worshipping communities, their music has become an international genre and is shared among Christians all over the world.[3] A key characteristic of Hillsong is its incredibly rapid growth over the last few decades, meaning that relatively new branches of it, such as the one in Oxford, are growing fast and in need of larger premises in which to meet. Firoozeh worships at Oxford Hillsong:

FW: The Oxford campus began, I think, in April 2015. It's just coming up for three years. They have about 750 people attending, two services in the cinema, in the Odeon. Craig, our pastor, is stepping out in faith and has booked the New Theatre, with 1400 seats, for Easter Day – encouraging everybody to bring a friend.

JA: Were you familiar with that size and kind of community before you started going to Hillsong?

FW: Because my sister is a vet in America and my father worked for British Airways, I've been to America many times, and I've been to these evangelical megachurches. In fact my sister's pastor is what they call a mega-pastor, and he's on the international set. I've been around that, it's not something that's completely alien to me, it's very big in the States. You can get attendances of 16,000 in stadiums – Billy Graham-style, coming up and giving your life to the Lord and a lot of worship. Now the difference that I have found is that, because Hillsong is obviously so new, I've never experienced pastors with English accents. Craig and Anna are in their mid-thirties now. They're English. He is a Bicester boy. He was a professional footballer at one stage and then had an injury. Then he was a builder for ten years and worked on building sites around Bicester. He's not from a Christian family. He and Anna have really stepped out in faith to do this and he's dyslexic, so when he's reading, he's open about the fact that this is challenging. Oxford is known as one of the most intellectual cities in the world, and he's leading the fastest-growing church in this city, and he's a dyslexic builder.

JA: So that's countercultural to some types of church today?

FW: It is countercultural and also it reminds us that anything is possible with God. It's incredibly Christ-centred. I've worked in prisons, I've worked in all sorts of different environments and, excuse my French, but I do think I have a really good nose for being able to detect bullshit. But they are very passionate, genuinely Christ-centred pastors, otherwise I wouldn't go.

It is incredibly well organised, and the community outreach is absolutely staggering. And as far as I know there are only one and a half people that are paid! That's Craig and then the youth pastor gets paid for three days a week. Anna doesn't get paid and there are so many volunteers, they are falling over themselves.

JA: Are Craig and the youth pastor paid by the congregation?

FW: I'm not really sure about that. Within Pentecostal churches there is a tradition of tithing. I don't know about anyone else but I always tithed and I do give. Of the charities that I tithe to, Hillsong is not one of the charities to whom I tithe, but I do give monthly to Hillsong.

JA: When you go to a service, what form does it take?

FW: You are greeted, and there's a coffee shop. It is very welcoming. As soon as you arrive there's music and a band. It's in a cinema but I understand that in all the Hillsong Campuses there's a lot of graphics.

JA: So they use the screens?

FW: A lot. For scripture and for videos that they make to show you how to get involved with groups, because there's the weekly congregation, and then everyone is encouraged to join some sort of group. I'm one of the eldest at forty-six. There are a lot of young people. It's very international and I like that. There's a basketball group, between thirteen and seventeen different Bible study groups just for women around Oxfordshire. I run one and I go to one as well. There's these things called Connect Groups so that, wherever you are, geographically, there will be people your age who attend Hillsong – there's one in our village. On WhatsApp you can just say if you're going or not. I have been to a few and I've met a few people. A Polish girl whose mother was dying of cancer, she came to live with us for a bit. Now she's working for Open Doors. It's a way of connecting and people do it out of generosity. The pastoral care is pretty good because of the groups. There's a group for people who are looking after foster children; there's a running group; there's a group for people who want to meet in Costa on Wednesday mornings; there's a group for students at one of the colleges, there's so many groups.

It seems that the atmosphere in the cinema on a Sunday morning is deeply enriched by the group work done during the week. Remembering Robin

Dunbar's sociological research on group sizes, as we saw in chapter five, the way that such a large congregation is sustained is by the dynamics and sense of social cohesion achieved in the midweek smaller groups, where people bond closely over their various chosen activities. The success of Hillsong as a structure seems to be sustained by regular social gatherings of manageable-sized groups. So I wondered how all this fed into the main Sunday worship, especially with regard to music.

JA: How much does music play a part in the services?

FW: Well, thinking about it, Jonathan, I am probably the most unmusical person you'll probably ever find – unashamedly. It's just not my thing. I don't think God gave me the gene that other people have, but I enjoy music a lot, but I don't really know anything about it.

In a service, they have three or four songs with the band, which are interspersed with praise reports and prayer. Praise reports are about what's going on in church this week, and what's going on globally. The music and visuals are so creative. What happens on the screens is staggering. Another example of this is the Colour Conference, which is a women's conference that's been held annually for twenty years on three different continents now and about ten different cities. Twelve thousand Christian women go and the speakers are incredible. It does take a lot to impress me in that kind of arena, but it is very moving, compelling, strengthening and purposeful. It is very genuine about Christ and being his hands and feet in this world. But the artisans they got involved to do this, the dreamers, the pastors, the stage-set, the lighting, the electricians, the creativity, the videos, the dancers, the singers – unbelievable, and not very many of them are paid. They are volunteers.

JA: Is there a similar multi-media experience in Hillsong? You've got the band, you've got the screen and the preaching, and they interact, do they?

FW: I don't know how shows work, and when I say 'show' I don't mean to do it any disservice, but there is an order of play. There's probably eight in the technical crew at the back of the cinema and Craig will make a reference to a particular passage of scripture and suddenly it will appear on screen. Most people will either have a Bible in their hand or a Bible app. Many people are taking notes, like at Colour Conference. I wouldn't be sitting there without a notebook.

The multi-media presentation uses modern technology and the convenient location of the cinema to produce a multi-sensory experience of sound, vision, drama and emotional engagement within the communal experience. But the essential note-taking also demonstrates that the Word is centre-stage. I wonder how much of the Sunday experience is enhanced by congregational participation.

JA: How much do you participate, vocally or otherwise, in the worship?

FW: In every way. My friend Anne was going to come today but she couldn't, so I said to her: 'What would you say to Jonathan?' In her French-Swiss accent she said, 'You can tell him, never would I sing in church, but I do at Hillsong.' She sings at Hillsong because the music is very loud, and she feels comfortable. Likewise at the Colour Conference there's 12,000 women. It's huge, and it's an encouraging atmosphere. It brought tears to my eyes the first time I went, because I thought, 'This is my tribe!' These beautiful women from all over the world, everybody is there together and I love these women. It's absolutely fantastic. But there's also that privacy, partly because the music is so loud – at Hillsong here they have noise-cancelling headphones for babies, and there's a crèche at the back. My friend Anne has never put her arms up in the air to worship before or jumped about in a service, but she does now. At the same time there's also an atmosphere of being able to be private.

The importance of community, even 'tribe', comes across strongly in Firoozeh's words, and the worship music enables people to be liberated from their inhibitions and to sing loudly, even if their singing is not good, because of the sheer volume, both of people and the loudness of the music. But also, paradoxically, that atmosphere also leads to a sense of privacy. The stimulant of sound, vision and communal worship allows the individual to be both extrovertly worshipping and to experience a more introspective encounter. The relationship dynamic in the large group gathering is both tribal and individual.

Donald Miller has noted that what he calls 'new-paradigm churches' are post-denominational, their doctrine firmly taken from early Christian narratives about Jesus and his disciples, while at the same time using the latest technology and cultural idioms of the postmodern age.[4] Firoozeh also sees herself, unsurprisingly given her background, as part of an international tribe of fellow believers, particularly women Christians. If we consider Dunbar's theories on social numbers, then it would be impossible for one person to know the 12,000 other women at the Colour Conference, but the sense of identity and belonging is nevertheless extremely powerful – powerful enough, in fact, to reduce one to tears. How can this be explained? Perhaps it cannot, but Ingalls attempts to do so by suggesting there is (to use Benedict Anderson's term) an 'imagined community.[5] She writes that the sense of community, in such a charismatic evangelical gathering, and between evangelical communities across the world, is because it is a 'body of people too large to meet face to face who are nevertheless united by a shared discursive framework that has been enabled by various mass media technologies'.[6]

Firoozeh is connected with believers from all over the globe. Some she knows and some she does not but they are united in one spirit and one aim within their charismatic faith. The church groups, both small and large, the conferences and the connections made through social media are all important in sustaining a community that has no permanent church building as a home. Simon Coleman explains it thus:

> These Christians are concerned to prompt the 'flow' of people, ideas and material objects across the globe, and the idea of cementing interconnections between believers united in 'Spirit' is powerfully articulated by them in sermons, oral testimonies and literature. Conferences, prayer networks and media are valued partly because they sustain a sense of participation in impermanent, free-flowing structures.[7]

Gesa Hartje-Döll's research on Hillsong, as well as other evangelical and charismatic churches, suggests there is one industry that unites them all globally, and that is the Christian music recording business.[8] This is borne out in Firoozeh's own testimony:

FW: There's over forty Hillsong albums. They recently won a Grammy in contemporary Christian music for one of their songs. I asked my friend Allie, 'What would you say about Hillsong music?' and she looked at me and said, 'It's the words.' For her it's the words. She's often just weeping because they really move her. That's the same for me as well. I think there's other things involved but for her and me that's very dominant.

JA: So the music is carrying those words and really communicating those words.

FW: I don't know because I'm not really into music that much, but I think the music has changed a lot. So they have more reflective and softer albums as well as the other more funky ones. I think the most recent one is a bit more, not electronic, but maybe more appealing to a younger audience. They also have one for children, albums for children.

JA: Is this Hillsong in general or just the Oxford band?

FW: This is Hillsong in general. All the Hillsong campuses play the music from Hillsong, which is written in Hillsong, Australia.

JA: But they play it live?

FW: Yeah.

JA: So you don't have recorded music playing over the speakers?

FW: Only when it's accompanying something you're watching on screen. They're always trying to incorporate the younger people. They're really young on stage.

The centralised nature of the Hillsong musical compositions, which are incorporated into Hillsong campus worship worldwide, helps to secure a sense of global community. Nevertheless, it is clear from Firoozeh's experience and that of her friend Allie, that the words come first and it is the words of belief that are being carried and communicated by the music. This is one example of a church where word-centred religion has not waned and where propositional belief is 'carried' by the music into the hearts of the believers. In the Hillsong community we see not only music and faith at work, but music and belief.

In contrast to Firoozeh's charismatic Sunday worship, she also has a son, Sacha, who is in Magdalen Chapel Choir and he sings traditional choral music in services six times a week. I could not help asking, therefore, what Firoozeh thought of the differences between her Hillsong experience and that of the worship in Magdalen College Chapel.

FW: I love it, yes. I was very much brought up in traditional English worship in boarding schools and in schools around the world. I love it, but I feel sometimes, not just here, that people are not listening to God's word and the communication of the Bible. They are more concerned with the delivery and how well somebody read the lesson and it really upsets me because it's not like that at Hillsong. At Hillsong everybody can have a say, it doesn't matter if you trip, and there's no fear about being authentically yourself. Even I, who do a lot of public speaking, am a little bit intimidated to do a reading here. I believe that Christ died to set me free, and I want to step into that potential and that freedom more and more. That's what I encourage in the counselling room, I encourage that in all ways. Where I feel fear, that's not from God. We are told over four hundred times in the Bible not to fear. So I feel annoyed if somebody says, 'Oh, didn't they read well!' and I think, 'Did you hear it? It was Jeremiah. Did you hear God's words?' This is the character of God they're trying to communicate, not whether somebody stammered on a word, and that upsets me. I want everyone to be thinking about what God is communicating.

JA: It's interesting because this is what people also got very cross about at the Reformation: that the Word of God had got lost in complex ceremony and music. There seems to be an interesting comparison between what you say and what happened five hundred years ago. Is it the same with the music, do you think? Do people ask, 'Did they perform that well'?

FW: They make mistakes all the time at Hillsong and nobody would comment. The words are powerful, the music is powerful. Sometimes they'll be a bit off – but it speaks to the heart. I think there's a really big difference between doing scripture A Level, and experiencing a revelation through scripture. I've seen the Holy Spirit do in twenty minutes what twenty years in therapy would not do. I feel, very much, out of all my ways of worship, I really feel the Spirit of the Lord, tangible, at Hillsong.

JA: And that affects your experience, doesn't it? Whether you're participating in your heart with the spirit of the worship?

FW: With the Spirit you feel these are my brothers and sisters in Christ and we are all over the world. It's not about us; it's more about Him and being able to serve. I feel that the truest success is being able to discern what God's voice is on your heart and to be able to follow that. But what I love about Magdalen is the singing. It strengthens me. But I do also like that sensation I get with Quakers that's more reflective, it's more contemplative. There certainly is that among Hillsong, but not at the weekly meetings, not in the quiet reflection kind of way, but it's certainly encouraged every day – continuous dialogue with God is encouraged, so every day spend an hour with your Bible.

The Word of God and the Holy Spirit are paramount in Firoozeh's global community of worshippers. As Mark Porter has observed, 'cosmopolitanism has now become an appropriate model for the current reality of everyday interactions with Contemporary Worship Music'.[9] Firoozeh's experience of such worship is highly focused on the revelation of God through Jesus Christ, the Word and the Spirit. The role of music in that context is to communicate and illuminate that revelatory word.

The magisterial reformer Ulrich Zwingli comes to mind as Firoozeh talks about the power of the Spirit in worship and in Bible study. Zwingli emphasised the importance of Scripture above all other authorities, but also the importance of the Spirit above the material world, citing John, chapter six, verse 63: 'It is the Spirit that gives life, the flesh is of no avail.' As we saw in chapter one, Zwingli's extremism led him to abandon music in church altogether, preferring to hear God's word without accompaniment. Such extremes are not necessary for Firoozeh, but she does, it seems, feel part of a global community where ideas are shared, where believers are united in the Spirit worldwide, and where local worshipping communities speak of their faith authentically to each other. The structure of worshipping in a cinema, attending large conferences, engaging in local prayer networks and other groups, and the use of a wide range of modern media are all ways in which people participate, even though there is no permanent building attached to the church. The community may be free-flowing but the sense of common belief is strong. They may not have a permanent home or structure, but the words of Jesus, the stories of the early Church and the theology of the Spirit give a weight and authority to the church.

In this sense, Firoozeh and the Hillsong Church are countercultural to the secularisation of society, Church decline and increased biblical illiteracy. In a post-secular society, religion and belief has not gone away. On the contrary, we live in an age where unbelieving secularists must live alongside, and in dialogue with, those who hold strong scriptural beliefs as well as those whose faith is less defined and on the margins.

CONCLUSION

> The relationship with God, not God as an object to pin down, dissect and endlessly talk about, but as the subject to whom we relate most deeply and peacefully, is the most important relationship of all. God is not the object of our knowledge: God is the cause of wonder.[1]

> This World is not Conclusion.
> A Species stands beyond –
> Invisible, as Music –
> But positive, as Sound –
> It beckons, and it baffles –
> Philosophy, don't know –
> And through a Riddle, at the last –
> Sagacity, must go –
> To guess it, puzzles scholars –
> To gain it, Men have borne
> Contempt of Generations
> And Crucifixion, shown –
> Faith slips – and laughs, and rallies –
> Blushes, if any see –
> Plucks at a twig of Evidence –
> And asks a Vane, the way –
> Much Gesture, from the Pulpit –
> Strong Hallelujahs roll –
> Narcotics cannot still the Tooth
> That nibbles at the soul –[2]

This book has been dedicated to a re-examination of the relationship between music and faith, between modernity and postmodernity, between atheism and belief, between implicit and explicit theology. As such I have emphasised that a life of faith is more about journey than destination. The world is not conclusion, Emily Dickinson wrote, and maybe there should be no conclusion to these conversations, just more conversations. I cannot claim to have reached a definite destination but I can offer some assertions, findings and conjectures.

I have traced a line of continuity between the late medieval experience of religion, through the logocentricism of the Reformation and modern world, to a twenty-first-century Western culture of decline in biblical illiteracy and an incline in the search for non-religious spirituality. I have made a careful distinction between the process or action of faith, deeply embedded in praxis, with propositional, doctrinal belief – between the implicit theology of faith and the explicit theology of the creed. Artists in music and poetry are now discovering a new vocabulary to express spirituality, a language removed from Reformation logocentricism or Enlightenment rationalism. My conclusions have been that music is often a powerful expression of faith because it is not constrained by ideology, reason or cognitive assent. But I also conclude that music can, paradoxically, take us both beyond logocentric rationalism and deeper into an understanding of scripture, doctrine and tradition. It opens up a process and relationality of encounter and experience. That experience may not be explicable in terms of a necessarily known reality but it can both go beyond language *and* illuminate, as well as helping to transcend, our own individualist concerns. As Mark Oakley has suggested in the opening quotation of this conclusion, whatever we call God is known through relationship and experience, and is not simply an object of knowledge:

> Like any relationship of worth it can be the most turbulent. I now see that the opposite of faith is not doubt but certainty, because faith must grow and change ... for many of us this relationship we call faith is an unsettling business that can be reverent one day and rebellious the other, devotional in the morning and deadened by a sense of dereliction by the late hours. Nothing can mask the face of God so much as religion, and yet it is in the beauty and space, the poetry and the ritual of our religion that mere relevance is exchanged for the deeper draw of resonance. That is why poetry keeps my priesthood alive.[3]

For Mark Oakley it is the resonance of poetry within the beautiful space of ritual that keeps his faith alive, rather than the seduction of 'quick clarity and sound-bite theology'.[4] And so it is with music. If the ultimate concern beyond ourselves is what we call God, then He or She is unknowable by means of reason, but music is one incarnational and embodied means of encountering the numinous and the mystical. This intuitive way of knowing is an idea that is growing in today's post-secular world. However, there are those who would object to such a loose and vague definition of faith. Therefore I will place my views within the light of current thinking on the role of music in faith.

THE POST-SECULAR DEBATE

At the outset of this book I mentioned the legacy of Reformation logocentricism which had a significant influence upon the devotional life of believers. We saw how Jeremy Begbie is part of the legacy of this Reformation, which leaves little place for more experiential encounters with the divine through the natural world, including the arts and nature. Begbie's scriptural and doctrinal priorities do not seem to match the experience of so many in the postmodern and post-secular West, where biblical literacy is in decline. In his short exposition on 'Natural Theology and Music,' Begbie criticises Brown's insufficient recognition of 'the way in which the mainstream Church has never replaced Scripture with (or subsumed Scripture seamlessly into) post-biblical tradition.'[5] Begbie prefers Anthony Monti's interpretation of music and natural theology, where God can be best understood through the Trinity, where the revelation of God through Jesus Christ, as revealed in the Scriptures is not replaced by natural encounter but that natural theology 'finds its fulfilment in, rather than substitutes itself for, the revelation of the Triune God.'[6]

David Brown and Gavin Hopps's notion of the 'extravagance' of music, which strays outside limits and is an art open to the divine, has an emphasis upon embodiment, physicality, emotion, imagination and metaphor. As Frank Burch Brown mentions in his foreword to their book, 'open to the divine' means making a move towards a 'mystery that is beyond conceptualization, and that is not reducible to norms susceptible to definite indoctrination.'[7] As such, their work, along with Frank Burch Brown, is critical of Begbie's insistence that the only accessible means to the divine are essentially verbal: 'Repeatedly, Begbie tiptoes up to the point of giving music room for genuine theological innovation, only to back away.'[8]

Begbie prefers to trust 'norms with bounds he sees as pre-determined exclusively by Scripture and by classic Christian doctrine.'[9] For Brown, Burch and Hopps, an encounter with spiritual reality can come through secular as well as religious means.[10]

Brown and Hopps argue in favour of 'the ability of music, for all its context-dependent character, to engender an awareness of something "other" (transcendence), which is at the same time incapable of complete description (ineffable).'[11] That means acknowledging that God can be found, or God can find us, beyond Scripture and in the everyday: 'For some Christians, everything is a matter of faith in the God who is revealed in Scripture, with all else firmly subordinate.'[12] But this is wrong, they argue, because it is not the attitude of the Bible itself, where encounter is often seen through nature, artefacts, music, etc.; because the generosity of God, as witnessed through the incarnation, is part of a much wider divine engagement with the world; because religious decline in the West is not solely due to the hostile attack from atheists, but also because of dogmatic Christians who have refused to acknowledge the 'potentially ubiquitous presence of the divine in the world'; and because 'to assign a role to what lies beyond Scripture need not necessarily be seen as undermining a continuing indispensable biblical contribution.'[13]

Encounter with God beyond the limits of Scripture, for Brown and Hopps, is of course two-way. There is the move from humanity to God and the move from God to humanity. From the human side, music brings order and 'allows insight into a particular way of conceiving the world that presumes a divine ground'; music brings a sense of the sublime and transcendent, 'a sense of wonder' where 'we presume to move beyond the internal object to a sense of majestic presence of a kind encountered in worship'; music brings a sense of immanence 'grounded in ... a profound reality that unites subject and object'; and music brings a sense of being carried into a more-than-human timelessness, a deep peace.[14] In this sense, Begbie is wrong, they say, in his 'attempt to establish in advance of the interpretation an abstract checklist of what constitutes Christian beauty "as such".'[15] For Begbie, music is music created by God and built into creation's capabilities and purposes. But Brown and Hopps consider a post-secular society can involve a process of 're-enchantment' of contemporary culture, which 'involves a widening or more visible diffusion of religious concerns,'[16] while also acknowledging Charles Taylor's description of a weakening of culture, through fragmentation, pluralisation and fragilisation.[17] Post-secularism, for Brown and Hopps, 'announces a fluid and porous "in-between" zone, which repudiates all forms of fundamentalism, whether secular or religious, but which entertains, in a partial or "weakened" sense, the possibility of both perspectives.'[18] This rejection of fundamentalism allows, for Brown and Hopps, music to be an art 'open to the divine' in a more wonderful sense than Begbie will allow. There is a stalemate between Begbie's insistence upon scriptural, Trinitarian, doctrinal interpretation of music and Brown and Hopps's insistence that divine encounter is possible through many and various types of music without the need for doctrinal scrutiny. So how can this impasse be resolved?

MUSIC, FAITH AND BELIEF

A distinction between faith and belief might be a means of starting to build a bridge between these two opposing sides. But not, I think, if we associate belief with absolutism, as Ellis does, then we dismiss all potential for developing faith through explicitly scriptural, revelatory means.[19] For Ellis, 'God is, for us, a matter of potential, not knowledge, and thus profoundly uncertain. Our response to God is thus closely aligned to our response to uncertainty itself. To respect God's holiness is thus to respect uncertainty.'[20] Ellis here dismisses only 'absolute' beliefs, found mostly in churches with the most rigid of dogmatic systems. In that sense, his objections are akin to new atheism and its rejection of a kind of fundamentalist evangelical dogmatic religion, which many Christians do not in fact adhere to or even recognise. The claim of absolutism means that Ellis fails to acknowledge the potential of faith experiences that can lead to a deeper understanding or belief (faith seeking understanding) and also that, within the single Greek word *pistis*, there are multiple meanings, of which trust, confidence, relationship, faith and encounter are a few and belief another that cannot be excluded. Ellis's 'strong agnosticism'[21] and rejection of all kinds of revelation leads to, it seems to me, a deeply impoverished, if not meaningless, Christianity.

While left-hemisphere dominance in the brain and rational thought have dictated the Christian conversation in recent centuries, and indeed more attention needs to be given to the activity of the right hemisphere's ability to 'know' more intuitively and experientially, that does not mean that we should dismiss everything in the realm of reason, logic and positive belief. If we ignore the explicit, then we, like Ellis, will hold the view that God cannot be an objective reality, and is reduced to only a 'glimpse of potential integration within our own experience.'[22] What we end up with is nothing more than an individualist approach to life, echoing Carl Jung's philosophy that 'there is only one way and that is your way. You seek the path? I warn you away from my own. It can also be the wrong way for you. May each go his own way.'[23]

On the other hand, if we acknowledge cognitive propositional belief as important for explicit theological appraisal of music, we might also allow that experiential faith can give insights into a more implicit way of knowing, that is not only complementary to explicit understanding but also essential to its existence. If, for Martin Luther, music was a second greatest gift to creation, after theology, it was because music gives shape to our unvoiced thoughts and, like the natural world around us, as well as our practices and habits of life, demonstrates our implicit and valuable beliefs. If faith is about process and journey, where God is experienced and known in a way beyond verbal expression, then belief is a rational assent to creedal propositions that may be cognitively 'known' but not fully understood. Knowledge of the Trinity, in this life, is an aspiration, not a destination. We might, therefore, express belief in a creed, hoping one day that the mystery of the Trinity will become fully known to us. But through praxis, we live out a faith seeking understanding and, in that journey of seeking, we gradually come to find that we have been found by God. In the Christian faith the only decisive and full disclosure of God's self occurs not in words, laws and doctrines, but in a person: Jesus. In that personification there is surely secured a kind of perceptive openness, occasionality and contextuality about how we may grasp and know God, not least also in the possibilities of fleshly and sensory reality, and especially in music.

SUMMARY OF FINDINGS

In part one of this book, we found that, although European late medieval religion may seemingly have little in common with twenty-first-century spirituality, there are some parallels in terms of biblical illiteracy, the hunger for spiritual nourishment through the arts and the aesthetic, and an emphasis on experience and encounter above textual and intellectual comprehension.

At the beginning of the sixteenth century, the textual and philological concerns of the Renaissance humanists called for greater clarity of text in both musical composition and rendition, which could reveal the Word of God to the greatest effect. For Luther, music revealed a cosmological order at the heart of all things, but for Zwingli music was merely a distraction and could not be trusted as a medium of divine revelation. The jewel of fine singing conveying a knowledge beyond words is thriving in the West and continues to offer largely inclusive access to its mysterious power. But in a post-secular age, as this book has attempted to reveal, that access permeates into all aspects of society, from other art forms, such as art, poetry and literature; sciences, such as evolutionary psychology and neuropsychiatry; through persecution, revolution and the oppression of religion; and to those of all faiths, and of none, from atheists and agnostics to Christian evangelists.

Ronald Blythe and Elisabeth Dutton helped us to see that hymns, psalms and spiritual songs connect our society with our cultural heritage of faith. They are transmitters of meaning to believers and non-believers, with their explicit theology carried by the implicit resonance of musical faith.

Janet Boulton's extraordinary connections of visual art with liturgical experience and musical sound create a wonderful symbiosis – art responding to art – with each discipline contributing, in her work, to the others in a responsive and relational way. The conversation with Janet revealed a fascination with light and darkness (*Tenebrae*) borne out of personal experience and religious conversion. Her 'Eye Music' and *Tenebrae* pictures resonate with the pain and joy of the world and with the sound of God's presence within the ambiguity of life's journey. Music floats across the paper into the liturgical space in which prayer is offered. Janet's personal encounter with the darkness and the revelation of God's light and love in the present reality of the liturgy is evident in her art. Janet's art teaches us lessons, in today's post-secular society, of how to live with the tension of powerlessness and struggles for existence alongside the joyous fruitfulness of faith and creative endeavour, especially when engaged in interdisciplinary collaboration. The mixture of manuscript notation, penned by anonymous monastics long ago, sung by clerics and clerks in churches and chapels as part of devotional worship and Janet's modern-day artworks links together centuries of traditions in Western Christianity, including artists, musicians, theologians and priests, and brings them together in the life of one human being and her response of faith.

In part two we turned to science and society, finding sacred music to be of great interest, not only in objective scientific terms but in personal and subjective ways. Robin Dunbar's work helps to demonstrate that, although the printed word has dominated society for many generations, the search for spiritual encounter and relationship through non-verbal means is as strong as ever. Robin's own enthusiasm for sacred music is echoed by his scientific findings that communal singing, even with people one does not know, has a beneficial effect on mood, brain activity and on social cohesion.

June Boyce-Tillman and Sarah Morgan's work on the community choir revealed that, for many people today, the social bonding which used to take place in the parish church choir, in some cases, has migrated to the village hall or other location for the local community choir. But for many thriving cathedrals and chapels, the professionalised choir is still the norm and the positive psychological and social effects of participation, whether vocally, as a musician, or as a listener, is a provable scientific phenomenon related to our evolutionary past. Such research refutes the notion that music is an added extra to nature with no servable purpose (auditory cheesecake, as Steven Pinker put it). On the contrary, communal singing and dancing, especially within religious ritual, has been at the heart of human experience from the beginning and continues to provide strong socially cohesive effects.

Quinton Deeley's research on religious ritual, trance states and music took the scientific conversation one stage further and into the realm of neuropsychiatry. Quinton's research involved measuring brain activity in people who are in trance states. As such he is interested in the mental and physical processes involved in our human experience of encounter and relationship, with the world around us and with each other, as well as experiences that shape our perception and reception of reality. Music, when used in ritual, is a psychological and neurological stimulant. In the religious context, music is part of a more powerful and persuasive experience than mere cognitive belief alone.

Both Dunbar and Deeley do not assent to any religious belief and yet both acknowledge the value of faith in a post-secular culture and how music is a universal characteristic of human existence, experience, encounter and relationships. This is true, even when faith, and the music of faith, becomes the object of persecution in a society that is ideologically opposed to religion. My exploration of communism and sacred music, through the experiences of Michael Bourdeaux and Balázs Déri, revealed the irrepressibility of music and faith in society, regardless of the official state politics. Michael's knowledge of Soviet Russia demonstrated how choirs, churches and monasteries kept sacred music alive within the liturgy of Orthodox Christianity. Music helped people keep faith, if secretly, against an opposing ideology. Love of music and a sense of faith in something beyond ourselves is impossible to eliminate. We reach out for the transcendent, numinous and unknowable experience with intuitive faith. Balázs Déri's work in Hungary showed how sacred music could thrive publicly in churches and in concert halls, especially the distinctive sound of plainchant in his Schola Hungarica choir. He learned his sacred music as a boy and continued to be employed as a church musician through the 1960s and '70s. In today's Hungary he looks forward to greater progress for liturgical reform revival in his country. Culture, art, poetry and music remained valued sources of hope even in oppressive communist countries.

In the third part of the book, I turned to consider the value of sacred music for those with different beliefs, from atheism to evangelicalism. The value of music was evident when we explored the importance of aesthetic and cultural connections to faith for non-believers, especially through music. The particularly aggressive form of atheism that attacks what it sees as religious belief systems, namely new atheism, can be dismissed, once it is acknowledged that religion is more often not just about belief but about communal practice. In the light of this, new atheist argument falls down. John Gray offers us alternative definitions of atheism that are much closer to the world of faith, such as an atheism that denies a creator-god yet does not replace monotheistic concepts with an unrealistically elevated and pious view of humanity, and an atheism that is close to the apophatic or negative theology of

Eastern Christian thought – the kind that asserts the unknowability, mystery and ineffability of the divine. It is into this realm of the unsayable, with regard to divinity, that sacred music speaks so keenly.

The phenomenon of 'belonging without believing,' as promoted by Davie, Day and Mountford, explains how many today are connected with church for cultural, historical, aesthetic, moral and social reasons, but not necessarily because of religious belief. I would suggest that this is far from being a recent development. Music is at the heart of this 'Anglo-Choral' world of architecture, art and incense, and was so long before Reformation modernity. But equally the sacred in music is being consumed outside the church by the concert-goer and the iTunes listener. This Spinoza-esque atheism revolves around the ineffable transcendent mystery of a non-creating God, of whom we can say nothing. What we cannot say concerning a non-existent God (as an atheist), we likewise cannot say for a God in which we have faith (as an apophatic Christian). The distinction between sacred and secular is so thin as to become invisible.

Neither are science and rationality opposed to this search for the unknowable, for they can positively promote an exploration of the world where truth and beauty can be found in the process of encounter, experience and relationship. In the mathematics of music, relationship between melody, rhythm and harmony are communicated through the relationship between composer, performer and listener, and resonate with a deep sense of physical coherence in the universe which, paradoxically, is seemingly able to lift us out of the material plain to a more numinous level of experience. The process of faith, if we are to understand it properly, involves encounter with the world around us and each other, has nothing to fear from scientific exploration, especially the fundamentally physical and mathematical discipline of music, whose essence is to be found deep within the origins of the universe.

For those who do declare a Christian belief, the spiritual experience encountered through music is not a mere decoration to the Christian life but *is* the Christian life. For clergy Nicholas Brown, Christopher Campling and Nick Baines, contact with the divine is made just as effectively through musical revelation as through doctrinal cognition. Nicholas Brown sees music, particularly within the liturgy, as a means to something greater than itself – a form of communication that leads to an experience of God. Christopher Campling sees a close connection between music and prayer, and music as the perfect sacrament. The blend of prayer, sacrament, faith and music produces a spiritual experience, wherever those elements are present. Nick Baines's definition of the role of the Church as a place in which we have the space to find that we have been found by God expresses the essence of how music helps people to discover the divine and to realise that the divine has found them.

In my final chapter, I spoke to two lay Christians of contrasting faiths and backgrounds. Shanika Ranasinghe spoke openly about her difficulty in connecting with God in the way that she was once able to do. She also made a clear distinction between the performance of sacred music in secular and liturgical contexts, the latter of which provided, for Shanika, greater spiritual nourishment. Shanika's discovery of classical choral music, plainsong and Anglican liturgy made a significant impact upon her psyche and spiritual life. Through musical and intellectual development Shanika continues to seek spiritual nourishment in liturgical music and hopes to encounter the divine again.

Such an encounter is not so elusive for Firoozeh Willans, with her strong conviction of belief, non-denominational religious stance and international outlook. The Word of God, the Holy Spirit and a sense of a global community of worshippers are all important in helping Firoozeh to authentically articulate her faith. The community, music and worship of Hillsong Church helps her in this mission.

St Paul tells us that the righteous are justified to God by faith – or should that be belief? The distinction has been made throughout this book. Some of those I interviewed, such as Firoozeh, have strong beliefs and convictions in the fundamentals of Christian doctrine. For others, faith is more fluid. But if faith is largely characterised by its properties of praxis, then our justification to God – of being put right with God – is brought about by how we relate to the divine, rather than what we say we believe about God. Relationship is about process, experience, encounter and time. Music, and especially sacred choral music, is in many ways the embodiment of all those things, as it brings composers, performers, listeners and worshippers into a linear, chronological process of encounter and community. If the greatest commandments are to love God and to love one another, then perhaps music is the best place to start that process of love, with each other and in search of the unknown divine, the source of all love.

A LIFE OF FAITH

I began with a true human story of love, which was both a reflection of divine love and also a means of divine discovery. At the heart of this book, through the conversations and the theological reflections upon them, is a simple question that is difficult to answer: how do we know, encounter or experience the divine? For many a reform-minded church throughout the Western world the answer will lie in the revelation of God's self-giving love to the world, through its creation, and its subsequent redemption of fallen humanity, through Jesus Christ, as related to us in the Scriptures. But for a growing number of theologians, philosophers, clergy, laity and those on the margins of religious experience, music offers a connection with the inexplicable, numinous mystery of human existence. My distinction between faith and belief becomes an important one in a post-secular, post-biblical world, where the process of 'faithing' is not the same as believing. The process of moving towards the spiritual life, through faith, *can* be hampered by overzealous preaching that God is *only* revealed to humanity through the scripturally based doctrine of the Trinity. A truth that we are bidden to *believe* rather than encounter. As David Brown reflects:

> Yet, if God in Christ allowed himself to be battered by human beings on the cross, why should we be so hesitant about the possibility that God might also be willing to open his presence to understanding – and misunderstanding – everywhere, a range of experiences complementing and interacting with one another, instead of their always needing to await the pronouncements of theologians on their legitimacy or otherwise?[24]

But, as Rowan Williams has opined, if we bypass revelation through the Scriptures we might end up avoiding doctrine altogether. As Wittgenstein asserted, the Gospels come with an imperative: 'But the question is, what makes us able to learn to recognize such an imperative, let alone respond to it?'[25] I have suggested, in the opening of this book, that an implicit, intuitive knowledge of God is not only just as valid as a logocentric explicit knowledge but also an essential complement to and illumination of it. The implicit has more in common with a life of faith than the explicit has with an acknowledgement of cognisant belief. Where we begin our exploration of the divine, or where we go to discover that God has already found us, is not dogmatically fixed, as Williams writes, 'the challenge to start from somewhere other than claims to revelation is not necessarily nonsensical or impious.'[26]

We may believe that God is Father, Son and Holy Spirit, but to 'know' this as truth needs a great deal more than blind belief. It requires experience, encounter and relationship with that self-sacrificial, self-giving, reconciling love. So is Begbie's insistence upon Trinitarian doctrine to scrutinise and explain the experience of music necessarily a constraint? I do not think so. But doctrinal belief can only be a small vocalisation or response of 'Yes' to a much deeper experience of the unfathomable mystery of the love of God. This experience must be *lived* – it must be *faithed*.

Thus, I am a long way from suggesting that we need to adopt a secularised version of an ineffable, numinous or mysterious encounter which, as Meerten ter Borg has argued, is only the use of the imagination and, while it might help us to hope and plan for the future, it ultimately makes humans 'aware of the ultimate hopelessness of their situation.'[27] A life of faith, rather, leads us to know that there is more than imagined hope to human experience – a reality of the divine who is willing to encounter humanity everywhere, not in a vague imagined transcendence of an unknowable otherness, but in a genuine immanence, where God can act through the natural world that He has created. There are many examples of faith encounter with God through music, and I hope this book has demonstrated some of them. For the 'Word of God cannot be grasped ... It can only be held lightly and poetically.'[28] We must be attuned to both *Scientia* and *Sapientia*, both rational knowledge and intuitive wisdom. This wisdom is often found in communal experience of music, whether through psalms or hymns, which can encapsulate Christian spiritual experience and historical understanding.

Music and faith are so closely aligned that the experience of one can evoke the other, or the two can be virtually indistinguishable. Music deepens, nourishes and enhances faith. It can also challenge and disturb our faith. Faith enriches music, accompanies it and embraces it. Music and faith are lived out together in time and space, in our bodies, minds and spirits. Music can give insights into the divine through embodied process that cannot be experienced through belief alone. Religious practice, ritual, performance and engagement are all part of the story, and music is part of a bigger picture of divine gift and encounter through nature, a gift that God continues to give and one that is available everywhere.

I end this exploration with a poem by Seamus Heaney that encapsulates something of the importance of listening, of fresh encounter with sound that takes hold of us, with a world of surprise and joy, and how, through the ordinary, natural world around us, we can be made rich in the experience of our senses and transported heavenwards.

THE RAINSTICK BY SEAMUS HEANEY

Upend the rainstick and what happens next
Is a music that you never would have known
To listen for. In a cactus stalk

Downpour, sluice-rush, spillage and backwash
Come flowing through. You stand there like a pipe
Being played by water, you shake it again lightly

And diminuendo runs through all its scales
Like a gutter stopping trickling. And now here comes
A sprinkle of drops out of the freshened leaves,

Then subtle little wets off grass and daisies;
Then glitter-drizzle, almost-breaths of air.
Upend the stick again. What happens next

Is undiminished for having happened once.
Twice, ten, a thousand times before.
Who cares if the music that transpires

Is the fall of grit or dry seeds through a cactus?
You are like a rich man entering heaven
Through the ear of a shower. Listen now again.[29]

NOTES

INTRODUCTION

1. Pope Benedict XVI, 'General Audience in the Paul VI Hall,' Vatican City, 21 May 2008.
2. M. Symmons Roberts, 'Contemporary Poetry and Belief,' in P. Robinson (ed.), *The Oxford Handbook of Contemporary British and Irish Poetry* (Oxford, 2013), pp. 694–706. Here at p. 702.
3. Ibid.
4. R. Dawkins, *Science in the Soul: Selected Writings of a Passionate Rationalist*, ed. G. Somerscales (London, 2017), pp. 212–13.
5. U. Eco, *Art and Beauty in the Middle Ages*, trans. H. Bredin (New Haven, 1958, reprinted 1986), p. 4.
6. C. Page, 'Music and the Beyond,' in F. Stone-Davis (ed.), *Music and Transcendence* (Farnham, 2015), pp. 13–21. Here at pp. 13 and 21.
7. D. Brown and G. Hopps, *The Extravagance of Music* (London, 2018), p. 1 and *passim*. See also the introduction by Frank Burch Brown, p. v.
8. Ibid.
9. G. Steiner, *Real Presences* (London, 1989), pp. 216–17; P. Bohlman, 'Is All Music Religious?,' in J.M. Spencer (ed.), *Theomusicology. A Special Issue of Black Sacred Music. A Journal of Theomusicology* (Durham, NC, 1994), pp. 3–12. Here at p. 9; J. Begbie, *Resounding Truth: Christian Wisdom in the World of Music* (Grand Rapids, MI, 2007), pp. 16–17.
10. J. Boyce Tillman, *Experiencing Music – Restoring the Spiritual: Music as Well Being* (Bern, 2016), p. 49.
11. Giles Fraser, *The Guardian*, 28 February 2014.
12. https://www.theguardian.com/world/2018/mar/21/christianity-non-christian-europe-young-people-survey-religion, accessed 12 October 2018; http://www.biblesociety.org.uk/uploads/content/projects/Bible-Society-Report_030214_final_.pdf, pp. 11–14, accessed 12 October 2018.
13. D. MacCulloch, *Silence: A Christian History* (London, 2013), p. 231.
14. Sarah Coakley's *God, Sexuality and the Self: An Essay on 'The Trinity'* (Cambridge, 2013) began a move towards a more pastoral, applied and practical theology, in which the practices and habits of life are treated as demonstrative and revelatory of actual belief. My thanks to James Crockford for this observation.
15. M. Percy, 'Afterword: Theology and Music in Conversation,' in M. Ingalls, C. Landau and T. Wagner (eds), *Christian Congregational Music: Performance, Identity and Experience* (Farnham, 2013), pp. 217–22. Here at p. 217.
16. In Charlotte Brontë's *Jane Eyre*.
17. See pp. 14–16, 169–75.
18. I. Mobsby, *God Unknown: The Trinity in Contemporary Spirituality and Mission* (Norwich, 2008), p. xii.
19. Ibid., p. xiii.

20. I. Mobsby, 'The Place of New Monasticism in a Post-Secular Culture': lecture delivered at the *Diocesan Spirituality Advisors' Conference*, Launde Abbey, Leicestershire, 10 April 2018.
21. N. Ammerman, *Sacred Stories, Spiritual Tribes: Finding Religion in Everyday Life* (New York, 2013), quoted in I. Mobsby, 'The Place of New Monasticism in a Post-Secular Culture'; N.T. Ammerman, 'Spiritual But Not Religious? Beyond Binary Choices in the Study of Religion', *Journal for the Scientific Study of Religion* 52 (2013), pp. 258–78. Here at p. 258 and *passim*.
22. Mobsby, *God Unknown*, p. 1.
23. Ibid.
24. Brian Mountford's *Christian Atheist: Belonging without Believing* (Winchester UK, Washington USA, 2010) explores the continued appeal of 'Christian' arts without the need for belief at all. See chapter seven below on 'Music, Faith and Atheism'.
25. Mobsby, *God Unknown*, pp. 1–2.
26. R. Williams, 'Keeping Time', in *Open to Judgement: Sermons and Addresses* (London, 1994), pp. 247–50. Here at p. 249.
27. We will consider natural theology in more detail below, pp. 26–9.
28. Mobsby, *God Unknown*, p. 2.
29. J. Arnold, *Sacred Music in Secular Society, passim*. See also Brown and Hopps, *Extravagance of Music* and F. Burch Brown, *Religious Aesthetics: A Theological Study of Making and Meaning* (Basingstoke, 1990), among others.
30. J.D.G. Dunn, *The Living Word* (Minneapolis, 2nd edn, 2009), chapter two: 'The Gospels as Oral Tradition', pp. 21–36; Mobsby, *God Unknown*, p. 7.
31. Ibid.
32. P. Rollins, *The Orthodox Heretic and Other Impossible Tales* (London, 2009), p. xi.
33. Ibid., pp. 12–13.
34. P. Rollins, *How (Not) to Speak of God* (London, 2006), p. 12.
35. M. McCarthy, 'Spirituality in a Postmodern Era', in J. Woodward and S. Pattison (eds), *The Blackwell Reader in Pastoral and Practical Theology* (Oxford, 2000), pp. 199–200. See also B. Quash, 'Making the Most of Time', *Studies in Christian Ethics* 15 (2002), pp. 97–114.
36. M. Zwerin, 'A Lethal Measurement', in R. Kostelanetz (ed.), *John Cage* (New York, 1970), p. 166.
37. J. Begbie, *Redeeming Transcendence in the Arts: Bearing Witness to the Triune God* (London, 2018), p. 3. See also Begbie, *Resounding Truth*, pp. 16–17.
38. Begbie, *Redeeming Transcendence*, p. 111.
39. Ibid., p. 117.
40. D. Brown, 'Review of J. Begbie, *Redeeming Transcendence in the Arts: Bearing Witness to the Triune God* (London, 2018)' in *Church Times*, 14 September 2018, p. 28. See also P. Sherry, *The Spirit of Beauty: An Introduction to Theological Aesthetics* (Oxford, 1992), who argues that a 'Trinitarian, and especially Pneumatological, approach to artistic endeavour can open up a spaciousness about attention, encounter, revelation, relationality that combats a Christo-Logo decisiveness'. I quote James Crockford's analysis here.
41. Brown, 'Review of Begbie, *Redeeming Transcendence*', p. 28.
42. See below, pp. 9, 13–16, 22–3, 146, 155, 221–3, 229.

43. https://www.collinsdictionary.com/dictionary/english/music, accessed 15 March 2018.
44. D. Aldridge, 'Music, Consciousness and Altered States', in D. Aldridge and J. Fachner (eds), *Music and Altered States: Consciousness, Transcendence, Therapy and Addictions* (London and Philadelphia, 2006), p. 9.
45. Arnold, *Sacred Music in Secular Society*, pp. 4–11.
46. E. Durkheim, *The Elementary Forms of the Religious Life: A Study in Religious Sociology* (London, 1915; Oxford, 2001), p. 47.
47. Dr Paula Gooder, talk given at Lambeth Palace, 21 March 2018. My thanks to Paula for the talk and for her subsequent help.
48. E.P. Sanders, *Paul: A Very Short Introduction* (Oxford, 2001), pp. 54–5.
49. I am extremely grateful to Dr Spencer Klavan, of Magdalen College, for his assistance with this knotty problem and for his helpful and expert ideas.
50. Spencer Klavan, Oxford, 25 May 2018.
51. O. Barfield, *Poetic Diction: A Study in Meaning* (London, 1928), pp. 62–3.
52. Ibid., pp. 72–3.
53. See https://boginsdotcom.files.wordpress.com/2012/09/feeling-into-words.pdf, accessed 14 October 2018; M. Guite, *Faith, Hope and Poetry* (London, 2012); M. Oakley, *The Splash of Words: Believing in Poetry* (London, 2016), which explores why poetry is essential to faith and how scripture, liturgy and theology are 'poetry in motion'.
54. A. Brown and L. Woodhead, *That was the Church that Was: How the English Church Lost the English People* (London, 2016), p. 67.
55. Ibid.
56. Ibid., p. 68.
57. K.A. Appiah, *BBC Radio 4 Reith Lectures 2016: Mistaken Identities: Creed, Country, Colour, Culture*. Lecture 1: Creed.
58. Ibid.
59. J. Begbie, *Redeeming Transcendence in the Arts*; Brown and Hopps, *The Extravagance of Music*.
60. Begbie, *Redeeming Transcendence*, p. 3.
61. Ibid., p. 4.
62. Boyce-Tillman, 'Postlude', in Morgan and Boyce-Tillman, *A River Rather than a Road*, p. 154.
63. Begbie, *Redeeming Transcendence*, p. 15.
64. See below, pp. 14, 22, 49, 171, 206, 222.
65. V. Jankélévitch, *Music and the Ineffable*, trans. C. Abbate (Princeton, 2003).
66. Begbie, *Redeeming Transcendence*, pp. 52–6.
67. Ibid., p. 117.
68. Ibid., pp. 118, 120 and 131.
69. Ibid., p. 153.
70. Ibid., p. 184.
71. Ibid.
72. My thanks go to James Crockford for this analysis.
73. Brown, 'Review of Begbie, *Redeeming Transcendence*', p. 28.
74. G. Davie, *Religion in Britain since 1945: Believing without Belonging* (Oxford, 1994), p. 3.
75. C. Taylor, *A Secular Age* (Cambridge, MA, 2007), p. 514.

76. G. Davie, *Religion in Britain since 1945*, pp. 69–70.
77. C. Taylor, *A Secular Age*, p. 522, referring to G. Davie, *Europe: The Exceptional Case* (London, 2002), p. 46.
78. Taylor, *A Secular Age*, p. 606.
79. Ibid., pp. 605–15.
80. Ibid., p. 712.
81. R.M. Ellis, *The Christian Middle Way: The case against Christian Belief but for Christian Faith* (Winchester UK, Washington USA, 2018), p. 5.
82. Ibid., p. 7.
83. Ibid., p. 19.
84. Taylor, *A Secular Age*, p. 772.
85. Ibid., p. 3.
86. Ibid., p. 43; J. Boyce-Tillman, *Experiencing Music*, p. 28.
87. Boyce-Tillman, *Experiencing Music*, p. 28. The term 'post-secular' has been credited to Jürgen Habermas.
88. R. Williams, *Faith in the Public Square* (London, 2012), p. 13, quoted in Boyce-Tillman, *Experiencing Music*, p. 28.
89. Boyce-Tillman, *Experiencing Music*, p. 28.
90. M. Warner et al., 'Editors' Introduction,' in *Varieties of Secularism in a Secular Age* (Cambridge, MA, 2010), p. 9, quoted in M. Moberg, K. Granholm and P. Nynäs, 'Trajectories of Post-Secular Complexity: An Introduction,' in P. Nynäs, M. Lassander and T. Utriainen (eds), *Post-Secular Society* (New Brunswick, 2012; new edn 2015), pp. 1–25. Here at p. 2.
91. The United States cannot be called post-secular as religion, especially Christianity, has continued to be a strong cultural and political force throughout the twentieth and twenty-first centuries. J. Habermas, 'Religion in the Public Sphere,' *European Journal of Philosophy* 14 (2006), pp. 1–25; J. Habermas, 'Notes on Post-Secular Society,' *New Perspectives Quarterly* 25 (2008), pp. 17–29, cited in M. Moberg, K. Granholm and P. Nynäs, 'Trajectories of Post-Secular Complexity,' p. 4.
92. Ibid.
93. Ibid., quoting Habermas, 'Notes on Post-Secular Society,' p. 20.
94. Moberg, Granholm and Nynäs, 'Trajectories of Post-Secular Complexity,' p. 4.
95. Ibid., p. 5.
96. Ibid., quoting M. Dillon, 'Can Post-Secular Society Tolerate Religious Differences?,' *Sociology of Religion* 71 (2010), p. 146.
97. Moberg, Granholm and Nynäs, 'Trajectories of Post-Secular Complexity,' p. 1.
98. B.S. Turner, 'Religion in a Post-Secular Society,' in *The New Blackwell Companion to the Sociology of Religion*, ed. B.S. Turner (Chichester, 2010), p. 650, quoted in Moberg, Granholm and Nynäs, 'Trajectories of Post-Secular Complexity,' p. 6.
99. Dillon, 'Can Post-Secular Society Tolerate Religious Differences?,' p. 142, quoted in Moberg, Granholm and Nynäs, 'Trajectories of Post-Secular Complexity,' p. 7; Turner, 'Religion in a Post-Secular Society,' p. 658.
100. R. Niebuhr, *Christ and Culture* (New York, 1951), p. 32.
101. A. Thomson, *Culture in a Post-Secular Context: Theological Possibilities in Milbank, Barth and Bediako* (Eugene, OR, 2014), pp. vii–viii.
102. G. Ward, *True Religion* (Oxford, 2003), p. vii, quoted in Thomson, *Culture in a Post-Secular Context*, p. 62.

103. Thomson, *Culture in a Post-Secular Context*, pp. 91–2.
104. W.A. Dyrness, *Poetic Theology: God and the Poetics of Everyday Life* (Grand Rapids, MI, 2010).
105. Thomson, *Culture in a Post-Secular Context*, p. 269.
106. Ibid., pp. 269–70.
107. Ibid., p. 270.
108. Ibid., p. 278.
109. Symmons Roberts, 'Contemporary Poetry and Belief', p. 696.
110. David Jones, 'Religion and the Muses', in idem, *Epoch and Artist* (London, 1941), p. 103; see also D. Jones, *The Anathemata* (London, 1952), p. 15; R. Harris, *The Image of Christ in Modern Art* (Farnham, 2013), p. 5.
111. Symmons Roberts, 'Contemporary Poetry and Belief', p. 696.
112. P. Blond (ed.), *Post-Secular Philosophy: Between Philosophy and Theology* (London, 1998), p. 9, quoted in Symmons Roberts, 'Contemporary Poetry and Belief', p. 696.
113. Ibid., p. 702.
114. Ibid., pp. 703–4.
115. Ibid., p. 704.
116. I. McGilchrist, *The Master and his Emissary* (New Haven and London, 2012), pp. 92–102 and *passim*.
117. I am grateful to James Crockford for these words, Oxford, October 2018.
118. Ibid.
119. Brown, 'Review of *Redeeming Transcendence*', p. 28.
120. Begbie, *Redeeming Transcendence*, p. 15.
121. Ibid., p. 52, citing V. Jankélévitch, *Music and the Ineffable*, trans. C. Abbatte (Princeton, 2003).
122. Begbie, *Redeeming Transcendence*, pp. 37–8.
123. J. Begbie, 'Foreword' to S. Guthrie, *Creator Spirit: The Holy Spirit and the Art of Becoming Human* (Grand Rapids, MI, 2011), p. vii.
124. Guthrie, *Creator Spirit*, p. xiv.
125. Ibid., p. xv.
126. Ibid., pp. xv–xvi. For the term 'humanization' Guthrie borrows from D. Staniloae, *The Experience of God: Orthodox Dogmatic Theology*, vol. 2, *The World: Creation and Deification*, trans. I. Ionata and R. Berringer (Brookline, MA, 2005).
127. Guthrie, *Creator Spirit*, p. xvi. See also Sherry, *The Spirit of Beauty*.
128. J. Boyce-Tillman, 'Prelude', in S. Morgan and J. Boyce-Tillman, *A River Rather than a Road: The Community Choir as Spiritual Experience* (Oxford; Bern, 2016), p. 25.
129. J. Boyce-Tillman, 'Postlude', in Morgan and Boyce-Tillman, *A River Rather than a Road*, p. 154.
130. Ibid.
131. R. Wuthnow, *After Heaven: Spirituality in America since the 1950s* (Berkeley, 1998), p. viii, quoted in Ibid., p. 156.
132. J. Boyce-Tillman, 'Postlude', in Morgan and Boyce-Tillman, *A River Rather than a Road*, p. 157.
133. K. Barth, *Theology and Church, Shorter Writings 1920–1928*, trans. L. Pettibone Smith (London, 1962), p. 157, quoted in Guthrie, *Creator Spirit*, pp. 6–7.
134. Ibid., p. 7.
135. Ibid., p. 16.

136. R. Scruton, *The Aesthetics of Music* (Oxford, 1997), p. 364; Guthrie, *Creator Spirit*, p. 17. See also R. Scruton, 'Music and the Transcendental', in Stone-Davis, *Music and Transcendence*, pp. 75–84.
137. R. Rohr, Blog, 10 January 2018.
138. M. Percy, 'Afterword: Theology and Music in Conversation', p. 217.
139. Ibid., p. 218.
140. Ibid.
141. D. MacCulloch, *A History of Christianity* (London, 2009), p. 9.
142. Ibid., p. 220.
143. A.W. Hall, 'Natural Theology in the Middle Ages', in R. Re Manning, J. Hedley Brooke and F. Watts (eds), *The Oxford Handbook of Natural Theology* (Oxford, 2013), p. 57.
144. Ibid.
145. S. Mandelbrote, 'Early Modern Natural Theologies', in *Handbook of Natural Theology*, p. 91.
146. Gifford Lectures website: http://www.giffordlecture.org, accessed 14 September 2018.
147. K. Barth, *The Knowledge of God and the Service of God according to the Teaching of the Reformation* (Gifford Lectures, 1937–8; Eugene, OR, 2005), pp. 8–9.
148. J. Barr, *Biblical Faith and Natural Theology* (Gifford Lectures, 1991; Oxford, 1993), pp. 2–3.
149. Quoted in R.T. Holder, 'Natural Theology', Faraday Paper, *The Faraday Institute for Science and Religion* 19 (April 2016), pp. 1–4. Here at p. 2.
150. Ibid., p. 3.
151. Ibid., p. 4.
152. Ibid.
153. As in the works of the sixth-century Syrian writer Dionysius the Areopagite. Explored in J. Arnold, *Dean John Colet of St Paul's: Humanism and Early Tudor Reform* (London, 2007), pp. 25–78.
154. Begbie, *Redeeming Transcendence*, p. 118.
155. Brown and Hopps, *The Extravagance of Music*, p. 9, citing P. Bannister, 'Kenosis in Contemporary Music and Postmodern Philosophy', *Contemporary Music and Spirituality*, ed. R. Scholl and S. van Maas (London, 2017), pp. 54–80. Here at pp. 56–7.
156. S. van Maas, *The Reinvention of Religious Music: Olivier Messiaen's Breakthrough Toward the Beyond* (New York, 2009), pp. 32–3 and 116.
157. J. Shepherd and K. Devine (eds), *The Routledge Reader on the Sociology of Music* (New York and London, 2015). The passing reference to religion is on p. 37.
158. P.B. Clarke (ed.), *The Oxford Handbook of the Sociology of Religion* (Oxford, 2009; paperback, 2011).

CHAPTER ONE

1. St Benedict.
2. Cardinal John Henry Newman, *The Dream of Gerontius*.
3. Brown and Hopps, *The Extravagance of Music*, p. 10, and pp. 10–24 for the whole section.
4. J. Begbie, *Resounding Truth*, p. 79.
5. Ibid., p. 80.
6. Ibid., p. 80, quoting Plato, *Timaeus*, 47d.

7. Ibid.
8. Ibid., p. 82.
9. J. Hankins, 'Humanism and Music in Italy', in A.M.B. Berger and J. Rodin (eds), *The Cambridge History of Fifteenth-Century Music* (Cambridge, 2015), pp. 231–62. Here at pp. 233 and 238.
10. Ibid., citing T. Mathiesen, 'Greek Views of Music', in W. Strunk and L. Treitler (eds), *Source Readings in Music History*, rev. edn (New York; London, 1998), p. 48 n. 4.
11. F. MacDiarmaid, '*De Utilitate Cantorum*: Unitive Aspects of Singing in Early Christian Thought', *Anglican Theological Review* 100 (2018), pp. 291–309. Here at p. 296, quoting Aristides Quintilianus, *On Music* 2.6.
12. MacDiarmaid, '*De Utilitate Cantorum*', p. 5, quoting Aristides Quintilianus, *On Music* 3.18, paraphrasing Plato, *Republic*, 403C.
13. MacDiarmaid, '*De Utilitate Cantorum*', p. 5.
14. N. van Deusen, '*Musica, De*', in *Augustine through the Ages: An Encyclopedia*, ed. A.D. Fitzgerald et al. (Grand Rapids, MI, 1999), pp. 574–7. Here at p. 575, quoted in Begbie, *Resounding Truth*, p. 84.
15. Begbie, *Resounding Truth*, p. 84.
16. Augustine, *Confessions*, 10:33, 49–50.
17. Brown and Hopps, *The Extravagance of Music*, p. 12, quoting Augustine in J. McKinnon (ed.), *Music in Early Christian Literature* (Cambridge, 1987), pp. 156–7.
18. Augustine, *De Musica*, 6:14–46 (cf. 6:4–7); C. Harrison, 'Augustine and the Art of Music', in J.S. Begbie and S.R. Guthrie (eds), *Resonant Witness: Conversations between Music and Theology* (Grand Rapids, MI, 2011), pp, 27–45. Here at pp. 31–9 and 45.
19. Ibid., pp. 31–2; B.L. Horne, 'A Civitas of Sound: On Luther and Music', *Theology* 88 (1985), pp. 21–8.
20. Augustine, *Confessions*, 9.6.14, quoted in Begbie, *Resounding Truth*, p. 86.
21. Augustine, *On Psalm 149*.
22. Augustine, *Confessions*, 10.33.50.
23. Harrison, 'Augustine and the Art of Music', pp. 41–2, and Begbie, *Resounding Truth*, p. 86.
24. Augustine, *Confessions* 10.33.49, quoted in Harrison, 'Augustine and the Art of Music', p. 42, and Begbie, *Resounding Truth*, pp. 320–1 n. 36.
25. C. Bower, 'Transmission of Ancient Music Theory into the Middle Ages', pp. 136–67. Here at p. 147, quoted in Begbie, *Resounding Truth*, p. 88.
26. Ibid., p. 89.
27. Ibid., p. 94.
28. Eco, *Art and Beauty*, p. 17.
29. Amalarius, *On the Liturgy*, 3.3, trans. Eric Knibbs. I am very grateful to Dr Matthew Cheung-Salisbury for his insights on Amalarius and Durandus. See M. Cheung-Salisbury, *Worship in Medieval England* (Leeds, 2018) for a fuller exploration of medieval liturgical music and ideas.
30. Ibid., 3.11.
31. Ibid., 3.21.
32. *Rationale Divinorum Officiorum* V.1, trans. Timothy Thibodeau (Colombia, 2007).
33. Ibid., Durandus (V.2.v).
34. Eco, *Art and Beauty*, p. 118.
35. Ibid.

36. E. Duffy, *The Stripping of the Altars* (New Haven and London, 1992), p. 4.
37. Ibid., p. 37.
38. Ibid., p. 38.
39. Ibid., p. 52.
40. G. Richardson, 'Craft Guilds and Christianity in Late-Medieval England: A Rational Choice Analysis,' *Rationality and Society* 17 (2005), pp. 139–89 [hereafter Richardson, 'Craft Guilds']. Here at p. 164.
41. R.N. Swanson, 'Medieval Liturgy as Theatre: The Props,' in *The Church and the Arts*, ed. Wood., 239–54. Here at p. 239.
42. Ibid., p. 240.
43. Ibid., p. 241.
44. Ibid., p. 245; J.C. Cox, *Catalogue of the Muniments and Manuscript Books pertaining to the Dean and Chapter of Lichfield; Analysis of the Magnum Registrum Album; Catalogue of the Muniments of the Lichfield Vicars = Collections for a History of Staffordshire*, 6/ii (1886), p. 201, Shrewsbury Public Library, MS 2 [SPL], fol. 92r.
45. SPL, fol. 93r.
46. Swanson, 'Medieval Liturgy as Theatre,' p. 249.
47. Ibid., p. 251; Cox, *Catalogue of the Muniments*, pp. 205–6, 212–13.
48. Swanson, 'Medieval Liturgy as Theatre,' p. 253.
49. Interview with Elisabeth Dutton.
50. Swanson, 'Medieval Liturgy as Theatre,' p. 253.
51. J. Muller, *The Letters of Stephen Gardiner* (Cambridge, 1933), p. 488.
52. K. Carleton, 'John Marbeck and the *Booke of Common Praier Noted*,' in D. Wood (ed.), *The Church and the Arts* (Oxford, 1992), p. 255.
53. Ibid.
54. P. Matheson (ed.), *Collected Letters and Writings of Thomas Müntzer* (Edinburgh, 1988), p. 166.
55. Carleton, 'John Marbeck,' p. 257.
56. Ibid., e.g. Luther's *Deutsche Messe* of 1525.
57. Carleton, 'John Marbeck,' p. 263. J. Marbeck, *The Book of Common Praier Noted* (London, 1550), Sig. A.ii.
58. Carleton, 'John Marbeck,' p. 263; J. Marbeck, *The Book of Common Praier Noted* (London, 1550), pp. 1015–20.
59. Carleton, 'John Marbeck,' p. 263.
60. Zwingli, quoted in C. Garside, *Zwingli and the Arts* (New Haven, 1966), p. 44; Begbie, *Resounding Truth*, p. 114.
61. Quoted in Garside, *Zwingli and the Arts*, p. 51, and Begbie, *Resounding Truth*, p. 115.
62. Begbie, *Resounding Truth*, p. 115.
63. Garside, *Zwingli and the Arts*, p. 37; Begbie, *Resounding Truth*, p. 116.
64. Begbie, *Resounding Truth*, p. 117.
65. Garside, *Zwingli and the Arts*, p. 74; Begbie, *Resounding Truth*, p. 117.
66. Brown and Hopps, *The Extravagance of Music*, pp. 10–11.
67. J. Irwin, '"So Faith Comes from What is Heard": The Relationship between Music and God's Word in the First Two Centuries of German Lutheranism,' in J. Begbie and S. Guthrie (eds), *Resonant Witness: Conversations between Music and Theology* (Grand Rapids, MI, 2011), pp. 65–82. Here at p. 69.
68. F. Burch Brown, 'Introduction' to Brown and Hopps, *the Extravagance of Music*, p. vii.

69. http://www.biblesociety.org.uk/uploads/content/projects/Bible-Society-Report_030214_final_.pdf, p. 11.
70. http://www.biblesociety.org.uk/uploads/content/projects/Bible-Society-Report_030214_final_.pdf, p. 13.
71. http://www.biblesociety.org.uk/uploads/content/projects/Bible-Society-Report_030214_final_.pdf, p. 14ff.
72. https://bachtrack.com/classical-music-statistics-2014, accessed 25 January 2018.
73. https://www.theaudienceagency.org/asset/1303, accessed 25 January 2018.
74. Brown and Hopps, *The Extravagance of Music*, p. 12.
75. J. Butt, 'Bach's Metaphysics of Music', in J. Butt (ed.), *The Cambridge Companion to Bach* (Cambridge, 1997), pp. 46–71. Here at pp. 46 and 54, quoted in A. Monti, *A Natural Theology of the Arts: Imprint of the Spirit* (Aldershot, 2003), p. 119.
76. S.L. Sorgner and O. Fürbeth (eds), *Music in German Philosophy*, trans. S.H. Gillespie (Chicago, 2010), p. 12, quoted in Brown and Hopps, *The Extravagance of Music*, p. 14.
77. F. Schleiermacher, *On Religion: Speeches to its Cultured Despisers*, trans. R. Crouter (Cambridge, 1996), pp. 78 and 75, quoted in Brown and Hopps, *The Extravagance of Music*, pp. 22–3.
78. Brown and Hopps, *The Extravagance of Music*, pp. 2–3.

CHAPTER TWO

1. Ephesians 5:19.
2. C. Gibbs, 'Hereford Cathedral: *The Traherne Windows*', in A. Johnson and J. Reed (eds), *Glory, Azure and Gold: The Stained-Glass Windows of Thomas Denny* (London, 2016), p. 57.
3. *The Salutation* is one of the poems set to music as part of the five-movement cantata for solo tenor or soprano and string orchestra *Dies Natalis* ('Day of Birth'), Op. 8, composed in 1938–9 by Gerald Finzi (1901–56). The cantata sets four texts by Thomas Traherne.
4. R. Blythe, *Divine Landscapes: A Pilgrimage through Britain's Sacred Places* (London, 1986; paperback edn Norwich, 1998), pp. 217–18.
5. R. Blythe, *The Time by the Sea: Aldeburgh, 1955–1958* (London, 2013), pp. xiii–xiv.
6. Ibid., pp. 113ff.
7. Ibid, p. 122.
8. Blythe, *Divine Landscapes*, p. 219.
9. Ibid.
10. S.E. Lehmberg, 'The Reformation of Choirs: Cathedral Musical Establishments in Tudor England', in D.J. Guth and J.W. McKenna (eds), *Tudor Rule and Revolution: Essays for G.R. Elton from his American Friends* (Cambridge, 1982), p. 47.
11. A.R.B. Fuller, 'The Minor Corporations of the Secular Cathedrals of the Province of Canterbury Excluding the Welsh Sees between the Thirteenth Century to 1585 with Special Reference to the Minor Canons of St Paul's Cathedral from their Origin in the Fourteenth Century to the Visitation of Bishop Gibson in 1724' (unpublished MA Thesis, London, 1947), p. 124; similarly at other secular cathedrals: N. Orme, *The Minor Clergy of Exeter Cathedral, 1300–1548* (Exeter, 1980), p. xviii.
12. Fuller, 'Minor Corporations', p. 124.

13. D. Lepine, *A Brotherhood of Canons Serving God: English Secular Cathedrals in the Later Middle Ages* (Woodbridge, 1995), p. 130.
14. Fuller, 'Minor Corporations,' p. 124, quoting BL, Lansdowne MS 364, fol. 6v.
15. F. Harrison, *Life in a Medieval College: The Story of the Vicars Choral of York Minster* (London, 1952), p. 24.
16. S.E. Lehmberg, *The Reformation of Cathedrals: Cathedrals in English Society 1485–1603* (Princeton, NJ, 1988), p. 182.
17. R. Rex, *Henry VIII and the English Reformation* (Basingstoke, 1993), p. 47; see also Lehmberg, *Cathedrals*, pp. 218–23 and 264–5; M. Bowker, *The Henrician Reformation: The Diocese of Lincoln under John Longland, 1521–1547* (Cambridge, 1981), pp. 34–7.
18. H. Kim, 'Erasmus on Sacred Music,' *Reformation and Renaissance Review* 8 (2006), pp. 277–300, quoting D. Erasmus, *Declarationes ad censuras Lutetiae vulgatus sub nomine facultatis theologie Parisiensis* (Basil, 1532).
19. B. Weiss and L.C. Pérez (eds), *Beginnings and Discoveries: Polydore Vergil's De Inventoribus Rerum. An Unabridged Translation and Edition with Introduction, Notes and Glossary* (Nieuwkoop, 1997), p. 395.
20. Elizabethan Injunctions, 1559, quoted in P. Le Huray, *Music and the Reformation in England, 1549–1660* (Oxford, 1967), p. 33.
21. A. Peel and L. Carlson (eds), *Elizabethan and Non-Conformist Texts, Volume II: The Writings of Robert Harrison and Robert Browne* (London, 1953; reprinted 2003), p. 415.
22. D.E. Saliers, *Music and Theology* (Nashville, TN, 2007), p. 35.
23. Augustine, *Enarrationes in Psalmos* 148.14, quoted in Blythe, *Divine Landscapes*, p. 220.
24. Ibid., pp. 220–1.
25. C.S. Lewis, *The Screwtape Letters* (London, 1942), p. 50, quoted in D. Conomos, 'C.S. Lewis and Church Music,' in A. Andreopoulos and G. Speake (eds), *Rightly Dividing the Word of Truth: Studies in Honour of Bishop Kallistos of Diokleia* (London, Bern, 2016), pp. 213–34. Here at p. 217.
26. Bishop Kallistos of Diokleia, 'C.S. Lewis: an "anonymous Orthodox"?,' *Sobornost* 1, ii (1995), pp. 14–15.
27. Andrew Louth, 'The Reception of Dionysius in the Byzantine World: Maximus to Palamas,' in *Dionysius the Areopagite*, ed. S. Cokely and C.M. Stang (Oxford: Blackwell, 2009), pp. 64–6.
28. C.E. Lutz, *Remigii Autissiodorensis Commentum in Martianum Capellam*, vol. 2 (Leiden, 1962), p. 304f. *Musica enim vera simper in caelo est.*
29. Conomos, 'C.S. Lewis and Church Music,' p. 218.
30. R. Green and W. Hooper, *C.S. Lewis: A Biography* (New York, 1974), p. 104.
31. C.S. Lewis, 'Answers to Questions on Christianity' (1944), originally a pamphlet, later included in the collection, *God in the Dock*, ed. W. Hooper (Grand Rapids, MI, 1970), p. 62.
32. C.S. Lewis, 'Christianity and Culture,' in W. Hooper (ed.), *Christian Reflections* (London, 1998), p. 3.
33. Letter to Eric Routley, 16 July 1946, in W. Hooper (ed.), *C.S. Lewis, Collected Letters II: Books, Broadcasts and War 1931–1949* (London, 2004), p. 720.
34. Conomos, 'C.S. Lewis and Church Music,' p. 222.
35. *The Presbyter: A Journal of Reformed Churchmanship* 6:2 (1948), pp. 15–20. Here at p. 20.

36. C.S. Lewis, *On Church Music*, ed. Walter Hooper (HarperCollins, 1967, reissued 1980), pp. 120–6.
37. Conomos, 'C.S. Lewis and Church Music', p. 226.
38. Lewis, *On Church Music*, p. 122.
39. Conomos, 'C.S. Lewis and Church Music', p. 227.
40. Lewis, *On Church Music*, p. 126.
41. *God in the Dock*, pp. 328–9.
42. This useful phrase was included in Dimitri Conomos's draft of his article, 'C.S. Lewis and Church Music', and I am grateful to him for sending me a copy. The words do not appear in the final printed article.
43. Blythe, *Divine Landscapes*, p. 221.
44. Ibid., p. 238.
45. Ibid., p. 222.
46. Ibid., p. 242.
47. Ibid., p. 245.
48. Ibid., pp. 246–7.
49. J. Boyce-Tillman, *Experiencing Music*, p. 226.
50. 1970s Alistair Hardy Archive quoted in Ibid.
51. *Desert Island Discs*, 28 November 2014, quoted in Boyce-Tillman, *Experiencing Music*, p. 226.
52. A. Bennett, *Hymn*, Radio 4 broadcast 22 December 2001, quoted in Ibid., p. 227.
53. R. Knowles-Wallace, 'Congregational Singing and Everyday Life', Keynote presentation at Hymns in Liturgy and Life, International Conference of Hymn Societies (Cambridge, 26 July–1 August 2015), quoted in Boyce-Tillman, *Experiencing Music*, p. 248.
54. Boyce-Tillman, *Experiencing Music*, pp. 260–1.
55. Arnold, *Sacred Music in Secular Society, passim.*
56. K. Jenkins, *Redefining the Hymn: The Performative Context, Occasional Paper, Third Series* 4 (Hymn Society of Britain and Ireland, 2010), pp. 9–10, quoted in J. Boyce-Tillman, 'Tune your Music to your Heart: Reflections for Church Music Leaders', in M. Ingalls, C. Landau and T. Wagner (eds), *Christian Congregational Music: Performance, Identity and Experience* (Farnham, 2013), pp. 49–65. Here at p. 51.
57. L.J. Clark, *Music in Churches: Nourishing Your Congregation's Musical Life* (The Alban Institute, 1994), p. 5, quoted in J. Boyce-Tillman, 'Tune your Music to your Heart', p. 51.
58. J. Boyce-Tillman, 'Tune your Music to your Heart', p. 63.
59. D.E. Saliers, *Music and Theology* (Nashville, TN, 2007), p. 35.
60. Ibid.
61. Ibid., p. 40.

CHAPTER THREE

1. Rembrandt.
2. http://www.janetboulton.co.uk, accessed 4 July 2017.
3. Ibid.
4. 'An Introduction to the Eye Music Series' by Joe Scarffe, in J. Boulton, *Eye Music* (Uniform Books, 2014), pp. 3–6. Here at p. 3.
5. Ibid., p. 4.

6. Ibid., p. 5.
7. Ibid., p. 9.
8. Ibid., p. 10.
9. Ibid., pp. 10–11.
10. Ibid., p. 11.
11. 'Matisse has taught the eye to hear.' R. Castleman, *Introduction to Henri Matisse* (New York, 1985). 'One day I must be able to improvise freely on the keyboard of colours: the row of watercolours in my paintbox.' P. Klee, *Painting Music* (New York, 1997). 'Music is a visual art as well as a sounding one. One way to see this is in notation.' S. Shaw-Miller, *Sighting Music* (Chichester, 2007).
12. Scarffe, 'An Introduction to the Eye Music Series', p. 12.
13. http://www.magd.ox.ac.uk/libraries-and-archives/news/new-exhibition-fragments-of-note, accessed 15 March 2018.
14. Translation of *Stabat Mater*.
15. *In Sorrow's Footsteps*, The Marian Consort, premiere recording, Merton College, 2018. Delphian Records.

INTERLUDE I

1. This chapter was originally printed as an article in *The Church Times*, 20 January 2017, pp. 22–3.
2. http://medievalconventdrama.org.
3. Interview with Elisabeth Dutton, 2016.

CHAPTER FOUR

1. Pope Benedict XVI, Paul VI Audience Hall, Vatican City, 16 April 2007.
2. A. Mesoudi, *Cultural Evolution: How Darwinian Theory can Explain Human Culture and Synthesize the Social Sciences* (Chicago, 2011), p. 1.
3. J.W. Davidson, 'Music as Social Behaviour', in E. Clarke and N. Cook (eds), *Empirical Musicology: Aims, Methods, Prospects* (Oxford, 2004), pp. 57–75. Here at p. 57.
4. Ibid.
5. Ibid., *passim*.
6. https://www.psy.ox.ac.uk/team/robin-dunbar, accessed 16 June 2017.
7. D. Weinstein, J. Launay, E. Pearce, R.I.M. Dunbar and L. Stewart, 'Singing and Social Bonding: Changes in Connectivity and Pain Threshold as a Function of Group Size', *Evolution and Human Behavior* 37 (2016) pp. 152–8. Here at p. 152.
8. Ibid., p. 152.
9. Ibid., p. 157.
10. Natural Voice Practitioners Network: http://www.naturalvoice.net, quoted in Morgan and Boyce-Tillman, *A River Rather than a Road*, p. 24.
11. Morgan and Boyce-Tillman, *A River Rather than a Road*, pp. 24 and 26.
12. Wellbeing Community Choir: https://www.facebook.com/wellbeingchoir, quoted in Morgan and Boyce-Tillman, *A River Rather than a Road*, p. 28.
13. https://www.manchestereveningnews.co.uk/news/greater-manchester-news/choir-brought-hope-survivors-manchester-14672046, accessed 22 May 2018.
14. Ibid.

15. Ibid.
16. Morgan and Boyce-Tillman, *A River Rather than a Road*, p. 31.
17. Ibid.
18. Ibid., p. 153.
19. E. Pearce, J. Launay and R.I.M. Dunbar, 'The Ice-Breaker Effect: Singing Mediates Fast Social Bonding', *Royal Society Open Science* 2: 150221 (2015). http://dx.doi.org/10.1098/rsos.150221; downloaded from http://rsos.royalsocietypublishing.org, accessed 17 November 2016.
20. Ibid.
21. B. Tarr, J. Launay, E. Cohen and R. Dunbar, 2015: 'Synchrony and Exertion During Dance Independently Raise Pain Threshold and Encourage Social Bonding', *Biology Letters* 11: 20150767; Downloaded from http://rsbl.royalsocietypublishing.org on 21 October 2016.
22. Such as R. Sosis and E.R. Bressler, 'Cooperation and Commune Longevity: A Test of the Costly Signaling Theory of Religion', *Cross-Cultural Research* 37 (2003), pp. 211–39.
23. E. Pearce, J. Launay and R.I.M. Dunbar, 'The Ice-Breaker Effect: Singing Mediates Fast Social Bonding', *Royal Society Open Science* 2 (2015), pp. 150–221.
24. http://www.sundayassembly.com/story, accessed 21 June 2016: 'The Sunday Assembly was started by Sanderson Jones and Pippa Evans, two comedians who were on the way to a gig in Bath when they discovered they both wanted to do something that was like church but totally secular and inclusive of all – no matter what they believed. The first ever Sunday Assembly meeting took place on January 6th 2013 at The Nave in Islington. Almost 200 people turned up at the first meeting, 300 at the second and soon people all over the world asked to start one. Now there are over seventy Sunday Assembly chapters in eight different countries where people sing songs, hear inspiring talks, and create community together. Why do we exist? Life is short, it is brilliant and it is sometimes tough. We build communities that help everyone live life as fully as possible.'
25. Pope Benedict XVI, *The Spirit of the Liturgy* (San Francisco, 2014), pp. 145–6; Arnold, *Sacred Music in Secular Society*, and J. MacMillan, 'Sacred Music can Heal our Broken Culture', 22 November 2012: http://www.aosm.org.uk/index.php/archive/item/sacred-music-can-heal-our-broken-culture, accessed 10 April 2018.
26. R. Dunbar, 'Altogether', *Times Higher Education* 43, 11 November 2010.
27. McGilchrist, *Master and his Emissary*, p. 102.
28. Ibid., p. 103.
29. Ibid.

CHAPTER FIVE

1. Heinrich Heine.
2. Anicius Manlius Severinus Boethius, *Fundamentals of Music*, ed. C.V. Palisca, trans. C.M. Bower (New Haven, 1989), p. 8.
3. Storr, *Music and the Mind*, p. 1.
4. Ibid., p. 24.
5. Such as Ibid., pp. 34–7; O. Sacks, *The Man who mistook his Wife for a Hat* (London, 1985), pp. 7–21; O. Sacks, *Awakenings* (London, 1973); O. Sacks, *Musicophilia: Tales of Music and the Brain* (London, 2007).

6. Sacks, *Musicophilia*, p. xii.
7. R. Jourdain, *Music, the Brain and Ecstasy: How Music Captures our Imagination* (New York, 1997).
8. Ibid., p. 328.
9. Ibid.
10. Ibid., p. 331.
11. Ibid.
12. M. Critchley, 'Ecstatic and Synaesthetic Experiences During Musical Perception,' in M. Critchley and R.A. Henson (eds), *Music and the Brain: Studies in the Neurology of Music* (London, 1997), p. 217.
13. D. Aldridge, 'Music, Consciousness and Altered States,' in D. Aldridge and J. Fachner (eds), *Music and Altered States: Consciousness, Transcendence, Therapy and Addiction* (London, 2006), pp. 9–14. Here at p. 13.
14. Ibid.
15. G. Rouget, *Music and Trance: A Theory of the Relations between Music and Possession* (Chicago, 1985), p. 10, quoted in J. Fachner, 'Music and Altered States of Consciousness: An Overview,' in Aldridge and Fachner (eds), *Music and Altered States*, pp. 15–37. Here at p. 20.
16. J.J. Pilch, 'Music and Trance,' in Aldridge and Fachner (eds), *Music and Altered States*, pp. 38–50. Here at p. 47; M.J. Kartomi, 'Music and Trance in Central Java,' *Ethnomusicology* 17, pp. 163–208.
17. Pilch, 'Music and Trance,' p. 47.
18. Kartomi, 'Music and Trance in Central Java,' p. 166.
19. http://www.quintondeeley.co.uk, accessed 16 March 2018.
20. Q. Deeley, E. Walsh, D.A. Oakley, V. Bell, C. Koppel, M.A. Mehta and P.W. Halligan, 'Using Hypnotic Suggestion to Model Loss of Control and Awareness of Movements: an Exploratory fMRI Study,' *PLoS One* 8, no. 10 (2013): e78324; Q. Deeley, D.A. Oakley, E. Walsh, V. Bell, M.A. Mehta and P.W. Halligan, 'Modelling Psychiatric and Cultural Possession Phenomena with Suggestion and fMRI,' *Cortex* 53 (2014), pp. 107–19.
21. Q. Deeley, 'The Religious Brain: Turning Ideas into Convictions,' *Anthropology & Medicine* 11, no. 3 (2004), pp. 245–67.
22. E. Walsh, D.A. Oakley, P.W. Halligan, M.A. Mehta and Q. Deeley, 'The Functional Anatomy and Connectivity of Thought Insertion and Alien Control of Movement,' *Cortex* 64 (2015), pp. 380–93; E. Walsh, D.A. Oakley, P.W. Halligan, M.A. Mehta and Q. Deeley, 'Brain Mechanisms for Loss of Awareness of Thought and Movement,' *Social Cognitive and Affective Neuroscience* 12, no. 5 (2017), pp. 793–801.
23. G. Rouget, *Music and Trance: A Theory of Relations between Music and Possession* (Chicago, 1985).
24. Ibid., p. 72.
25. T.K. Oesterreich, *Possession, Demoniacal and Other: Among Primitive Races, in Antiquity, the Middle Ages and Modern Times* (London, 2013).
26. I. McGilchrist, *The Master and His Emissary* (New Haven and London, 2012).
27. V. Turner, 'Body, Brain, and Culture,' *Zygon* 18 (1983), pp. 221–45.
28. Deeley, 'The Religious Brain,' pp. 245–67.
29. Ibid.
30. Ibid. Examples of emotionally evocative stimuli widely sampled in ceremonial ritual include: motion, colour, luminosity, emotive facial expressions of masks, accentuated

sexual characteristics (cosmetics, oils), sudden loud noises (fireworks, bells), prosodic accentuations of language (singing, chanting), pain (flagellation, circumcision), temperature (baptism by immersion), smells (incense, perfumes), taste (ritual foods), and multi-sensory repetitious stimuli which activate arousal systems.

31. J. Gray, *Seven Types of Atheism* (London, 2018), p. 158.
32. Storr, *Music and the Mind*, p. 187.
33. Ibid., p. 188.

CHAPTER SIX

1. Dietrich Bonhoeffer.
2. BBC Radio 4, *FutureProofing: Faith*. https://www.bbc.co.uk/programmes/b0b17fkh, accessed 25 May 2018.
3. Ibid.
4. Ibid.
5. M. Bourdeaux, 'Religion Revives in all its Variety: Russia's Regions Today', *Religion, State and Society* 28 (2000), pp. 9–21. Here at p. 9.
6. Ibid., p. 13.
7. T. Eagleton, *Culture and the Death of God* (New Haven, 2014), p. 88.
8. Ibid., p. 90.
9. W.J. Vanden Heuvel, *The Future of Freedom in Russia* (West Conshohocken, PA, 2000), p. 165.
10. Such as *Sacred Songs and Solos* (1877), a hymn collection by Ira David Sankey and Dwight Lyman Moody, which became known as Sankey and Moody's Songs, or The Sankey-Moody Hymnbook, even though the tunes and words are by other authors.
11. The Ordinary of the Mass are the different movements, such as Kyrie, Gloria, Sanctus, Benedictus and Agnus Dei. The Propers are seasonal words which change throughout the year's liturgical calendar.
12. Pope Benedict XVI, *The Spirit of the Liturgy*, p. 145.
13. Ibid., p. 142.

INTERLUDE II

1. This chapter was first published as an article in *The Church Times*, 22 July 2017, pp. 20–1. Many thanks indeed to Caroline Chartres who commissioned and edited the article.
2. A. Charters, *John Sanders: Friend for Life* (Milton Keynes, 2009), pp. 100–1.

CHAPTER SEVEN

1. Mark 9:24.
2. By 'Process' I do not mean 'Process Theology', which concerns whether God can be changed by temporal processes.
3. A. Day, *Believing in Belonging: Belief and Social Identity in the Modern World* (Oxford, 2011), p. 3.
4. Ibid., p. 48.

5. Ibid., p. 202.
6. Ibid.
7. Gray, *Seven Types of Atheism*, p. 1.
8. Ibid., pp. 2–3.
9. Ibid., p. 4.
10. Ibid., p. 5.
11. Ibid., p. 9.
12. Ibid., p. 7.
13. Ibid.
14. Ibid., p. 142.
15. Mountford, *Christian Atheist*, p. 1.
16. Ibid. pp. 2–5.
17. Ibid., p. 7.
18. J. Shaw, 'Twenty-Third Eric Symes Abbott Memorial Lecture', 8 May 2008, published by King's College London and quoted in Mountford, *Christian Atheist*, p. 8.
19. Ibid., p. 9.
20. Ibid., pp. 13–14.
21. Ibid.
22. Ibid., pp. 18–19.
23. Ibid., p. 20.
24. J. Cottingham, *The Spiritual Dimension* (Cambridge, 2005), p. 136; H. Küng, *Mozart – Traces of Transcendence* (London, 1992), p. 35; Mountford, *Christian Atheist*, pp. 20–1.
25. Ibid., p. 20.
26. Ibid., p. 25.
27. Ibid., p. 37.
28. Ibid., p. 85.
29. R. Dawkins, *The God Delusion* (London, 2006), p. 86, quoted in Mountford, *Christian Atheist*, pp. 21–2.
30. Begbie, *Redeeming Transcendence*, pp. 40–76.
31. Dawkins, *Science in the Soul*, pp. 1–2.
32. Ibid., p. 3.
33. Ibid.
34. Ibid., p. 5.
35. Quoted in Ibid., pp. 212–13.
36. Ibid., p. 213.
37. Ibid.
38. 'Atheists for Jesus', in *Free Inquiry*, December 2004-January 2005, quoted in Ibid., p. 275.
39. Quoted in Ibid., p. 275.
40. Ibid., p. 279.
41. Ibid., p. 280.
42. R. Scruton, *The Face of God: The Gifford Lectures 2010* (London, 2012), pp. 177–8.
43. Ibid., p. 1.
44. Ibid., p. 70.
45. Ibid., pp. 70–1.
46. Ibid., pp. 173–4.
47. Ibid., p. 176.

48. Ibid., pp. 176–7.
49. Mountford, *Christian Atheist*, p. 22.
50. I. Murdoch, *The Sovereignty of Good* (London, 1970), pp. 64–5, quoted in Mountford, *Christian Atheist*, p. 23.
51. Mountford, *Christian Atheist*, p. 79.
52. Ibid., p. 115.
53. C.A. Duffy, *Mean Time* (London, 2012 edn), p. 48, quoted in Mountford, *Christian Atheist*, p. 119. *Prayer* by Carol Ann Duffy is reprinted courtesy of Faber and Faber.
54. Ibid., p. 119.
55. Ibid., p. 129.
56. Ibid., p. 56.
57. Boyce-Tillman, *A River rather than a Road, passim.*
58. D. MacCulloch, *A History of Christianity* (London, 2009), p. 9, quoted in Mountford, *Christian Atheist*, p. 58.
59. Ibid., p. 67.
60. Ibid., pp. 69–73.
61. Ibid., p. 111.
62. Quoted in Ibid., p. 113.
63. Eagleton, *Culture and the Death of God*, p. 146.
64. Durkheim, *The Elementary Forms of the Religious Life*, p. 18.
65. Eagleton, *Culture and the Death of God*, pp. 146–7.
66. See the end of chapter five above.
67. H. Jacobson, *The Reader* 29, University of Liverpool, p. 30, quoted in Mountford, *Christian Atheist*, p. 97.
68. R. Gilbert, *Science and the Truthfulness of Beauty: How the Personal Perspective Discovers Creation* (London, 2018), p. 145.
69. Ibid., p. 11.
70. Ibid., p. 11; D'Arcy Thompson, *On Growth and Form*, abridged edn ed. J. Tyler Bonner (Cambridge, 1961; Canto edn, 1992), pp. 172–201.
71. Interview with Frank Wilczek by Michael Berkeley for BBC Radio 3, *Private Passions*, broadcast 27 September 2015, http://www.bbc.co.uk/programmes/b06db6tx, quoted in Gilbert, *Science and the Truthfulness of Beauty*, p. 11.
72. Ibid.
73. Ibid., p. 12.
74. Ibid., p. 12.
75. Ibid.

CHAPTER EIGHT

1. Romans 10:15; Isaiah 52:7; and libretto by Charles Jennens for Handel's *Messiah*.
2. M.L. Heaney, *Music as Theology: What Music Says about the Word* (Eugene, OR, 2012), p. 1.
3. Ibid.
4. Begbie, *Redeeming Transcendence*, pp. 1–13 and *passim*.
5. Heaney, *Music as Theology*, p. 5.
6. G. Steiner, *Real Presences*, p. 218, quoted in Ibid., p. 6.
7. Heaney, *Music as Theology*, p. 11.

8. Ibid., p. 10.
9. Ibid., p. 25.
10. Ibid., p. 310.
11. F. Schleiermacher, *On Religion and the Natural Order* (London, 1965).
12. C. Campling, *The Food of Love: Reflections on Music and Faith* (London, 1997), p. 19.
13. Ibid., p. 20.
14. In Brown and Hopps, *The Extravagance of Music*, p. 212; F. Burch Brown, *Good Taste, Bad Taste, and Christian Taste: Aesthetics in Religious Life* (Oxford, 2000).
15. Brown and Hopps, *The Extravagance of Music*, pp. 189–207.
16. N. Baines, *Finding Faith: Stories of Music and Life* (Edinburgh, 2008), pp. 24, 26, 36 and 46–7.
17. Ibid., pp. 30–1.
18. Ibid., pp. 32, 33 and 34.
19. Ibid., p. 34.
20. Ibid., pp. 64–5.
21. Ibid. pp. 72–4.
22. Ibid., p. 180.
23. Ibid., p. 181.

CHAPTER NINE

1. Johann Sebastian Bach.
2. Martin Luther.
3. G. Hartje-Döll, '(Hillsong) United Through Music: Praise and Worship Music and the Evangelical "Imagined Community"', in M. Ingalls, C. Landau and T. Wagner (eds), *Christian Congregational Music: Performance, Identity and Experience* (Farnham, 2013), pp. 137–52. Here at pp. 137–8.
4. D.E. Miller, 'Postdenominational Christianity in the Twenty-First Century', *Annals of the American Academy of Political and Social Science* 558 (1998), pp. 197 and 203, cited in Hartje-Döll, '(Hillsong) United Through Music', pp. 140–1.
5. B. Anderson, *Imagined Communities: Reflection on the Origin and Spread of Nationalism*, revised edn (London, 1983/2006).
6. M.M. Ingalls, 'Awesome in this Place: Sound, Space, and Identity in Contemporary North American Evangelical Worship', unpublished PhD Thesis, University of Pennsylvania (2008), p. 13, quoted in Hartje-Döll, '(Hillsong) United Through Music', p. 142.
7. S. Coleman, *The Globalization of Charismatic Christianity: Spreading the Gospel of Prosperity* (Cambridge, 2000), p. 67, quoted in Hartje-Döll, '(Hillsong) United Through Music', p. 142.
8. Hartje-Döll, '(Hillsong) United Through Music', *passim*.
9. M. Porter, *Contemporary Music and Everyday Music Lives* (Abingdon, 2017), p. 155.

CONCLUSION

1. M. Oakley, 'Batter my Heart: The Poetry and Theology of John Donne', *Church Music Quarterly* (June 2018), p. 13.

2. 'The World is not Conclusion' by Emily Dickinson; R. Franklin (ed.), *The Poems of Emily Dickinson* (New Haven, 1998), p. 384. *Conclusion* by Emily Dickinson is reprinted courtesy of Harvard University Press.
3. Ibid.
4. Ibid.
5. J. Begbie, 'Natural Theology and Music', in J. Hedley Brooke, R. de Manning and F. Watts, *The Oxford Handbook of Natural Theology* (Oxford, 2013), pp. 566–80. Here at pp. 567–9, assessing D. Brown, *God and Enchantment of Place: Reclaiming Human Experience* (Oxford, 2004).
6. Begbie, 'Natural Theology', p. 571; A. Monti, *A Natural Theology of the Arts: Imprint of the Spirit* (Aldershot, 2003), p. 9.
7. Burch Brown, 'Introduction to Brown and Hopps', in *The Extravagance of Music*, p. ix.
8. Ibid., p. x.
9. Ibid.
10. Ibid.
11. Brown and Hopps, *The Extravagance of Music*, pp. 5–6.
12. Ibid., p. 36.
13. Ibid., pp. 37–9.
14. Ibid., pp. 134–6.
15. Ibid., p. 207.
16. Ibid., p. 251.
17. Taylor, *A Secular Age*, p. 8.
18. Brown and Hopps, p. 251.
19. Ellis, *The Christian Middle Way*, p. 19.
20. Ibid., p. 159.
21. Ibid., p. 161.
22. Ibid., p. 288.
23. Ibid., p. 293.
24. Brown, 'Review of Begbie', *Church Times*, p. 28.
25. R. Williams, *The Edge of Words: God and the Habits of Language* (London, 2014), p. 3.
26. Ibid., p. 17.
27. M. Ter Borg, 'A Function for Religion in the Survival of the Human Species' in *The Oxford Handbook of the Sociology of Religion*, p. 197.
28. Williams, *Edge of Words*, quoting M. Leunig, *The Lot: In Words* (Camberwell, Australia, 2008), p. 237.
29. S. Heaney, *The Spirit Level* (London, 1996), p. 1. *The Rainstick* by Seamus Heaney is reprinted courtesy of Faber and Faber, and Farrar, Straus and Giroux.

BIBLIOGRAPHY

Aldridge, D., 'Music, Consciousness and Altered States,' in D. Aldridge and J. Fachner (eds), *Music and Altered States: Consciousness, Transcendence, Therapy and Addictions* (London and Philadelphia, 2006), pp. 9–14.

Ammerman, N.T., *Sacred Stories Spiritual Tribes: Finding Religion in Everyday Life* (New York, 2013).

Ammerman, N.T., 'Spiritual but not Religious? Beyond Binary Choices in the Study of Religion,' *Journal for the Scientific Study of Religion* 52 (2013), pp. 258–78.

Anderson, B., *Imagined Communities: Reflection on the Origin and Spread of Nationalism* (rev. edn, London, 1983/2006).

Anicius Manlius Severinus Boethius, *Fundamentals of Music*, ed. Claude V. Palisca, trans. C.M. Bower (New Haven, 1989).

Arnold, J., *Dean John Colet of St Paul's: Humanism and Early Tudor Reform* (London, 2007).

Arnold, J., *Sacred Music in Secular Society* (Farnham, 2014).

Baines, N., *Finding Faith: Stories of Music and Life* (Edinburgh, 2008).

Bannister, P., 'Kenosis in Contemporary Music and Postmodern Philosophy,' in R. Scholl and S. van Maas (eds), *Contemporary Music and Spirituality* (London, 2017), pp. 54–80.

Barfield, O., *Poetic Diction: A Study in Meaning* (London, 1928).

Barr, J., *Biblical Faith and Natural Theology* (Gifford Lectures, 1991; Oxford, 1993).

Barth, K., *The Knowledge of God and the Service of God according to the Teaching of the Reformation* (Gifford Lectures, 1937–8; Eugene, OR, 2005).

Barth, K., *Theology and Church, Shorter Writings 1920–1928*, trans. L. Pettibone Smith (London, 1962).

Begbie, J., 'Foreword' to S. Guthrie, *Creator Spirit: The Holy Spirit and the Art of Becoming Human* (Grand Rapids, MI, 2011), pp. vii–viii.

Begbie, J., 'Natural Theology and Music,' in J. Hedley Brooke, R. de Manning and F. Watts, *The Oxford Handbook of Natural Theology* (Oxford, 2013), pp. 566–80.

Begbie, J., *Redeeming Transcendence in the Arts: Bearing Witness to the Triune God* (London, 2018).

Begbie, J., *Resounding Truth: Christian Wisdom in the World of Music* (Grand Rapids, MI, 2007).

Bennett, A., *Hymn*, Radio 4 broadcast, 22 December 2001.

Bishop Kallistos of Diokleia, 'C.S. Lewis: an "Anonymous Orthodox"?,' *Sobornost* 1, ii (1995), pp. 14–15.

Blond, P. (ed.), *Post-Secular Philosophy: Between Philosophy and Theology* (London, 1998).

Blythe, R., *Divine Landscapes: A Pilgrimage through Britain's Sacred Places* (London, 1986; paperback edn, Norwich, 1998).

Blythe, R., *The Time by the Sea: Aldeburgh, 1955–1958* (London, 2013).

Bohlman, P., 'Is All Music Religious?,' in *Theomusicology. A Special Issue of Black Sacred Music. A Journal of Theomusicology*, ed. J.M. Spencer (Durham, NC, 1994), pp. 3–12.

Bourdeaux, M., 'Religion Revives in all its Variety: Russia's Regions Today', *Religion, State and Society* 28 (2000), pp. 9–21.
Bower, C., 'Transmission of Ancient Music Theory into the Middle Ages', pp. 136–67.
Bowker, M., *The Henrician Reformation: The Diocese of Lincoln under John Longland, 1521–1547* (Cambridge, 1981).
Boyce Tillman, J., *Experiencing Music – Restoring the Spiritual: Music as Well Being* (Bern, 2016).
Boyce-Tillman, J., *A River Rather than a Road: The Community Choir as Spiritual Experience* (Oxford; Bern, 2016).
Boyce-Tillman, J., 'Tune your Music to your Heart: Reflections for Church Music Leaders', in M. Ingalls, C. Landau and T. Wagner (eds), *Christian Congregational Music: Performance, Identity and Experience* (Farnham, 2013), pp. 49–65.
Brown, A. and Woodhead, L., *That was the Church that was: How the English Church Lost the English People* (London, 2016).
Brown, D., *God and Enchantment of Place: Reclaiming Human Experience* (Oxford, 2004).
Brown, D., 'Review of J. Begbie, *Redeeming Transcendence in the Arts: Bearing Witness to the Triune God* (London, 2018)', in *Church Times*, 14 September 2018, p. 28.
Brown, D. and Hopps, G., *The Extravagance of Music* (London, 2018).
Burch Brown, F., *Good Taste, Bad Taste, and Christian Taste: Aesthetics in Religious Life* (Oxford, 2000).
Burch Brown, F., *Religious Aesthetics: A Theological Study of Making and Meaning* (Basingstoke, 1990).
Butt, J., 'Bach's Metaphysics of Music', in J. Butt (ed.), *The Cambridge Companion to Bach* (Cambridge, 1997), pp. 46–71.
Campling, C., *The Food of Love: Reflections on Music and Faith* (London, 1997).
Carleton, K., 'John Marbeck and the *Booke of Common Praier Noted*', in D. Wood (ed.), *The Church and the Arts* (Oxford, 1992), pp. 255–65.
Castleman, R., *Introduction to Henri Matisse* (New York, 1985).
Charters, A., *John Sanders: Friend for Life* (Milton Keynes, 2009).
Clark, L.J., *Music in Churches: Nourishing Your Congregation's Musical Life* (The Alban Institute, 1994).
Clarke, P.B. (ed.), *The Oxford Handbook of the Sociology of Religion* (Oxford, 2009; paperback, 2011).
Coakley, S., *God, Sexuality and the Self: An Essay on 'The Trinity'* (Cambridge, 2013).
Coakley, S. and Stang, C.M. (eds), *Dionysius the Areopagite* (Oxford, 2009).
Coleman, S., *The Globalization of Charismatic Christianity: Spreading the Gospel of Prosperity* (Cambridge, 2000).
Conomos, D., 'C.S. Lewis and Church Music', in A. Andreopoulos and G. Speake (eds), *Rightly Dividing the Word of Truth: Studies in Honour of Bishop Kallistos of Diokleia* (London, Bern, 2016), pp. 213–34.
Cottingham, J., *The Spiritual Dimension* (Cambridge, 2005).
Cox, J.C., *Catalogue of the Muniments and Manuscript Books pertaining to the Dean and Chapter of Lichfield; Analysis of the Magnum Registrum Album; Catalogue of the Muniments of the Lichfield Vicars – Collections for a History of Staffordshire*, 6/ii (1886).
Critchley, M., 'Ecstatic and Synaesthetic Experiences During Musical Perception', in M.D. Jones, *Epoch and Artist* (London, 1941).

Critchley, M. and Henson, R.A. (eds), *Music and the Brain: Studies in the Neurology of Music* (London, 1997).

Davidson, J.W., 'Music as Social Behaviour', in E. Clarke and N. Cook (eds), *Empirical Musicology: Aims, Methods, Prospects* (Oxford, 2004), pp. 57–75.

Davie, G., *Europe: The Exceptional Case* (London, 2002).

Davie, G., *Religion in Britain since 1945: Believing without Belonging* (Oxford, 1994).

Dawkins, R., *The God Delusion* (London, 2006).

Dawkins, R., *Science in the Soul: Selected Writings of a Passionate Rationalist*, ed. G. Somerscales (London, 2017).

Day, A., *Believing in Belonging: Belief and Social Identity in the Modern World* (Oxford, 2011).

Deeley, Q., 'The Functional Anatomy and Connectivity of Thought Insertion and Alien Control of Movement', *Cortex* 64 (2015), pp. 380–93.

Deeley, Q., 'The Religious Brain: Turning Ideas into Convictions', *Anthropology & Medicine* 11, no. 3 (2004), pp. 245–67.

Deeley, Q., Oakley, D.A., Walsh, E., Bell, V., Mehta, M.A. and Halligan, P.W., 'Modelling Psychiatric and Cultural Possession Phenomena with Suggestion and fMRI', *Cortex* 53 (2014), pp. 107–19.

Deeley, Q., Walsh, E., Oakley, D.A., Bell, V., Koppel, C., Mehta, M.A. and Halligan, P.W., 'Using Hypnotic Suggestion to Model Loss of Control and Awareness of Movements: an Exploratory fMRI Study', *PLoS One* 8, no. 10 (2013): e78324.

Deusen, N. van, '*Musica, De*', in A.D. Fitzgerald et al. (eds), *Augustine Through the Ages: An Encyclopaedia* (Grand Rapids, MI, 1999), pp. 574–6.

Dillon, M., 'Can Post-Secular Society Tolerate Religious Differences?', *Sociology of Religion* 71 (2010), pp. 139–56.

Duffy, C.A., *Mean Time* (London, 2012 edn).

Duffy, E., *The Stripping of the Altars* (New Haven and London, 1992).

Dunbar, R., 'Altogether', *Times Higher Education* 43, 11 November 2010.

Dunn, J.D.G., *The Living Word* (Minneapolis, 2nd edn, 2009).

Durkheim, E., *The Elementary Forms of the Religious Life: A Study in Religious Sociology* (Oxford, 2015; 2001 edn).

Dyrness, W.A., *Poetic Theology: God and the Poetics of Everyday Life* (Grand Rapids, MI, 2010).

Eagleton, T., *Culture and the Death of God* (New Haven, 2014).

Eco, U., *Art and Beauty in the Middle Ages*, trans. H. Bredin (New Haven 1958, reprinted 1986).

Ellis, R.M., *The Christian Middle Way: The case against Christian Belief but for Christian Faith* (Winchester, UK; Washington, USA, 2018).

Erasmus, D., *Declarationes ad censuras Lutetiae vulgatus sub nomine facultatis theologie Parisiensis* (Basel, 1532).

Fachner, J., 'Music and Altered States of Consciousness: An Overview', in D. Aldridge and J. Fachner (eds), *Music and Altered States: Consciousness, Transcendence, Therapy and Addiction* (London, 2006), pp. 15–37.

Franklin, R. (ed.), *The Poems of Emily Dickinson* (New Haven, 1998).

Fuller, A.R.B., 'The Minor Corporations of the Secular Cathedrals of the Province of Canterbury Excluding the Welsh Sees between the Thirteenth Century to 1585 with Special Reference to the Minor Canons of St Paul's Cathedral from their Origin in the Fourteenth Century to the Visitation of Bishop Gibson in 1724' (unpublished MA Thesis, London, 1947).

Garside, C., *Zwingli and the Arts* (New Haven, 1966).

Gibbs, C., 'Hereford Cathedral: *The Traherne Windows*', in A. Johnson and J. Reed (eds), *Glory, Azure and Gold: The Stained-Glass Windows of Thomas Denny* (London, 2016), p. 57.

Gilbert, R., *Science and the Truthfulness of Beauty: How the Personal Perspective Discovers Creation* (London, 2018).

Gray, J., *Seven Types of Atheism* (London, 2018).

Green, R. and Hooper, W., *C.S. Lewis: A Biography* (New York, 1974).

Guite, M., *Faith, Hope and Poetry* (London, 2012).

Habermas, J., 'Notes on Post-Secular Society', *New Perspectives Quarterly* 25 (2008), pp. 17–29.

Habermas, J., 'Religion in the Public Sphere', *European Journal of Philosophy* 14 (2006), pp. 1–25.

Hall, A.W., 'Natural Theology in the Middle Ages', in R. Re Manning, J. Hedley Brooke and F. Watts (eds), *The Oxford Handbook of Natural Theology* (Oxford, 2013), pp. 57–74.

Hankins, J., 'Humanism and Music in Italy', in A.M.B. Berger and J. Rodin (eds), *The Cambridge History of Fifteenth-Century Music* (Cambridge, 2015), pp. 231–62.

Harris, R., *The Image of Christ in Modern Art* (Farnham, 2013).

Harrison, C., 'Augustine and the Art of Music', in J.S. Begbie and S.R. Guthrie (eds), *Resonant Witness: Conversations between Music and Theology* (Grand Rapids, MI, 2011), pp. 27–45.

Harrison, F., *Life in a Medieval College: The Story of the Vicars Choral of York Minster* (London, 1952).

Hartje-Döll, G., '(Hillsong) United Through Music: Praise and Worship Music and the Evangelical "Imagined Community"', in M. Ingalls, C. Landau and T. Wagner (eds), *Christian Congregational Music: Performance, Identity and Experience* (Farnham, 2013), pp. 137–52.

Heaney, M.L., *Music as Theology: What Music Says about the Word* (Eugene, OR, 2012).

Heaney, S., *The Spirit Level* (London, 1996).

Holder, R.T., 'Natural Theology', Faraday Paper, *The Faraday Institute for Science and Religion* 19 (April 2016), pp. 1–4.

Horne, B.L., 'A Civitas of Sound: On Luther and Music', *Theology* 88 (1985), pp. 21–8.

Ingalls, M.M., 'Awesome in this Place: Sound, Space, and Identity in Contemporary North American Evangelical Worship' (unpublished PhD Thesis, University of Pennsylvania, 2008).

Irwin, J., '"So Faith Comes from What is Heard": The Relationship between Music and God's Word in the First Two Centuries of German Lutheranism', in J. Begbie and S. Guthrie (eds), *Resonant Witness: Conversations Between Music and Theology* (Grand Rapids, MI, 2011), pp. 65–82.

Jankélévitch, V., *Music and the Ineffable*, trans. C. Abbatte (Princeton, 2003).

Jenkins, K., *Redefining the Hymn: The Performative Context, Occasional Paper, Third Series* 4 (London, 2010).

Jones, D., *The Anathemata* (London, 1952).

Jourdain, R., *Music, the Brain and Ecstasy: How Music Captures our Imagination* (New York, 1997).

Kartomi, M.J., 'Music and Trance in Central Java', *Ethnomusicology* 17 (1973), pp. 163–208.
Kim, H., 'Erasmus on Sacred Music', *Reformation and Renaissance Review* 8 (2006), pp. 277–300.
Klee, P., *Painting Music* (New York, 1997).
Knowles-Wallace, R., 'Congregational Singing and Everyday Life', Keynote presentation at *Hymns in Liturgy and Life, International Conference of Hymn Societies* (Cambridge, 26 July–1 August 2015).
Küng, H., *Mozart – Traces of Transcendence* (London, 1992).
Kwame Anthony Appiah, *BBC Radio 4 Reith Lectures 2016: Mistaken Identities: Creed, Country, Colour, Culture*. Lecture 1: Creed.
Le Huray, P., *Music and the Reformation in England, 1549–1660* (Oxford, 1967).
Lehmberg, S.E., *The Reformation of Cathedrals: Cathedrals in English Society from 1485–1603* (Princeton, NJ, 1988).
Lehmberg, S.E., 'The Reformation of Choirs: Cathedral Musical Establishments in Tudor England', in D.J. Guth and J.W. McKenna (eds), *Tudor Rule and Revolution: Essays for G.R. Elton from his American Friends* (Cambridge, 1982), pp. 45–69.
Lepine, D., *A Brotherhood of Canons Serving God: English Secular Cathedrals in the Later Middle Ages* (Woodbridge, 1995).
Leunig, M., *The Lot: In Words* (Camberwell, Australia, 2008).
Lewis, C.S., 'Answers to Questions on Christianity' (Oxford, 1944).
Lewis, C.S., 'Letter to Eric Routley' (16 July 1946), in W. Hooper (ed.), *C.S. Lewis, Collected Letters* II: Books, Broadcasts and War 1931–1949 (London, 2004), p. 720.
Lewis, C.S., *On Church Music*, ed. W. Hooper (London, 1967, reissued 1980).
Lewis, C.S., *The Presbyter: A Journal of Reformed Churchmanship* 6:2 (1948).
Lewis, C.S., *The Screwtape Letters* (London, 1942).
Louth, A., 'The Reception of Dionysius in the Byzantine World: Maximus to Palamas', in *Modern Theology* 24 (2008), pp. 585–99.
Lutz, C.E., *Remigii Autissiodorensis Commentum in Martianum Capellam*, Vol. 2 (Leiden, 1962).
Maas, S. van, *The Reinvention of Religious Music: Olivier Messiaen's Breakthrough Toward the Beyond* (New York, 2009).
MacCulloch, D., *A History of Christianity* (London, 2009).
MacDiarmaid, F., '*De Utilitate Cantorum*: Unitive Aspects of Singing in Early Christian Thought', *Anglican Theological Review* 100 (2018), pp. 291–309.
Mandelbrote, S., 'Early Modern Natural Theologies', in *Handbook of Natural Theology*, pp. 75–99.
Marbeck, J., *The Book of Common Praier Noted* (London, 1550), Sig. A.ii.
Matheson, P. (ed.), *Collected Letters and Writings of Thomas Müntzer* (Edinburgh, 1988).
McCarthy, M., 'Spirituality in a Postmodern Era', in J. Woodward and S. Pattison (eds), *The Blackwell Reader in Pastoral and Practical Theology* (Oxford, 2000), pp. 199–200.
McGilchrist, I., *The Master and his Emissary* (New Haven and London, 2012).
McKinnon, J. (ed.), *Music in Early Christian Literature* (Cambridge, 1987).
Mesoudi, A., *Cultural Evolution: How Darwinian Theory can Explain Human Culture and Synthesize the Social Sciences* (Chicago, 2011).
Miller, D.E., 'Postdenominational Christianity in the Twenty-First Century', *Annals of the American Academy of Political and Social Science* 558 (1998), pp. 196–210.
Moberg, M., Granholm, K. and Nynäs, P., 'Trajectories of Post-Secular Complexity: An

Introduction', in P. Nynäs, M. Lassander and T. Utriainen (eds), *Post-Secular Society* (New Brunswick, 2012; new edn 2015), pp. 1–26.
Mobsby, I., *God Unknown: The Trinity in Contemporary Spirituality and Mission* (Norwich, 2008).
Mobsby, I., 'The Place of New Monasticism in a Post-Secular Culture': an unpublished lecture delivered at the *Diocesan Spirituality Advisors' Conference*, Launde Abbey, Leicestershire, 10 April 2018.
Monti, A., *A Natural Theology of the Arts: Imprint of the Spirit* (Aldershot, 2003).
Morgan, S. and Boyce-Tillman, J., *A River Rather than a Road: The Community Choir as Spiritual Experience* (Oxford, Bern, 2016).
Mountford, B., *Christian Atheist: Belonging without Believing* (Winchester UK, Washington USA, 2010).
Muller, J., *The Letters of Stephen Gardiner* (Cambridge, 1933).
Murdoch, I., *The Sovereignty of Good* (London, 1970).
Niebuhr, R., *Christ and Culture* (New York, 1951).
Oakley, M., 'Batter my Heart: The Poetry and Theology of John Donne', *Church Music Quarterly* (June 2018), p. 13.
Oakley, M., *The Splash of Words: Believing in Poetry* (London, 2016).
Oesterreich, T.K., *Possession, Demoniacal and Other: Among Primitive Races, in Antiquity, the Middle Ages and Modern* (London, 2013).
Orme, N., *The Minor Clergy of Exeter Cathedral, 1300–1548* (Exeter, 1980).
Page, C., 'Music and the Beyond', in F. Stone-Davis (ed.), *Music and Transcendence* (Farnham, 2015), pp. 13–21.
Pearce, E., Launay, J. and Dunbar, R.I.M., 'The Ice-Breaker Effect: Singing Mediates Fast Social Bonding', *Royal Society Open Science* 2 (2015), pp. 150–221 and *Royal Society Open Science* 2: 150221: http://dx.doi.org/10.1098/rsos.150221.
Peel, A. and Carlson, L. (eds), *Elizabethan and Non-Conformist Texts, Volume II: The Writings of Robert Harrison and Robert Browne* (London, 1953; reprinted 2003).
Percy, M., 'Afterword: Theology and Music in Conversation', in M. Ingalls, C. Landau and T. Wagner (eds), *Christian Congregational Music: Performance, Identity and Experience* (Farnham, 2013), pp. 217–22.
Pilch, J.J., 'Music and Trance', in D. Aldridge and J. Fachner (eds), *Music and Altered States: Consciousness, Transcendence, Therapy and Addictions* (London and Philadelphia, 2006), pp. 38–50.
Pope Benedict XVI, 'General Audience in the Paul VI Hall', Vatican City, 21 May 2008.
Pope Benedict XVI, 'Paul VI Audience Hall', Vatican City, 16 April 2007.
Pope Benedict XVI, *The Spirit of the Liturgy* (San Francisco, 2014).
Porter, M., *Contemporary Music and Everyday Music Lives* (Abingdon, 2017).
Quash, B., 'Making the Most of Time', *Studies in Christian Ethics* 15 (2002), pp. 97–114.
Rex, R., *Henry VIII and the English Reformation* (Basingstoke, 1993).
Richardson, G., 'Craft Guilds and Christianity in Late-Medieval England: A Rational Choice Analysis', *Rationality and Society* 17 (2005), pp. 139–89.
Rollins, P., *How (Not) to Speak of God* (London, 2006).
Rollins, P., *The Orthodox Heretic: and Other Impossible Tales* (London, 2009).
Rouget, G., *Music and Trance: A Theory of the Relations between Music and Possession* (Chicago, 1985).
Sacks, O., *Awakenings* (London, 1973).

Sacks, O., *The Man who mistook his Wife for a Hat* (London, 1985).
Sacks, O., *Musicophilia: Tales of Music and the Brain* (London, 2007).
Saliers, D.E., *Music and Theology* (Nashville, TN, 2007).
Salisbury, M. Cheung, *Worship in Medieval England* (Leeds, 2018).
Sanders, E.P., *Paul: A Very Short Introduction* (Oxford, 2001).
Sankey, I.D. and Moody, D.L., *Sacred Songs and Solos* (London, 1877).
Scarffe, J., 'An Introduction to the Eye Music Series', in J. Boulton, *Eye Music* (Uniform Books, 2014), pp. 3–6.
Schleiermacher, F., *On Religion and the Natural Order* (London, 1965).
Schleiermacher, F., *On Religion: Speeches to its Cultured Despisers*, trans. R. Crouter (Cambridge, 1996).
Scruton, R., *The Aesthetics of Music* (Oxford, 1997).
Scruton, R., *The Face of God: The Gifford Lectures 2010* (London, 2012).
Scruton, R., 'Music and the Transcendental', in F. Stone-Davis (ed.), *Music and Transcendence* (Farnham, 2015), pp. 75–84.
Shaw-Miller, S., *Sighting Music* (Chichester, 2007).
Shepherd, J. and Devine K. (eds), *The Routledge Reader on the Sociology of Music* (New York and London, 2015).
Sherry, P., *The Spirit of Beauty: An Introduction to Theological Aesthetics* (Oxford, 1992).
Sorgner, S.L. and Fürbeth, O. (eds), *Music in German Philosophy*, trans. S.H. Gillespie (Chicago, 2010).
Sosis, R. and Bressler, E.R., 'Cooperation and Commune Longevity: A Test of the Costly Signaling Theory of Religion', *Cross-Cultural Research* 37 (2003), pp. 211–39.
Staniloae, D., *The Experience of God: Orthodox Dogmatic Theology*, vol. 2, *The World: Creation and Deification*, trans. I. Ionata and R. Berringer (Brookline, MA, 2005).
Steiner, G., *Real Presences* (London, 1989).
Swanson, R.N., 'Medieval Liturgy as Theatre: The Props', in D. Wood (ed.), *The Church and the Arts* (Oxford, 1995), pp. 239–54.
Symmons Roberts, M., 'Contemporary Poetry and Belief', in P. Robinson (ed.), *The Oxford Handbook of Contemporary British and Irish Poetry* (Oxford, 2013), pp. 694–706.
Tarr, B., Launay, J., Cohen, E. and Dunbar, R.I.M., 'Synchrony and exertion during dance independently raise pain threshold and encourage social bonding', *Biology Letters* 11: 20150767 (2015); downloaded from http://rsbl.royalsocietypublishing.org on 21 October 2016.
Taylor, C., *A Secular Age* (Cambridge, MA, 2007).
Ter Borg, M., 'A Function for Religion in the Survival of the Human Species', in *The Oxford Handbook of the Sociology of Religion* (Oxford, 2009; paperback edn, 2011), pp. 194–209.
Thompson, D., *On Growth and Form*, abridged edition ed. J. Tyler Bonner (Cambridge, 1961; Canto edn, 1992).
Thomson, A., *Culture in a Post-Secular Context: Theological Possibilities in Milbank, Barth and Bediako* (Eugene, OR, 2014).
Turner, B.S., 'Religion in a Post-Secular Society', in B.S. Turner (ed.), *The New Blackwell Companion to the Sociology of Religion* (Chichester, 2010), pp. 649–67.
Turner, V., 'Body, Brain, and Culture', *Zygon* 18 (1983), pp. 221–45.
Vanden Heuvel, W.J., *The Future of Freedom in Russia* (West Conshohocken, PA, 2000).
Walsh, E., Oakley, D.A., Halligan, P.W., Mehta, M.A. and Deeley, Q., 'Brain Mechanisms

for Loss of Awareness of Thought and Movement', *Social Cognitive and Affective Neuroscience* 12 (2017), pp. 793–801.

Ward, G., *True Religion* (Oxford, 2003).

Warner, M. et al., 'Editors' Introduction', in *Varieties of Secularism in a Secular Age* (Cambridge, MA, 2010).

Weinstein, D., Launay, J., Pearce, E., Dunbar, R.I.M. and Stewart, L., 'Singing and social bonding: changes in connectivity and pain threshold as a function of group size', *Evolution and Human Behavior* 37 (2016) pp. 152–8.

Weiss, B. and Pérez, L.C. (eds), *Beginnings and Discoveries: Polydore Vergil's De Inventoribus Rerum. An Unabridged Translation and Edition with Introduction, Notes and Glossary* (Nieuwkoop, 1997).

Williams, R., *The Edge of Words: God and the Habits of Language* (London, 2014).

Williams, R., *Faith in the Public Square* (London, 2012).

Williams, R., 'Keeping Time', in *Open to Judgement: Sermons and Addresses* (London, 1994), pp. 247–50.

Wuthnow, R., *After Heaven: Spirituality in America since the 1950s* (Berkeley, 1998).

Zwerin, M., 'A Lethal Measurement', in R. Kostelanetz (ed.), *John Cage* (New York, 1970), p. 166.

WEBSITES

http://www.aosm.org.uk/index.php/archive/item/sacred-music-can-heal-our-broken-culture

https://bachtrack.com/classical-music-statistics-2014

https://www.bbc.co.uk/programmes/b06db6tx

https://www.bbc.co.uk/programmes/b0b17fkh

http://www.biblesociety.org.uk/uploads/content/projects/Bible-Society-Report_030214_final_.pdf, pp. 11–14.

https://boginsdotcom.files.wordpress.com/2012/09/feeling-into-words.pdf

https://www.collinsdictionary.com/dictionary/english/music

https://www.facebook.com/wellbeingchoir

https://www.giffordlecture.org

http://www.janetboulton.co.uk

http://www.magd.ox.ac.uk/libraries-and-archives/news/new-exhibition-fragments-of-note

https://www.manchestereveningnews.co.uk/news/greater-manchester-news/choir-brought-hope-survivors-manchester-14672046

http://medievalconventdrama.org

http://www.naturalvoice.net

https://www.psy.ox.ac.uk/team/robin-dunbar

http://www.quintondeeley.co.uk

http://www.sundayassembly.com/story

https://www.theaudienceagency.org/asset/1303

https://www.theguardian.com/world/2018/mar/21/christianity-non-christian-europe-young-people-survey-religion

INDEX